CORNEILLE'S IRONY

CORNEILLE'S IRONY

NINA EKSTEIN

ROOKWOOD PRESS

Charlottesville

2007

ISBN
978-1-886365-25-4
1-886365-25-3

This book is printed on acid-free paper.

EMF Critiques

EDITORS
Anne L. Birberick and Russell J. Ganim

FOUNDING EDITOR
David Lee Rubin

COPY EDITOR
Katherine Saunders Nash

PRODUCTION
Angel Applications

COVER DESIGN
Dallas Pasco

For Roland

Table of Contents

Part I: Evident Irony

Chapter 1 (1)

Introduction
An Ironic Corneille? (2)—Irony: A Brief Overview (3)
Intention and Reception (5)—Signals (9)
The Dramatic Context (11)—Directions (13)

Chapter 2 (16)

Dramatic Irony
Stage-Centered Dramatic Irony (17)—Authorial Dramatic Irony (19)
Combining Stage-Centered and Authorial Dramatic Irony (24)
Œdipe (25)

Chapter 3 (31)

Verbal Irony
Signs (32)—Types of Verbal Irony in Corneille's Theater (33)
Nicomède (41)—Pulchérie: Duplicity and Irony (48)

Chapter 4 (55)

Situational Irony
Types of Situational Irony in Corneille's Theater (57)
Irony of Fate (60)—Oracles (63)

Part II: Signals of Possible Irony
Introduction (75)

CHAPTER 5 (77)

REDUPLICATION

Repetition (77)—Coincidence (79)—Symmetry (81)
Echoic Mention (83)—Sabine in *Horace* (90)

CHAPTER 6 (101)

EXAGGERATION

Parody (105)—Alazon (113)—Eirôn (115)

CHAPTER 7 (124)

GAPS

Incongruity (124)—Double Register (128)
Character Contradictions (134)—Antithesis and Paradox (139)
Cinna (143)

CHAPTER 8 (150)

MARGINS

Margins Between Plays (150)—Prologue and Play (158)
Sources (165)—Authority (169)

CHAPTER 9 (180)

CONCLUSION

Works Cited (188)

Index (198)

Acknowledgments

I would like to thank Susan Read Baker for having patiently and pains-takingly read my manuscript, Perry Gethner for always generously providing me with useful information and good counsel, Harriet Allentuch for having insisted that Corneille was fascinating, Trinity University for its support, and Babette Guajardo for all her help with my work. I would also like to thank Katherine Nash for her careful editing; David Lee Rubin, Russell Ganim, and Anne Birberick for their support for my work; and the anonymous reviewers whose suggestions were extremely helpful. Above all, I want to thank my husband, Roland Champagne, for having read the manuscript numerous times, for his excellent advice, for his patience, and for giving me the time and encouragement to undertake this project.

An early version of part of chapter 8 appeared as "Knowing Irony: The Problem of Corneille" in *Le Savoir au dix-septième siècle*, edited by John D. Lyons and Cara Welch. I am grateful to Gunter Narr Verlag for the permission to reprint it here. Another part of chapter 8 was delivered as a paper entitled "Le Pratique ironique de l'appel à l'autorité dans les paratextes du théâtre de Corneille" at the Colloque International pour le Quatrième Centenaire de la Naissance de Pierre Corneille, Rouen, June 2006. It will appear in the *Actes* of the conference and I am grateful to Myriam Dufour-Maître for the permission to use it here.

CORNEILLE'S IRONY

PART I
EVIDENT IRONY

CHAPTER I
INTRODUCTION

Pierre Corneille's consecrated position in the canon of French literature endures as we reach the 400th anniversary of the playwright's birth. His plays continue to be read, performed, studied, and admired throughout the world. While his work has received somewhat less attention than his rival Racine's in the last generation or two, it remains a competition of giants, who between them virtually own the terrain referenced by the words "French tragedy." Among the many defining characteristics of Corneille's theatrical output, the most salient may be diversity. In the thirty-two plays written entirely by him, there is a remarkable range of plot, source, tone, rhetorical strategy, and dramaturgical technique. In undertaking a work on any author, whatever the particular focus, one inevitably seeks to convey one's vision of the specificity of that author's genius. While I am much influenced by Georges Forestier's excellent study of the genesis and structure of Corneille's plots, I personally locate the specificity of his genius at the level of his language and rhetoric. I am repeatedly struck by the tremendous subtlety and complexity of his language, with its crisscrossing network of references and levels of elevation. I do not believe that Cornelian expression has received its due. My focus in this study—irony—in no way suffices to account for that linguistic subtlety and complexity. It does, however, allow for an understanding of a dimension that informs his language and that furthermore has received little attention. Irony is by no means, however, a purely linguistic feature. As we shall see, it operates on numerous levels, encompassing both language and plot, as well as specifically dramatic features. In its many manifestations—dramatic irony, the irony of fate, echoic mention, parody, sarcasm, exaggeration, coincidence, *raillerie*, incongruity, reversal of fortune, changes of register, and contradiction, to name only some—irony is widely dispersed throughout Corneille's work. It is crucial to note from the outset that the presence of irony, however varied and wide-ranging, is rarely dominant. This study by no means offers a totalizing perspective: I do not subscribe to the notion that Corneille is above all an ironic playwright. Rather, my work is a reframing and an eclectic exploration of the problem of irony. I find that irony permeates Corneille's dramatic universe to an extent that varies widely, at times coloring a particular play more strongly, at other times sounding or merely suggesting a subtle note in a character or a scene. I will seek to highlight how irony, like a series

1

of threads, is woven into Corneille's œuvre. Through my efforts to elucidate the wide-ranging and subtle manifestations of irony within Corneille's works, I suggest new and different perspectives on the playwright's artistry, which at times complement and enrich other readings of his theater and at others, posit alternate interpretations. Indeed, irony itself, a term that refers to a broad range of radically different features, functions as a rich metaphor for Corneille's theater, in its complexity, its resistance to conclusive interpretation, and its enduring fascination.

An Ironic Corneille?

Corneille is not generally associated with irony. When D. C. Muecke opens his work on irony with a long list of distinguished authors "in whose work irony is significantly present," he includes Molière, Racine, and Pascal from seventeenth-century France, but not Corneille (*Irony* 3). I can identify three partial and tentative explanations why Corneille is usually not perceived as ironic. The first involves the image that tradition has handed down of Corneille the man. Alain Niderst provides an example of that perception when, in reference to the prologue to the *Toison d'or*, he refers to Corneille in terms of "son habituelle sincérité, un peu gauche, un peu lourde" (94). The three terms "sincérité," "gauche," and "lourde" embody the antithesis of the ironic personality. Niderst is not alone in his impression of the author. The issue of Corneille's character is pertinent here because irony is inextricably bound to authorial intent, as we shall see shortly. The second reason involves the long-standing preeminence of the notion of heroism in the critical discussion of Corneille's works. Cornelian heroism is for many, if not a forbidden domain for irony, then at least a problematic one, fostering a persistent blind spot. The relationship between the two is discordant, in that heroism depends on universal admiration for a single set of values, while irony calls into question what it targets and thus implies the possibility of alternative values. The ideals of heroism, honor, glory, and duty are so central to the traditional French ideological stakes in Corneille's theater that there is a general tendency to resist or even reject any possibility of irony in his plays.[1] D. H. Green argues against this inclination, however, in his discussion of irony in the medieval romance, asking the question "Is it conceivable that, alongside their manifest wish to legitimise chivalry, these authors may also have applied irony to this theme?" (51). He responds in the affirmative. Indeed, I will argue that the same holds true for Corneille, that he both glorifies heroism and at the same time treats this theme ironically. The third reason I have found, quite different in nature, involves the kind of irony favored by Corneille. Typically, the irony of fate is associated with tragedy. Irony of fate can be defined as situational irony with a clear divine or supernatural source. Œdipus is its classic victim. Despite the fact that Corneille wrote his own version of the Œdipus myth, the fact remains that this kind of irony is fundamentally alien to his view of the universe. Corneille has a strong predilection for characters who take control of their situation; the hand of God or fate or destiny is little felt in his dramatic universe. Even in the case of Corneille's two religious tragedies, *Polyeucte* and *Théodore*, where God's presence is a given, we do not find irony of fate *per se*.

Thus there are cogent reasons why Corneille is not usually associated with irony. Occasional comments by scholars suggest some recognition, however, that irony may play a role in his theater. Verbal irony is occasionally noted, especially in *Nicomède*.[2] Alice Rathé mentions Corneille's "goût de l'ironie" ("Cercle" 524), but does not examine it further. Both R. C. Knight and I. D. McFarlane suggest a larger role for irony than is commonly assumed. The former admits, "J'ai dit moi-même, il n'y a pas longtemps, en vantant l'éblouissante escrime de *Nicomède*, que c'était un exemple à peu près isolé [of irony] chez ce poète. Maintenant, au contraire, il me semble en découvrir presque partout" ("*Andromaque*" 21), while the latter suggests, "I wonder if we have not underplayed the role of irony in Corneille's drama" ("*Œdipe*" 47). Indeed, when one examines certain features of these plays, the ponderous atmosphere of mortal dilemmas and human courage is mated with a playful, ironic tone that lends depth, complexity, and surprise to Corneille's dramaturgy.

Knight poses a central question related to Corneille's intent: "We know he enjoyed teasing d'Aubignac. Can our unsociable, gawky 'pied plat' have had, not only a sense of drama, but enough sense of humour to take pleasure in disconcerting?" ("Quand" 32). To answer *yes* is to propose a significantly different understanding of what Corneille was about in his theater than is commonly accepted. The vision I will put forth is of an author far more playful and mocking than the dour standard-bearer of exalted values, a playwright who is both astonishingly complex and daring in his dramaturgy, who is also willing to take himself less than seriously at times.

IRONY: A BRIEF OVERVIEW

To ask the question, what exactly is irony? is daunting, because there are so many possible answers, and so many angles from which to consider this complex concept.[3] The subject of irony has received considerable renewed attention of late, particularly in France, with major works by Pierre Schoentjes (2001), Laurent Perrin (1996), and Philippe Hamon (1996), and in Canada, Linda Hutcheon's important *Irony's Edge* (1994). While all of these scholars struggle with the question of defining irony, as have countless others before them, there is general acknowledgement that, as Schoentjes puts it, "[I]l n'existe pas de conception unifiée et homogène de l'ironie" (9).

Corneille never used the term "ironie" or "ironique" in any of his plays or theoretical writings. The word "ironie" is, however, found in Antoine Furetière's dictionary (1690), tied to antiphrasis—what is implied is the opposite of a statement's literal meaning—the simplest form of irony.[4] Yet the concept of irony is transhistoric and far broader (Schoentjes 25). Ancient literature, such as the Bible, Homer's epics, or Greek tragedies, abounds with the kinds of situations that we would refer to as ironic, but which were not associated with the term until the middle of the eighteenth century. At the same time, the concept of irony can be said to have a history, one that foregrounds certain features at certain moments and has at times involved the expansion of the notion itself (e.g., nineteenth-century Romantic irony). Thus while one may assume that my interest in both irony and its manifestations in Corneille's work is a function of the postmodern moment in which I write, the concept of irony itself is one that was completely current in Corneille's world.

Not surprisingly, given the complexity of the concept, there exist numerous taxonomies of irony. The simplest and most universal one is the basic division between verbal and situational irony. As the term "verbal" suggests, verbal irony entails a speaker and the irony is located in his or her words. Situational irony involves some contradiction, opposition, or contrast between two contiguous elements (events, objects, etc.). Numerous other factors complicate our understanding of irony, however. How do we separate the semantics of irony from its syntax, from its pragmatics? Intention and reception are further considerations, as is the context in which irony appears.

A central feature of irony is doubling. All irony involves two elements, each in some relation to the other. The other can be either explicit or implicit, concrete (an earlier statement) or abstract (a norm). It is the relationship between the two, a relationship covered by terms such as gap (*écart*), opposition, contradiction, contrast, disparity, tension, distance, divergence, and incongruity, that creates the conditions necessary for irony, whether verbal or situational. In the former, it is the gap between what one says and either what was meant or what was said earlier that signals verbal irony. In the case of situational irony, the gap or tension can be spatial (e.g., an incongruous juxtaposition) or structural / temporal (e.g., a reversal of fortune).

Hutcheon posits three semantic characteristics of irony: the differential, the relational, and the inclusive (*Edge* 58). The opposition or gap is covered by her term "differential," and the need for two elements by "relational," but the third term, "inclusive," marks an additional feature necessary for our discussion of irony in Corneille. Irony is inclusive in the sense that the two elements are in play simultaneously. Rather than facing a simple choice between what X says and what X means, one accepts the fundamental ambiguity in an ironic statement of perceiving both concurrently. The irony comes from the undecidability and the tension between the two.[5] The two perspectives, while perfectly incompatible, are equally valid.[6] Thus neither meaning is privileged, at least not absolutely, over the other, as would be the case in allegory. In Hutcheon's view, the mind oscillates between two meanings and embraces both simultaneously (*Edge* 59–60). Inclusiveness contributes to interpretive uncertainty; indeed irony, as we shall see, often and even inherently entails doubt.

It is important to note that doubling by itself does not constitute irony, nor is every contradiction or gap ironic. A second step is necessary: one of the two elements must in some fashion be making a commentary on, even critiquing, the other. If the two elements are ordered temporally, then the latter comments on the former; if there is no temporal gap, as in the case of the inclusive undecibability described above, the commentary can be dialogic, running in both directions. This is the "edge" of irony referred to in the title of Hutcheon's book. The ironist is a moralist who passes judgment: the evaluative function of irony is universally recognized and helps to distinguish irony from other tropes (Hutcheon, *Edge* 39). Tied to irony's edge is the notion of questioning. Irony is profoundly, even etymologically, related to questioning: "L'ironie propose une interrogation et s'efforce de mettre les vérités en question" (Schoentjes 219). Irony as interrogation also extends to its apprehension and comprehension: the reader must question what the intended meaning of an ironic statement might be (Dupriez 264). Irony judges and irony questions. It also may serve to attack or defend—functions much favored by Corneille, as we shall see.

While irony is transhistoric in nature, and thus transnational as well, it nonetheless displays certain cultural characteristics. The French understanding of irony, as opposed to the Anglo-Saxon and Germanic traditions, in which irony is often perceived as a serious stance (Schoentjes 23), generally associates irony with *raillerie*, an attitude of mocking, derisive playfulness (Kerbrat-Orecchioni, "Trope" 119). Schoentjes underscores the notion of play: "L'ironie relève du ludique et son sérieux est celui du jeu" (212).[7] *Raillerie* ranges in tone from the light and playful to the biting. At the same time, it can be used to attack some target, extending from the self (self-deprecating irony) to the other and beyond, to more abstract authorities, principles, and values.

INTENTION AND RECEPTION

Did Corneille mean to be ironic? Did he mean to be playful? Does it matter what Corneille may have intended? And how can we possibly know with any certainty? Certainty is difficult to come by in discussions of irony, for the Greek term *éirônéia*, whatever other associations it may have, almost always conveys the notion of "dissimulation."[8] Inherent to irony is ambiguity, which ensures that what the author intended and how it is to be interpreted by the receiver are matters for speculation. The degree of speculation required varies enormously, however. Sarcasm, for example, leaves little doubt as to the speaker's ironic intent. In order to identify irony, authorial intent must be considered, but it is not the sole criterion for establishing the presence of irony in Corneille's works; I will also consider reception and signals, which provide complementary grounds for identification.

To discuss intention is to posit the existence of a unified subject as the origin and source of an instance of irony, a rather uncomfortable stance, as Hutcheon points out, "in a post-Derridean, post-Barthesian, and post-Foucaultian age" (*Edge* 11). There is, however, critical agreement that one cannot meaningfully discuss irony without reference to an intending subject. Catherine Kerbrat-Orecchioni sums up the role of intent: "On peut remarquer que l'étude de l'ironie littéraire est absolument indissociable d'une interrogation sur le sujet d'énonciation, cette instance qui, dissimulée derrière le texte, juge, évalue, ironise. Si l'on refuse ce type de problématique, le concept d'ironie se trouve du même coup frappé d'inanité" ("Problèmes" 41). It is obvious that the need to assign intention, while unavoidable and inevitable, brings with it serious problems. The first is epistemological: how can we possibly *know* what the speaker, specifically Corneille, intended? Second, how may we, pragmatically speaking, access that intent? The distance in time makes this task all the more difficult: as Schoentjes notes, it is one thing to talk about ironic intention in the context of a conversation with a friend, but quite another when one is reading the work of a long-dead author (147). The third problem is even more troubling: an analysis based on authorial intent presupposes that an author is conscious, and in complete control, of his/her text. Irony has lost a crucial dimension if its study can be reduced to a game of substitution and translation, in which the "real" meaning can be fully recuperated from the "hidden."[9] Accepting such faith in authorial intention implies, as Candace D. Lang points out, that "the truly multivalent text is unthinkable: discrepancies or incoherencies can only be interpreted as errors" (45). To read Corneille (or any other author) as merely encoding irony for the reader or spectator to decode is to diminish the art and complexity of his works. The question remains, as Hutcheon puts it, "[W]hat status should that intention have in theorizing ironic meaning?" (*Edge* 117).

The question of intent is complicated from another angle entirely when we consider the basic division of irony mentioned above: verbal and situational. In the case of verbal irony the presupposition of an intending ironist seems reasonable, but the same can not be said for situational irony. The line between situational irony and coincidence is difficult to locate. For example, one might say, "Isn't it ironic that I found a watch in the road on the same day you lost your watch in another city?" One certainly feels the hand of the gods and their ironic intent in the plight of Œdipus, as in the case of all irony of fate, but in a watch lost and a watch found? Whose intent is in play here? How one answers depends on one's view of the universe. A rationalist view would reject any ironizing intent on the part of either the watch or some divinity. It is not uncommon, however, to find the belief, held either consciously or unconsciously, that there is some intending force or deity at the source of all situational irony.[10] In the context of a work of literature, however, the intending force of situational irony is unquestionably present in the person of the author, and the watch lost and the watch found cannot be dismissed as a meaningless coincidence. Thus the distance between verbal and situational irony is considerably narrower in Corneille's theater than in "real life," and we may assume that all evident irony in the literary context has an intender, with the proviso that this intender may conceivably be unconscious of being ironic.[11]

In sum, I do not believe that the notion of the author can be dispensed with in the context of this study, much as it is my almost automatic inclination to do so. In the final analysis, it is precisely our judgment of the author's intentions that will lead us to perceive a given element as ironic or serious (Schoentjes 152). At the same time, I do not believe that the author's intentions can be fully recovered, and I certainly do not propose an exercise in the translation of the "hidden." I suggest an exploration of a different perspective on Corneille as a playwright and in so doing, I accept the presence of a fair degree of ambiguity and uncertainty.

I mentioned earlier the doubling that is a defining feature of irony; it extends as well to our discussion of knowledge of irony. Irony requires not only an ironist (with ironic intent) but also an interpreter, someone who perceives the irony. Irony's inherent ambiguity makes perception and interpretation crucial parts of ironic communication. Can an intended irony even be said to be ironic if it is not interpreted as such? The interpreter thus has a decidedly active role in the work of irony. For Hutcheon, interpretation is absolutely central, even at the expense of the intending ironist:

> To call something ironic is to frame or contextualize it in such a way that, in fact, an intentionalist statement has already been made—either by the ironist or by the interpreter (or by both).
>
> In other words, intentional/non-intentional

may be a false distinction: all irony happens intentionally, whether the attribution be made by the encoder or the decoder. Interpretation is, in a sense, an intentional act on the part of the interpreter. (*Edge* 118)

In the case of "real life" situational irony, the rationalist may well deny the existence of an intending ironist, but an intending ironist cannot dispense with the interpreter.

Having taken on the role of interpreter of Corneille's ironies, I am naturally buoyed by all authoritative assertions of that role's centrality. I would be remiss, however, not to consider the host of thorny issues raised by what we might call "reader-response" irony. The freedom to interpret irony itself leads to problems. Muecke states that "while we may legitimately question whether or not something has been said or done with ironical intent, we cannot question anyone's right to see something as ironic. We may question his sense or taste though" (*Irony* 43–44). Following that logic, I may call anything ironic, but it behooves me to argue my interpretation persuasively. To leave the existence of irony to the interpreter also allows for the undesirable possibility of a kind of contagion of ironic reading, one that sees irony everywhere.[12] Corneille himself gives a concrete example of the problem posed by the aggressive perception of irony in the absence of any signal of ironic intent. In *La Veuve*, Philiste resists believing that Clarice's expressions of affection are sincere, fearing that she is being ironic and thus merely toying with him: "[E]t par quelque signe / Qu'elle me découvre son cœur, / Je le prends pour un trait moqueur" (ll. 431–33).[13] The interpreter has much power, but that power is potentially dangerous and may lead to misinterpretation.

Even if the interpreter did not run rampant in the pursuit of irony, one would be hard pressed to avoid interpretive disagreement. Because irony is grounded in ambiguity, universal agreement would seem not only unlikely but almost undesirable in that it would signal the failure of the ironic element to raise doubt. Is it even fair to use the term "irony" if everyone recognizes it without disagreement? To illustrate the issue of interpretive uncertainty, I would like to give an example of possible irony in Corneille's theater that might arouse some disagreement, an example that is not my own, but belongs rather to Richard Goodkin. He refers to "the irony whereby Corneille might be said to mark the death of the founder of the Académie française [Richelieu] by opening his next play [*Pompée*] with a *malséant* description of putrid, rotting corpses" (95-96). Perhaps we might agree about the *possibility* of ironic intent on Corneille's part here, but the distance between the two domains (the minister's death and *Pompée*) is so large that it would be difficult to find the grounds upon which to build a convincing case. One would have to rely on our limited knowledge of Corneille's attitude towards Richelieu as well as our assumptions concerning the degree to which contemporary concerns (political and otherwise) figure in Corneille's plays, to say nothing of our suppositions concerning Corneille's proclivity for irony.[14] This particular example, in my opinion, is undecidable. What are we to do then, as Hutcheon asks, "with the obvious fact that ironies exist that are not intended, but are most certainly interpreted as such? Similarly, there are ironies you might intend, as ironist, but which remain unperceived by others" (*Edge* 10). Napoleon famously suggested an ironic stance on Corneille's part in Auguste's pardon of Cinna and Émilie. According to Jules Lemaître, "Napoléon, bon juge en ces matières, ne croyait pas à la clémence d'Auguste; et il allait jusqu'à dire que Corneille n'y croyait pas non plus" (295). Doubt and uncertainty are frequently unavoidable in a discussion of irony.

Making a convincing argument in favor of the presence of irony in various contexts will obviously be a central concern of this study. I hope that when I intepret as irony something that was likely not intended ironically, I will do so consciously and admit the liberty I take. It is difficult, if not impossible, to draw a clear line between what may be read as ironic and what cannot possibly be, for no final knowledge is achievable in the domain of irony. The tools at one's disposal are good judgment, reliance on signals and context, and lucidity concerning the pitfalls. The more that both intention and reception can be brought to bear on the question, the more likely that a compelling case for the presence of irony can be made. Irony is an especially complex form of communication, and therefore one that often courts the possibility of miscommunication.[15]

SIGNALS

There is a kind of middle ground between reception and intention, accessible to both parties involved: signs or signals of irony. The intending ironist employs certain cues or signs that indicate to the receiver the possibility of an ironic interpretation; correspondingly the receiver perceives such signals and consequently interprets ironically. Because of the inherent indirection of ironic communication, the possibility persists that the receiver will not notice the intended signal or that the perceived signal was not intended as such. Furthermore, one cannot rely entirely on specific signals in the text or speech act; irony may be situated on a far more global level. Nonetheless, signals provide a crucial basis on which to ground an assertion of irony.

The first category of ironic signals rely on the physical presence of both the ironist and the receiver. These may include the tone of voice, a smile or a look (or wink) of complicity, a gesture, or a facial expression. Such signals often, but by no means always, appear in conjunction with verbal irony.[16] They are completely alien to the dramatic text unless specified in the stage directions, a practice to which Corneille did not subscribe. In the performance of Corneille's plays, the director obviously has the freedom to mask, accentuate, or even create irony with such presence-based signals, but in such cases Corneille is not the intending source of the irony. Thus we will be unable to rely on this category of signals for indications of the presence or absence of intended irony.

The second group of signals involves those that have some basis in the text, and range broadly from the specific and local to the more global and imprecise. The desire for a specific typographical sign for ironic intent is long-standing but has never been fully realized.[17] Italics and quotation marks often serve this function, but they are subject to misinterpretation because both have other communicative functions as well. Overtly metalinguistic terms, such as "so to speak," "no doubt," etc., may function as localized signals of irony as well (Hutcheon, *Edge* 156). Such explicit signs are not characteristic of Corneille's theater and thus of limited interest here.

Far more broad and useful are Hutcheon's five categories of signals of irony: "(1) various changes of register; (2) exaggeration / understatement, (3) contradiction / incongruity; (4) literalization / simplification; (5) repetition / echoic mention" (*Edge* 156). This list, while it touches on the most important signals of irony (almost all of which we will return to in the discussion of specific ironies in Corneille's theater), is far from complete. It is the nature of irony to resist all efforts at exhaustiveness of description.[18] Less precise as a category of ironic signal, but no less true for its lack of precision, is context. Muecke speaks of "l'incompatibilité du sens littéral du texte avec son contexte" ("Analyses" 491), which is related to Hutcheon's third category (incongruity). One particular context that fairly often signals irony is the intertextual reference. The reader is invited to perceive the contrast between the implicitly paired texts, such as when Dorante, in the earlier editions of *Le Menteur*, makes explicit reference to *Le Cid* (1.1).

Most signals of irony do not offer certainty, but rather raise the possibility that an ironic reading might be appropriate. Overly clear signals of irony are often considered with disdain, which may explain why sarcasm is at times not included in discussions of verbal irony or why the repetition of "Brutus is an honourable man" in Shakespeare's *Julius Caesar* is considered excessive. Hutcheon sums it up well: "The problem is that, as soon as an irony signal becomes fixed and thus direct, it loses its usefulness as a marker of ironic indirection and often gets ironized itself" (*Edge* 149).

Thus we are left with the issues of unknowable intent on the part of the long-dead ironist, the potentially overzealous interpreter of irony, and

signals that raise the possibility of irony but offer no guarantees. While that
may appear to be an unpromising assessment of the terrain, there remains
enough space in the interplay of the three, particularly if framed more opti-
mistically—the intuition of intent, the informed and prudent judgment of
the interpreter, and signals of varying clarity—to discover much about the
role of irony in Corneille's theater. Green defends a comparable undertaking,
his *Irony in the Medieval Romance*, in terms that I would like to echo:

> I concede that there is such a thing as a false hunt for irony
> and that there is a danger of subjectively turning medieval
> literature into an image of our own modern concerns. Yet
> I also think that, by taking this into account and paying
> due regard to signals built into the text, it is possible to
> isolate from the examples where differences of opinion
> are still possible a number of cases where the presence of
> irony is much more likely. (35)

I acknowledge that it is incumbent upon me to make a convincing case—cases
actually, as irony takes so many forms—and that some difference of opinion
is inevitable. By relying on all three—intent, reception, and signals—in
varying combinations, I hope to enlarge and alter our perspective on the
works of Corneille.

The Dramatic Context

We alluded briefly above to the importance of context to the discussion of irony. The most immediate context here is the dramatic one. Irony in
everyday life and in theater are significantly different, although the theatrical performance shares the orality and physical presence of the real world.
Unlike everyday life, however, theater resembles irony in that both have an
intrinsically double nature which makes theater a privileged setting for the
latter. It is not an accident that irony is almost universal in theater, something
one would not say of other literary forms.[19] François Hédelin d'Aubignac
himself, in the single sentence he devotes to irony in his *Pratique du théâtre*
(1657), notes its theatrical nature: "L'ironie est encore une figure du Poëme
Dramatique, et de sa nature elle est théâtrale; car en disant par moquerie le
contraire de ce qu'elle veut faire entendre sérieusement, elle porte avec soi
un déguisement, et fait un jeu qui n'est pas désagréable" (4:318).

On the simplest level, the space itself of the theater is a double one, at
once physically real and yet completely fictional. Theatrical representation
reproduces the physical presence of "real life" and allows for the use of the first
category of ironic signals discussed above, such as intonation, facial expres-

sion, and gesture. It also favors the recreation of the basic ironic roles typical
in a natural-speech context: the ironist, the ironist's victim, and the receiver
for the irony.[20] When both Hamon (111) and Anne-Marie Paillet-Guth (20)
call theater a privileged context for irony, it is to these forms of doubling that
they refer. However, I believe one may go considerably further.

As has been often noted, the actor is double as well, simultaneously
him- or herself and the character being played. If the obvious gap between
the two is ignored or well-hidden, the audience may well not perceive any
irony, but if it is marked (one has only to think of Jack Nicholson in almost
any of his roles), one is left with a disturbing sense of undecidability. This
issue is brought to the fore in act 5 of *L'Illusion comique* where Clindor plays
the role of a *seigneur anglais* without the spectators (including his father Pridamant) being aware of the doubling. His resurrection after being killed on
stage reminds us forcefully, and precisely because we did not *notice* it, that
all actors (including the one playing Clindor) are double.

The relationship between irony and theater works in both directions;
not only does the theater resemble the situation of irony, but the opposite
is true as well. To the extent that one says one thing but means something
quite different (verbal irony), one may be engaged in role-playing. "Dans
une énonciation ironique, le locuteur se met lui-même (lui-même devenu
autre) en scène. L'ironie est donc d'essence théâtrale, plus orale qu'écrite"
(Géraud 16). It has long been noted that a significant number of Corneille's
characters are given to rather dramatic self-representation.[21] The thematics of
illusion and reality, of *être* and *paraître*, are examples of theatrical doubling
and lend themselves readily to irony.

The most important aspect of the double nature of the dramatic context involves the source of the words spoken on stage. There are essentially
two channels of communication in the theatrical speech act: from character
A to character B and from playwright to audience (see Ubersfeld 130). The
playwright and the character speak simultaneously through the same words,
but these same words can have different meanings if one interprets their
source to be one or the other. The potential for implicit dissonance between
the two voices, for ironic gaps between them, is a rich source of irony. The
result may be a kind of double intentionality, whereby the character has no
intention of being ironic and is unconscious of the ironic impact of his or
her words, while the playwright fully intends irony. As we shall see, Corneille
exploits this potential in numerous situations. Furthermore, the separation
between the two channels of communication may break down; while the
audience was never to my knowledge brought inside the world of the play in
the seventeenth century, it was not uncommon in comedy for the author to
address the public directly (*parabase*) or otherwise collapse the world of the

fiction into the world of the spectator, thereby "ironizing and subverting of the autonomy of the artifact" (Rosenmeyer 33). Whether through distance or complete absence of distance between the two channels of communication in theater, the double nature of dramatic speech is marked and thereby made ripe for ironic treatment.

DIRECTIONS

It is obvious from the preceding discussion that irony does not take a single form and that it cannot be located and isolated with utter certainty. The variety and complexity of irony coupled with the variety and complexity of Corneille's theatrical output is unlikely to produce a simple picture. I have chosen to use irony as the organizing principle for my study because, first, it allows for a deeper understanding of irony and the interpretive problems that it inevitably poses, and second, it is more organic, allowing for a global understanding of irony's place in Corneille's œuvre.

The study itself is divided into two parts, "Evident Irony" and "Signals of Possible Irony." "Evident Irony" entails a significant degree of certainty that irony is present. Thus, part 1 will establish the manifest and substantial presence of irony in Corneille's plays. I divide this part into three chapters that correspond to the categories typically associated with the term *irony*: dramatic, verbal, and situational. The paramount division lies between verbal and situational irony, that is, between irony intended by a speaker and conveyed by his or her words and irony that is rooted in a situation and signaled by an incongruity of some sort. I include and begin with dramatic irony, which is in large measure situational, because it is the form of irony most commonly associated with theater and it often entails a high degree of certainty. Part 2 focuses on possible ironies (those that elicit some doubt) and is organized by the various kinds of signals that allow us to perceive or suspect irony. While the terrain is indeed more precarious, it is also stimulating. I make reference to the basic division between verbal and situational irony in part 2, but because the signals of possible irony are sometimes predominantly situational (e.g., symmetry) and sometimes predominantly verbal (e.g., echoic mention), and most often both (e.g., repetition or incongruity), it is more fruitful to foreground the signals of possible irony instead.

In dealing with Corneille's theater, I expand the domain to include his prefaces, *examens*, and other paratextual material, as well as his theoretical writings on the theater in the *Trois Discours sur le poème dramatique*. Paratextual elements of all sorts are particularly conducive to signaling irony, because it is through them that the author indicates his or her intentions (Schoentjes 177) and establishes a communicative pact with the reader (Hamon 80). Indeed, the most important reason to include these texts is that they come directly from the playwright. Whereas Corneille is heard only indirectly in his plays through the voices of his characters, here his voice is unfiltered and direct.[22]

I have chosen to treat all plays equally in the sense that the attention paid to each will be strictly a function of the significance of the irony found or suspected therein. An ironic remapping of Corneille's œuvre will thus privilege *La Suite du Menteur* over *Le Cid*, for instance. In any event, it is not a question of weighing one play against another. Analyses will focus not on entire plays, but, varyingly, on different features of a work, and will appear in conjunction with the kinds of evident or possible irony in question. The considerable variety in the depth and length of these analyses will be a function of several factors: the nature of the irony being examined, the degree to which Corneille employs different kinds of irony, and the specific ends to which he uses it. While in some cases the use of irony may have implications for the interpretation of an entire play, I believe that going too far with what is often a localized feature will generally be counterproductive to understanding Corneille's theater better. Corneille did not write ironic plays; rather he employed irony, suggested irony, and even struggled with it (e.g., the irony of fate). My focus will thus be on irony as a local feature and on the broader implications for Corneille's theater as a whole.

[Margin handwritten note: i. irony as a local feature + implications for C's theater as a whole]

NOTES

[1]"Que dans une tragédie classique, l'ironie ne soit pas incompatible avec le sérieux de la générosité et de l'héroïsme, deux siècles avant le drame romantique, voilà ce que les contemporains, et à leur suite Voltaire, admettront difficilement" (Paillet-Guth 24).

[2]Paillet-Guth has written an enlightening article on the subject entitled "L'ironie dans *Nicomède.*" See also Yarrow (*Corneille* 170) and Fumaroli ("Rhétorique" 318).

[3]Berrendonner discusses "l'absence totale d'homogénéité des phénomènes rassemblés sous la définition traditionnelle de l'ironie" (177).

[4]Furetière defines irony thus: "Figure dont se sert l'orateur pour insulter à son adversaire, le railler, et le blasmer en faisant semblant de le loüer. L'ironie consiste dans le ton, aussi-bien que dans les paroles. Les contre-vérités sont les plus fortes ironies."

[5]Schoentjes states that "L'ironie met donc nécessairement en présence deux sens contradictoires dans une aire de tension; l'écart ironique naît du fait que l'ironie exprime toujours l'un *et* l'autre, le oui *et* le non" (93–94).

[6]This is related to Booth's "unstable irony" and Perrin's concept of "cynisme" (164). Jankélévitch describes Socrates's maieutic in a similar fashion: "Tous il [Socrate] les accule dans l'impasse, il les jette dans la perplexité de l'*aporia* qui est le trouble symptomatique engendré par l'ironie" (*L'Ironie* [1964] 12).

[7]According to Jankélévitch, "L'ironiste joue sérieusement, *severe ludit*, mais tantôt l'accent est sur *severe*, tantôt sur *ludit*" (*L'Ironie* [1964] 130).

[8]Not everyone interprets the Greek word in the same way. According to Tiefenbrun, "irony (*eironeia*) from the Greek originally meant 'dissimulation' especially through understatement. Irony involves the art of the hidden, the elusive, the oblique" (*Signs*

144). For Hutcheon as well *eironeia* suggests dissimulation (*Edge* 51). Gay-Crosier ascribes to "l'étymon grec *eirôneia*...la triple fonction de dissimulation, d'oblicité et d'écart" (85).

[9]Tiefenbrun entitles her book *Signs of the Hidden*. Epstein attacks her for this kind of reductionism: "Tieffenbrun [sic] treats the study of irony as an effort 'to penetrate the hidden,' as if the critic's task were to somehow restore transparency to the relationship between the sign and the truth it signifies, which has been deliberately obscured by the ironist" (31).

[10]"We virtually always think of irony as having an author, even in real life, as our names for such irony reveal: Irony of Fate, Irony of God, Irony of Things, etc. Not to think of an author here is the exception rather than the rule" (Knox 56). Murphy's Law is grounded in precisely such a belief: that there is an intending superior source involved in all situational irony.

[11]Stringfellow raises the possibility of unconscious irony, that is, saying something ironic without realizing that one is doing so (27).

[12]Booth points to the problem of such uncontrolled enthusiasm: "For the determined ironist any anomaly or incongruity is ironic, and almost any phenomenon can be seen as incongruous in some light or other: what is not incongruous viewed locally will be found so when placed in a larger context" (236).

[13]All references to Corneille, unless otherwise indicated, are to Couton's three-volume edition of the *Œuvres complètes*.

[14]Corneille's famous epigram following Richelieu's death serves to underline the difficulty of interpretive certainty in this case:

> Qu'on parle mal ou bien du fameux Cardinal,
> Ma prose ni mes vers n'en diront jamais rien:
> Il m'a fait trop de bien pour en dire du mal,
> Il m'a fait trop de mal pour en dire du bien. (1:1062)

[15]"It is almost a miracle that irony is ever understood as an ironist might intend it to be: all ironies, in fact, are probably unstable ironies" (Hutcheon, *Edge* 195).

[16]Perrin points out that tone can be used either to signal or to mask ironic intent (147–48).

[17]In 1899, Alcanter de Brahm famously proposed an inverted question mark as a universal sign of the presence of irony. While it had its supporters, this sign was never widely accepted.

[18]Perrin, in a brilliant and subtle examination limited to verbal irony, discusses at length several specific signals: untruths (*contre-vérités*), an overly weak argument, and a position taken to the point of absurdity (this last is related to Hutcheon's second category) (179–224). Booth proposes "cognitive dissonance" (35), while Morel talks about a logical *faille* as a signal of irony (57).

[19]"It is not easy to think of a play from Aeschylus to Arrabal in which there is no ironic structure or no ironic situations or events" (Muecke, *Irony* 71).

[20]See Kerbrat-Orecchioni for a discussion of the operation of these three roles ("Problèmes" 17). Knox finds this arrangement to be inherently dramatic (53).

[21]"La plupart de ses personnages ont en commun une tendance à se donner en représentation à eux-mêmes et aux autres" (Rousset, *Littérature* 217). See also Hubert's *Corneille's Performative Metaphors*.

[22]Jaouën draws the distinction succinctly: "Cette œuvre [de Corneille] 'déserte de son créateur,' selon la belle expression d'Octave Nadal, est pourtant le produit d'un auteur furieusement 'présent' par le biais de ses examens et de ses discours" (63).

Chapter 2
Dramatic Irony

The most immediately evident category of irony in theater is dramatic irony. In the simplest terms it involves a significant discrepancy of awareness between an onstage character and the audience. The irony is rooted both in the antiphrastic relationship of knowledge and ignorance and secondarily in the opposition between the two channels of communication discussed at the end of the preceding chapter (that is, from one onstage character to another and from playwright to audience). The classic example of dramatic irony is Sophocles' *Œdipus Rex*, in which the eponymous character searches for Laïus's murderer, ignorant of his own guilt, while the audience knows from the start what he will discover only at the end. Indeed, Corneille's version of the myth, which we will deal with at length in this chapter, is rich in examples of dramatic irony.

Examining dramatic irony in detail reveals a considerably more complex device than the above definition and example would suggest. First of all, dramatic irony has a very wide range: it may be tragic, as in the example of Œdipus, or comic, as when in *La Place Royale*, Angélique believes that Alidor will carry her off, while in fact the audience shares Alidor's knowledge that Cléandre is to take his place. Dramatic irony may provide a source of suspense, or be almost trivial; it may be heavy-handed or subtle. There are three basic roles that need to be set out in order to discuss the operation of dramatic irony in Corneille's theater. These are the ones we mentioned in the introductory chapter as typical of irony in a natural-speech context: the ironist (or intending source of the irony), the audience for the irony (the receiver), and the ironist's victim. They are not always all on stage nor are they always embodied by three different characters, but they form the framework for the mechanism of dramatic irony. What differentiates dramatic irony from other forms of verbal irony is that it invariably involves both channels of communication: from character A to character B and from playwright to audience.

Within the basic framework of ignorance and knowledge, certain rules apply. There must always be an onstage victim of the dramatic irony, a character who is completely ignorant of something that someone else knows, such as Œdipus or Angélique in the examples above. The audience, as the privileged but not necessarily sole receiver, must always know whatever it

16

is that the onstage victim is unaware of. Next, while there may indeed be multiple receivers (on stage and off) and even multiple victims of the irony, there is only one intending source. That source may be an onstage character, or it may be the author behind a character's words. It goes without saying that in the context of the theater, the author speaks behind all characters. The author's voice becomes salient to our discussion essentially when there is a clear disjunction between his voice and the voice of the character. When the intending source of the irony is the author alone and not the onstage character, then the irony involves double voicing as well as the double meaning inherent in all verbal irony. There are thus two speakers, the character and the playwright, operating on two channels, meaning different things with the same words. The mechanism at work is a kind of double entendre. The disjunction between an onstage speaking character and the author who is the intending source of irony is a common and fertile source of dramatic irony.

One way to group examples of dramatic irony involves the voice of the playwright. If that voice is heard through, but distinct from, the voice of a character, then a direct channel of communication has been established between author and audience that exists on a plane other than that of the play itself. We will call this situation authorial dramatic irony. If the dramatic irony is rooted in the situation on stage or in the words and intentions of a character, the audience is still the receiver, but indirectly so.[23] We will call this stage-centered dramatic irony. Both encompass a broad range of possibilities that Corneille exploits to varying degrees.

Stage-Centered Dramatic Irony

Stage-centered dramatic irony may be more or less global or localized. *Héraclius* is based almost entirely on a stage-centered dramatic irony revolving around identity.[24] Whereas *Œdipe* is ignorant of his own true identity, Héraclius knows who he is. Others (Pulchérie, Phocas, Martian), however, do not, and as Héraclius progresses the situation becomes so complex that the hero himself begins to doubt his own knowledge concerning his identity. Far more localized stage-centered dramatic irony occurs in *Polyeucte* when Sévère eagerly waits to see his beloved Pauline, alone unaware that she has married Polyeucte (2.1). Unnecessary to the action of the play, this example serves primarily as a means for Corneille to dramatize the contrast between Sévère's love and excitement at the scene's outset and his shock and despair once he learns the truth. Equally localized is the dramatic irony of the last scene of *Rodogune*, in which Antiochus does not know the identity of his brother's assassin while the audience does. In all cases, the disparity in knowledge works to engage the audience. In the last example in particular,

Corneille creates thick suspense through the use of dramatic irony, as the audience fears that Antiochus's ignorance may lead him to drink the poison his mother has prepared for him.

Stage-centered dramatic irony is often a staple of comedy. On numerous occasions one character will tell another something both the speaker and the audience know to be untrue. For example, in *La Veuve*, Doris and Alcidon share a scene in which each seeks to convince the other of the depth of her/his love, while the audience knows that the speakers feel no such thing (2.5). Similarly, in *La Suivante*, Théante talks of his love for Amarante, but he and the audience are aware that he really loves Daphnis (1.6). *Le Menteur* is based on a kind of apprenticeship for both the audience and Cliton, teaching both to move from the position of victim of irony to that of complicit receiver of the dramatic irony created by Dorante's lies. Corneille stands this situation on its head in *La Suite du Menteur*, where Cliton's hard-won knowledge—that Dorante regularly deviates from the truth—becomes ignorance once more because of the latter's transformation from amoral suitor to a man of noble virtue.

Dramatic irony is often related to role-playing. A double entendre may signal to the audience that the speaker is assuming a different persona, as when Cléopâtre seemingly accedes to Antiochus's impassioned pleas to forgive and accept Rodogune by saying, "La Nature est trop forte" (*Rodogune* l. 1362). The audience, but not Antiochus, grasps that Cléopâtre's own "Nature" is tied to ruthless ambition rather than maternal love for her son. Indeed, there are a number of moments in *Rodogune* when Cléopâtre's duplicitous words are a source of dramatic irony. Because of her frequent monologues, the audience has strong indications, that is to say knowledge, about when she is being sincere and when she is playing a role. Such dramatic irony is evident when Cléopâtre opens act 5, scene 3 with "Approchez, mes enfants (car l'amour maternelle, / Madame [Rodogune], dans mon cœur vous tient déjà pour telle…)" (ll. 1559–61), and when she says to Antiochus and Rodogune as they are about to drink from the poisoned cup, "Le temps presse, et votre heur d'autant plus se diffère" (l. 1596). *Attila*, a character with significant similarities to Cléopâtre, also engages in ironic role-playing evident to the spectator when he disingenuously suggests possible husbands (other than himself) for Ildione (*Attila* 4.4). We know he is aware that his interlocutor, Ardaric, is in love with her. This type of play-acting, in which the audience knows what the character is up to, is also fairly common in comedy, as when Alidor pretends to have written a love letter to Clarine, while the audience knows that he is seeking to provoke Angélique into breaking off with him (*La Place Royale* 2.1-2), or when Lysandre pretends to be in love with Hippolyte in order to make Célidée jealous (*La Galerie du palais* 3.5). Similarly, in *La Suivante,* Florame assures his beloved Daphnis that God must be the source of the apparent miracle granting them permission to marry (ll. 939–40), all the while knowing full well, as does the audience, that its true source is Daphnis's father's desire to marry Florame's sister. A particularly egregious example of dramatic irony that involves role-playing occurs in *Le Cid* when the king tells Chimène that Rodrigue is dead (4.5). The king, the spectators, and the courtiers on stage all know that he is alive and well; it is Chimène alone who is the ignorant victim. The king's fabrication is an almost comic manifestation of a more serious dramatic irony: Chimène alone does not know that the king has pardoned Rodrigue (4.3) and that her pleas for justice will fall on deaf ears.[25]

Nicomède provides an unusual example of stage-centered dramatic irony, distinctive because of the presence of an onstage receiver for the speaker's irony. In the second scene of the play, Attale is unaware that the stranger to whom he is speaking is Nicomède. The latter, one of the most deliberately ironic characters in Corneille's theater, takes advantage of Attale's ignorance to mock him for the benefit of his onstage receiver, Laodice. She is obviously cognizant of Nicomède's identity, as is the audience. Muecke finds this sort of dramatic irony, with all three roles embodied by onstage characters, to be more "powerful" than those cases in which the recipient is the audience alone (*Irony* 81).[26]

AUTHORIAL DRAMATIC IRONY

If the dramatic irony is authorial rather than stage-centered, then the receiver will invariably be the audience alone (whether physically present or reading). In authorial dramatic irony, the author establishes complicity between himself and the audience. The onstage speaker does not intend to be ironic. In fact, it is not unusual in such situations for the onstage speaker to be the victim of the author's irony. Thus, in an admirable economy of means, knowledge and ignorance can be united in the words of a single onstage character. Referring to Laodice as she tries to discourage Attale from pursuing the princesse, Arsinoé says to her son, "Qu'est-ce qu'en sa fureur une femme n'essaie?" (*Nicomède* l. 1503). Through the queen's words Corneille reminds the audience that "femme furieuse" suits Arsinoé far better than it does Laodice.

A major category of authorial dramatic irony involves the author's reliance on information that he knows his audience will bring to the play. As Elaine Aston points out, "[T]he more the reader knows of a character's story, the greater the opportunity for irony" (26). Much use of this device is made in *Œdipe*, where every spectator knows that Œdipe kills his father and marries his mother. The spectator of *Pompée* knows that César will never marry Cléopâtre, and when in *Médée* Cléone defends Créuse's insistence on keeping Médée's dress by saying, "de s'en voir parée elle brûle d'envie," the audience is quick to appreciate the double meaning of the word "brûle." Similarly, when Camille says to Horace after he has killed Curiace,

> Puissent tant de malheurs accompagner ta vie
> Que tu tombes au point de me porter envie,
> Et toi, bientôt souiller par quelque lâcheté
> Cette gloire si chère à ta brutalité
>
> (*Horace* ll. 1291–94)

the audience appreciates the ironically prophetic impact of her words because we, unlike the characters, know what will occur. The structure is repeated once again in *La Toison d'or* when Hypsipyle warns Médée about Jason: "Les lieux aident au choix, et peut-être qu'en Grèce / Quelque troisième objet surprendrait sa tendresse" (ll. 1296–97). What Hypsipyle foretells out of jealousy, the audience knows to be prophetically true. Because the audience's knowledge of what is to come makes such events seem inevitable, this form of dramatic irony has a deep structural link to what is called the irony of fate, a subject which will be discussed in detail in chapter 4. In fact, Corneille does not often employ this type of dramatic irony, particularly when it pertains to events that will transpire within the play, because, generally speaking, his dramaturgy is based on surprise. Obviously, dramatic irony works against surprise. Corneille seeks to astound his audience and arouse their admiration, goals that he does not often sacrifice for the sake of collusion between author and audience. This may explain why so few of his plays deal with subjects or even characters that would be well known to the audience.

There is an unusual and playful variant of this type of dramatic irony in *Sophonisbe*. The story of this queen was known to seventeenth-century audiences chiefly through Mairet's 1634 tragedy entitled *La Sophonisbe*. The play was so popular in fact that it was still being performed in 1663 when Corneille's *Sophonisbe* appeared. In the latter, Corneille seems to play on the audience's knowledge, not of Roman history, but of Mairet's version of the story. When Syphax says to his wife, "Mais que deviendrez-vous si je meurs au combat? / Qui sera votre appui si le sort des batailles / Vous rend un corps sans vie au pied de nos murailles?" (ll. 378–80), the audience expects his death and knows that Sophonisbe will turn happily to her former fiancé Massinisse. Corneille, however, converts what appeared to be dramatic irony into surprise: Syphax is not killed in battle as he is in Mairet's version, but returns, albeit defeated. The playwright defends his choice not to have Syphax die on the grounds of historical veracity, stating in his preface, "[L]a mort de Syphax était une fiction de M. Mairet" (3:383). One cannot help but espy a playful manipulation of expected dramatic irony at the expense of the audience.

In the most common form of dramatic irony in Corneille's theater, audience knowledge is based on information provided by the play itself. Examples include misinterpretation on the part of a speaker, as when Auguste says to Cinna and Maxime, "Je vois trop que vos cœurs n'ont point pour moi de fard" (*Cinna* l. 628), while the audience is aware that they are planning his assassination, or when Grimoald speaks of the traitorous Garibalde in terms of "des mains si fidèles!" (*Pertharite* l. 532), while the latter's perfidy is evident to the audience. In *Polyeucte*, Pauline frets at length about what may be transpiring at the scene of the sacrifice (3.1). Her ignorance leads her to worry about possible friction between Polyeucte and Sévère, while the audience's knowledge leads to a different preoccupation altogether: whether Polyeucte has carried through with a threat to overturn the idols. When the speaker is a minor character, the communication appears more direct between playwright and audience, as when Cléon says to Polyeucte, "Seigneur, Félix vous mande au Temple; / La victime est choisie, et le Peuple à genoux, / Et pour sacrifier on n'attend plus que vous" (ll. 627–29). The audience, unlike Polyeucte, knows that the young son-in-law will become the sacrificial victim. Similarly, when Oronte says to Cléopâtre in *Rodogune*, "Votre sincérité s'y fait assez paraître" (l. 1587), the audience's ability to read the word "sincérité" ironically is based solely on what we already know of Cléopâtre's personality. Because the speaker is a minor character, his ignorance is not itself of significance.

The complicity between author and audience seems in such cases to operate outside of the play's action. One might even perceive a threat to the theatrical illusion, as in the case where Philiste and Mélisse both make frequent reference to vision and eyes at precisely the moment when she has mistaken him for someone else as they speak in the dark (*La Suite du Menteur* 4.5).[27] The information or knowledge need not be absolutely certain for dramatic irony to occur. When Flavian comments to Tite, at a point when both are completely unaware that Bérénice has come to Rome, "Si vous la revoyiez, je plaindrais Domitie" (*Tite et Bérénice* l. 375), the audience automatically suspects that he will indeed see her, all the more so since Albin has hinted that he may have organized her return (ll. 343–46) and because of the title of the play.

A third kind of authorial dramatic irony comes to light when one rereads or reviews a play. It is a common feature of most literature to contain proleptic clues that are imperceptible at first, but that enhance a second exposure to the work. Again, examples in Corneille's theater are numerous and often quite playful. Arsinoé reacts to the news that Nicomède has escaped by saying to Attale, "Ah, mon fils, qu'il est partout des traîtres!" (l. 1755), unaware, as is the audience initially, that the "traître" in question is Attale. When Cléopâtre refers to Séleucus's likely sorrow at losing both throne and Rodogune by saying, "Mais j'en saurai sur l'heure adoucir l'amertume" (*Rodogune* l. 1384), we do not realize until later that "adoucir" will entail murdering him, nor can we appreciate the prophetic nature of Sertorius's words to Perpenna, "Et ma tête abattue ébranlerait la vôtre" (*Sertorius* l. 1422), until a second viewing. The most significant site for such retrospective dramatic irony is *Héraclius*. Much of what Héraclius says has a completely different meaning depending on whether one believes him to be Martian or Héraclius. That Corneille intended this dramatic irony is clear from what he says in his *Examen*:

> [M]ais je n'ai pu avoir assez d'adresse pour faire entendre les équivoques ingénieux, dont est rempli tout ce que dit Héraclius à la fin de ce premier acte, et on ne les peut comprendre que par une réflexion, après que la pièce est finie, et qu'il est entièrement reconnu, ou dans une seconde représentation. (2:359)

Corneille clearly delights in embedding such clues in his theater, thereby rewarding a second experience of his work with the complicitous pleasure of dramatic irony. This technique is all the more noteworthy in a playwright who is so committed to surprising his audience; evidently he takes pains to ensure that a rereading or second viewing will contain significant compensations for the loss of the element of surprise.

The fourth type of authorial dramatic irony is very similar to the first in that it depends on knowledge that the spectator brings to the play. It differs significantly, however, in that it depends on allusion to situations beyond the limits of the play's action. Such allusions may be more or less obvious. When Œdipe says, "Quel Énigme!" (l. 1693) in reference to the situation in Corinthe, and Corneille pointedly capitalizes "énigme," the Sphinx's riddle comes to mind immediately. *Pompée* is particularly rich in such external dramatic ironies, but their range from the obvious to the subtle is striking. At one extreme we find Cléopâtre saying, "Ainsi finit Pompée, et peut-être qu'un jour / César éprouvera même sort à son tour" (ll. 587-88). César's assassination is, of course, likely to be common knowledge for the play's audience. Somewhat less obvious is Marc Antoine's enthusiastic description of Cléopâtre's beauty (ll. 946-52); the audience may or may not know that he will later be her lover. More subtle are Cornélie's threats of future defeat

directed at César. As H. T. Barnwell points out, "All her references to her allies in North Africa and elsewhere have a hollow and ironic ring when we realize that, in terms of history, each name mentioned spells defeat" (*Pompée* 202). It is unclear how large a portion of the contemporary audience would have come to the play with that knowledge. When in *Sophonisbe* Lélius makes reference to Prusias and Attale as examples of Roman allies who rule their own kingdom with complete independence and authority (ll. 1748-52), the audience may espy irony by recalling Corneille's depiction of Prusias's servitude to Rome in *Nicomède*.

The traditional triangular structure of an ironist, victim, and receiver is particularly strong in this fourth type of authorial dramatic irony. Not only does the audience, who serves as the receiver, have knowledge unavailable to the characters, but some members of the audience may know more than others. While "Quel Énigme!" is awkwardly heavy-handed, there is some palpable pleasure in noticing the role of Marc Antoine, and even more in perceiving the implications of Cornélie's references. It is the pleasure of private complicity with the author. One should note that discerning this particular type of dramatic irony is not necessary to a full understanding of the play. While all irony runs the risk of not being understood and interpreted as intended, here the consequences of imperception are negligible, because the knowledge involved is extraneous to the play's action. Perceiving the irony in such situations is a kind of delicious bonus that operates much like intertextuality in general, affirming the spectator's intelligence, underscoring his or her complicity with the author, and enriching the aesthetic value of the work. For instance, one may understand Théudas's explanation of Pollux's whereabouts in act 5, scene 1 of *Médée* as nothing more than a means of removing the latter definitively from the stage: Jason's loyal friend "court à grande hâte aux noces de sa sœur / Dont bientôt Ménélas doit être possesseur" (ll. 1343–44). However, if one recalls that Pollux's sister is Helen, the coincidence of that doomed marriage with the union of Créuse and Jason adds something to the audience's experience: it is as if Corneille were winking at us, playfully embedding an allusion for only some to share. Thus, while we may call this a form of evident irony, it is only evident to the audience who brings the necessary knowledge to the play. For the others, this kind of authorial dramatic irony is simply invisible.

In most cases, the references made in this fourth type of authorial dramatic irony are related in some fashion to the action of the play, striking additional chords in the complex histories and legends that Corneille is bringing to the stage. Occasionally, however, Corneille eschews all relevance in favor of pure playfulness: in *Tite et Bérénice*, Bérénice suggests a number of possible brides for Tite: "Seigneur, faites-moi grâce, épousez Sulpitie, /

Ou Camille, ou Sabine, et non pas Domitie" (ll. 971–72). The presence on that list of both Sabine and Camille, the heroines of *Horace*, cannot be mere coincidence.[28] Corneille's playfully gratuitous reference to his earlier play will not be noted by all; perceiving it, however, may distract one from the serious tone of Bérénice's words in *Tite et Bérénice*, or it may encourage the audience to seek parallels between the heroines of *Tite et Bérénice* and those of *Horace*.

At times, uncertainty may arise as to whether dramatic irony was intended or not. Martian responds to the announcement that Pulchérie has made a choice concerning a husband with "Quel qu'il soit, il sera l'Arrêt de mon trépas" (*Pulchérie* l. 1519). Are we or are we not entitled to hear the comic shadow of a sexual innuendo coming from Corneille accompanying Martian's grave prediction, specifically, that sex at his age would kill him, given our knowledge of Martian's advanced age (and Corneille's in 1672)? Nothing prevents us from perceiving such dramatic irony, but its irrelevance to the play's action makes it difficult to defend.

Combining Stage-Centered and Authorial Dramatic Irony

While I have divided Corneille's dramatic irony into the two categories of stage-centered and authorial, they may in fact sometimes work in tandem. Cinna tries to dissuade Auguste from abdicating by saying, "Un plus puissant Démon veille sur vos années [than over César's], / On a dix fois sur vous attenté sans effet, / Et qui l'a voulu perdre au même instant l'a fait" (*Cinna* ll. 434–36). Cinna, at least consciously, does not believe that Auguste is divinely protected from assassination, for he is risking his own future in the plot to assassinate the emperor. Insofar as the audience knows that in act 2 Cinna has access to information that Auguste does not have, specifically that there is an assassination plot against the emperor, this is an example of stage-centered dramatic irony. At the same time, it is authorial dramatic irony, because Corneille can depend on his audience to know that Auguste will not be assassinated and thus that Cinna's words, unbeknownst to him, are in fact true. Cinna's assertion presents a complex, double-layered dramatic irony of which Auguste and Cinna are both in turn the victims.

Stage-centered and authorial dramatic irony are combined in a vertical, rather than horizontal, fashion when multiple receivers result from disparities in knowledge. In the case of *Héraclius*, on the one hand the reader knows the true identities of Héraclius and Martian because the list of characters is explicit (e.g., "HÉRACLIUS, fils de l'empereur Maurice, cru Martian fils de Phocus"). The spectator, on the other hand, is completely in the dark until the second act and thus cannot grasp the dramatic irony of the initial situation nor Héraclius's many double entendres. Thereafter, while the spectator's knowledge provides contrast with the ignorance of Phocas (or even Martian), it never equals the reader's knowledge, for the spectator will share Héraclius's own doubts about his identity, while the reader, assured by the author's voice in the list of characters, will not. The situation is even more complex in *L'Illusion comique* where there are three audiences: readers, spectators, and the privileged onstage spectator, Pridamant.[29] For most of the play, reader and spectator, by virtue of their positions exterior to the play's action, as well as their awareness of certain conventions (e.g., heroes of comedies are not executed in the third act), enjoy a position superior to that of Pridamant. In the last act, however, positions shift, and the spectator joins Pridamant in ignorance of the fact that Clindor and the others are merely playing roles in a play. The reader, again because of stage directions, comprehends the full situation and enjoys the dramatic irony of Pridamant's misinterpretation of the onstage murder.[30]

In essence, dramatic irony plays with two variables that appear to stand in a paradoxical relationship to each other: complicity and distance. Complicity between intending source and receiver is universal, whether those two roles are occupied by two onstage characters, the author and the audience, or some combination thereof, and it is rooted in shared, privileged knowledge. Distance between intending source and victim is necessary as well and is based on the disparity in knowledge between the two. In all cases, the two channels of dramatic communication are brought into play: whatever other relationships of complicity or distance obtain, there must be complicity between intending source of the dramatic irony and the receiver just as there must be distance between the receiver and the victim.

ŒDIPE

No other play in the Western tradition so famously embodies the notion of dramatic irony as Sophocles' *Œdipus Rex*. Every spectator knows what discoveries await Œdipus's quest for knowledge of Laïus's killer. But the dramatic irony of this play is not based solely on the information that the audience brings to the play. It is compounded by Œdipus's own curious combination of knowledge, ignorance, and blindness, for oracles have informed him that it is his fate to kill his father and marry his mother.

Corneille takes a different path with the same basic material. Despite the fact that it was quite unusual for the playwright to employ a subject that was well-known to his audience, Corneille assumes extensive audience foreknowledge when writing his play, and uses it to create dramatic irony. Where he differs radically from Sophocles is in the play of knowledge and ignorance within Œdipe himself. By reducing the prominence of the oracles (see Louvat and Escola, "Statut" 458 and Matzat 164), Corneille creates an

Œdipe who is a far more innocent victim of the gods' irony.[31] The irony of fate does not so much disappear as become a simple precondition of the play's action, not worthy of further attention. The second radical alteration that Corneille makes to the traditional myth involves the addition of surprise. On the one hand, there are the surprises occasioned by the existence of a daughter born to Jocaste and Laïus as well as this daughter's love for Thésée, himself an unexpected newcomer to this part of the Œdipus myth. On the other hand, the very inclusion of surprise within the unfolding of a well-known plot is itself startling. The conjunction of dramatic irony and surprise is a remarkable theatrical experiment, even if many have found that Corneille was not entirely successful in making the two work together. The playwright in no way masks the dramatic irony or diminishes it in favor of surprise. In fact, he multiplies the dramatic ironies almost excessively, thus calling attention to the basic clash between the predetermined and the unexpected.

A large portion, but by no means all, of the dramatic irony we encounter in *Œdipe* is based on the audience's foreknowledge of the underlying situation. At times Corneille is overbearing: Œdipe tells Dircé that he would rather suffer the sorry fate predicted for Dircé's brother rather than break his word promising her to Hémon (ll. 484-86). Œdipe, of course, is unaware that he is referring to himself.[32] There are many such examples in the play. Corneille shows a particular fondness for evocative vocabulary, especially *yeux* (thirty-six occurrences) and *œil* (six), which remind the audience of the fate that awaits Œdipe. The indications of dramatic irony in this domain are at times heavy-handed, as when Thésée says to Jocaste, "N'enfonçons toutefois, ni votre œil, ni le mien / Dans ce profond abîme, où nous ne voyons rien" (ll. 1171-72). This use of certain words to trigger dramatic irony extends even to the play's *Examen*, in which Corneille describes the experience of tackling a subject that had been so brilliantly rendered by his predecessors: "Comme j'ai pris une autre route que la leur, il m'a été impossible de me rencontrer avec eux" (3:19). As Goodkin notes, one immediately thinks of Œdipe and Laïus's meeting at the triple crossroads (151). Corneille thus incongruously juxtaposes Œdipe's confrontation with Laïus and his own encounter with his dramatic predecessors, especially Sophocles.

Corneille is often inventive in his use of audience foreknowledge. By initially separating the question of identity from that of Laïus's killer, Corneille places Jocaste in the woeful and novel situation of discovering that her second husband murdered her first, while at the same time knowing that either her son or her daughter must be sacrificed to the gods to rid the city of the plague. Dramatic irony comes to the fore when Jocaste reproaches the gods:

Et comme si leur haine impuissante, ou timide,
N'osait le faire ensemble inceste, et parricide,
Elle partage à deux un sort si peu commun,
Afin de me donner deux coupables, pour un.

(ll. 1541–44)

Jocaste refers to Thésée with the "le" in the second line, but we all know that
the true referent is Œdipe, that the incest in question is not between siblings
as she imagines, and that the gods have done precisely what she faults them
for being too timid to do.

Corneille is also surprisingly playful. The king begins the process of
recognition of who he is and what he has done, which the audience of course
already knows, with an informal, bantering tone suitable to a cocktail party.
After essentially asking Phorbas, "Haven't I seen you somewhere before?"[33]
and going so far as to pinpoint the time frame ("Il y pourrait avoir entre
quinze, et vingt ans," l. 1427), he exclaims, "Ah! je te reconnais, ou je suis
fort trompé. / C'est un de mes brigands à la mort échappé" (ll. 1431–32).
Corneille thereby accentuates the contrast between Œdipe's blindness and
the moment of recognition, but the casual tone is strangely inappropriate to
the circumstances. The dramatic irony becomes excessive when, in the course
of a description of the older man he killed at the crossroads, Œdipe says,
"On en peut voir en moi la taille, et quelques traits" (l. 1464), and hints at a
cri du sang: "Et tout mon cœur s'émeut de le voir aux abois" (l. 1468). The
author is also playful about dramatic irony when he has Jocaste accuse Dircé
of being a "fille dénaturée" (l. 294). The audience is thereby reminded that
Dircé is the only one of Jocaste's children to whom the adjective does *not*
apply. Furthermore, the tragic moment of recognition in Sophocles' play is
seemingly mocked by Corneille when Phorbas hems and haws about revealing
to Jocaste who killed Laïus: "Mais si je vous nommais quelque personne chère,
/ Hémon votre neveu, Créon votre seul frère, / Ou le prince Lycus, ou le Roi
votre époux…?" (ll. 1409–12). Corneille is seeking to build suspense into the
situation, as the onstage characters do not yet *know* Laïus's killer's identity,
but the parlor-game tone ("What if I said it were…?") coupled with audience
foreknowledge undermine the tragic potential of the scene. Furthermore,
Corneille overplays the dramatic irony of audience knowledge of Œdipe's
identity in a way that raises the possibility of parody.[34] Œdipe reacts to the
news that he is not the son of the king of Corinthe with "Je ne dois plus
qu'à moi tout ce que j'eus de rang" (l. 1720), a clear echo of Don Sanche.
In the earlier *Don Sanche d'Aragon*, the hero trumpets his self-reliance with
"pour mes parents je nomme mes exploits, / Ma valeur est ma race, et mon
bras est mon père" (ll. 252–53), itself an echo of *Don Quixote*, as Georges

Couton points out (Corneille 2:1439). The dramatic irony of Don Sanche's
true identity, while widely suspected, would only have been perceptible on
a second viewing or reading; here Œdipe's heroic pretentions are debased by
the dramatic irony of the audience's foreknowledge.

While Œdipe is not the intending source of the irony in the example
above, Thésée knowingly engages in dramatic irony when he pretends to be
Jocaste's son. He plays with the line between sexual and fraternal love at the
alarmed Dircé's expense ("J'ai mêmes yeux encore, et vous, mêmes appas," l.
1235), knowing full well, as does the audience, that he is not her brother.

As if the dramatic irony inherited from Sophocles' and Seneca's versions
of the play did not suffice, on three occasions Corneille takes advantage of
probable audience knowledge about events outside of the play's action to
create further dramatic irony. First, when Thésée insists, "Mais pour ce parricide, il est plus que certain / Que ce ne fut jamais un crime de ma main"
(ll. 1199–1200), the "jamais" may remind the audience that, in ironic coun-
terpoint to his assertion, he would indeed be responsible for his own father's
death by neglecting to change his ship's sails from black to white upon his
return from Crete. Second, Phorbas alludes to the substance of the Sphinx's
riddle when he discusses the unlikelihood that he might recognize an adult
Œdipe: "Je sais ainsi que vous que les traits de l'enfance / N'ont avec ceux
d'un homme aucune ressemblance" (ll. 1373–74). Finally, and none too
subtly, Corneille has Œdipe say to Thésée, "Prenez soin d'apaiser les discords
de mes fils" (l. 1875). Étéocle and Polynice will, as is well known, kill each
other. All three examples depend, in order to function as dramatic irony, on
the knowledge of Greek mythology that the audience brings to the play.

The sheer volume of examples makes it clear that, far from minimizing
the role of dramatic irony in his version of *Œdipe*, Corneille uses it extensively,
perhaps even excessively. What is fascinating is that dramatic irony should
normally function to reinforce the tragic environment, to make the irony of
fate the centerpiece of the play, but here it does not do so. Even more often
than he refers to the story of Œdipus that we all know, Corneille displaces that
story, changing it and downplaying the role of Œdipe while foregrounding
the notions of free will and romantic love so that the audience remains off
balance. Here and in other modifications that Corneille operates upon the
original material, he seems to be turning dramatic irony on its head. Counting
on his audience to know the Sophoclean or Senecan versions, he both fulfills
and scorns the expectations the audience brings to the play, retaining a broad
range of dramatic irony based on audience knowledge and yet dazzling us
with our own ignorance. At the same time, he incorporates into the framework of the inherited story a host of his own preoccupations with power, the
monarchy, and legitimacy. It is no wonder, then, that Bénédicte Louvat and

Marc Escola decribe *Œdipe* as "un inceste dramaturgique" ("Statut" 470).
Most astonishing, Corneille adopts the dramatic subject that exemplified
classical tragedy for Aristotle and many others and renders it untragic. That
this was perhaps not a wise choice is beside the point. Whether tragic or
not, the feature that enjoys pride of place in Corneille's play as well as in the
tragic versions of antiquity is dramatic irony.

*

Dramatic irony is ubiquitous in *Œdipe*, and relatively widespread in
Corneille's theater in general. The notion of the two channels of dramatic
communication is central to dramatic irony, and its centrality is accentuated in this body of plays by the the fact that the majority of examples are
authorial rather than stage-centered. Stage-centered irony camouflages the
role of the audience through the presence of an onstage receiver, just as it
invariably cloaks the role of the author behind that of the onstage intender
of the irony. In the case of authorial dramatic irony, the two channels are
distinct because they operate at cross-purposes. Attention is thereby focused
on the two channels and the inherent disparity between them, with the result
that the dramatic irony is more conspicuous. Most importantly, the broad
presence of dramatic irony provides clear evidence of Corneille's intention
to be ironic. While some of the dramatic ironies we noted require considerable knowledge on the part of the audience, most require merely that we
retain what we have seen and heard on stage. As such, this is evident irony,
of a sort that entails little or no doubt. The widespread and substantial use
that Corneille makes of dramatic irony, and particularly authorial dramatic
irony, also points to an appreciation of its potential for playful and pleasur-
able complicity between playwright and audience.

NOTES

[23]An exception occurs when the onstage intending source directly addresses the
audience, as discussed near the end of chapter 1 (*parabase*), an option that Corneille
does not favor. Corneille does employ *parabase* on two occasions: Cliton addresses
the audience in the final lines of both *Le Menteur* and *La Suite du Menteur*, but these
are not instances of dramatic irony.
[24]Schoentjes notes the affinity between irony and hidden identity (58).
[25]"Crois que dorénavant Chimène a beau parler, / Je ne l'écoute plus que pour la
consoler" (*Le Cid* ll. 1265–66).
[26]Paillet-Guth explains the frequency of scenes involving three characters in this play
as a function of this classic ironic triangle (20). Forestier discusses the centrality of
the same mechanism in Rotrou's *L'Heureux naufrage* ("Ironie" 555).
[27]Philiste: "Ah! s'il en est besoin, j'en jure, et par vos yeux" (l. 1435); Mélisse: "Vous
revoir en ce lieu m'en persuade mieux" (l. 1436).
[28]Stegmann includes the following note in his edition of the play: "Aucun de ces
noms ne figure dans ses sources historiques. Corneille ne cherchait pas bien loin des

noms vraisemblables" (*OC* 743).

[29] I am deliberately excluding Alcandre because he is the onstage director rather than a mere spectator. Clearly, the discrepancy in knowledge between him and Pridamant creates its own potential for dramatic irony.

[30] In fact the situation is complicated further by different editions. The editions published between 1644 and 1668 convey the information to the reader (e.g., "Isabelle représentant Hippolyte") while the 1682 edition does not, thus placing the reader in the same position as the spectator.

[31] A curious aspect of this reduction is Thésée's suggestion that the oracle of Delphi may be corrupt: "Delphes a pu vous faire une fausse réponse, / L'argent put inspirer la voix qui les prononce, / Cet organe des Dieux put se laisser gagner" (ll. 1173–75). This is part of Corneille's concerted effort to parcel out blame in different directions so as to disculpate Œdipe.

[32] Dircé responds predictably, highlighting the ironic potential typical of all oracles: "On ne sait pas toujours ce qu'un serment hasarde, / Et vous ne voyez pas ce que le Ciel vous garde" (ll. 489–90). Oracles will be discussed at length in chapter 4.

[33] Œdipe's actual words are

> Mais dessus ce vieillard plus je porte les yeux,
> Plus je crois l'avoir vu jadis en d'autres lieux.
> Ses rides me font peine à bien reconnaître.
> Ne m'as-tu jamais vu?
>   (ll. 1423–26)

[34] The relationship between irony and parody will be discussed in chapter 6.

Chapter 3
Verbal Irony

One of the distinguishing features of irony in Corneille's theater is the relative frequency of verbal irony. Seymour Chatman's definition provides a useful starting point for discussion of its operation: "Verbal irony is purposefully generated by a human speaker, intentionally communicated to an audience as a subtext at odds with the ostensible message" (118). Foregrounded here are the three conditions for verbal irony. First, it has a clear and human source. In terms of the theater, this means that there is no double voicing: the source of the irony is understood to be the character who utters the statement in question. While we all know that Corneille is the original source of the words spoken on stage, he disappears completely behind his character in the case of verbal irony. The disjunction that we noted in authorial dramatic irony between playwright and character does not occur in verbal irony. Second, as indicated by the word "purposefully," there is a clear intent to produce verbal irony, and that intent is attributable to the character speaking. Third, verbal irony occurs in a communicative context: one character speaks ironically to another. While the audience is ultimately the theatrical audience, just as Corneille is ultimately the source of all verbal irony, the receiver for verbal irony is first and foremost a character on stage. Thus verbal irony takes place without reference to either external audience or ironist (Corneille); it is complete on stage. In *La Suite du Menteur*, Dorante demeans his valet Cliton by telling Cléandre, "[Q]uand il [Cliton] a dessein de se mettre en crédit, / Plus il y fait d'effort, moins il sait ce qu'il dit" (l. 830). Cliton responds, "On appelle cela des Vers à ma louange" (l. 831). The valet's characterization of Dorante's words is obviously ironic: what he says is quite different from what he means. Often, as in this example, we find the basic triangular structure of ironist (Cliton), victim of the irony (Dorante), and receiver (Cléandre) embodied on stage.

All definitions of verbal irony concur in including a significant disjunction between the apparent meaning of a statement and its intended meaning. Thus while the intending source of verbal irony is not double, the utterance itself most definitely is. The relationship between what Chatman calls the subtext and the ostensible message may be of several sorts. It is important to keep in mind that in this chapter the focus will be limited to the kinds of disjunction that signal evident irony. Others exist as well, and we will

31

consider them in part 2. Perrin divides verbal ironies into two categories: *contre-vérité* and *exaggération*. *Contre-vérité* is essentially antiphrasis—whereby what is implied is the opposite of a statement's literal meaning—while *exaggération* involves taking a stance to the point of absurdity in order to mark one's distance from what is seemingly avowed (189). Other relationships between apparent and intended meanings may exist as well; the constant feature is disjunction. Vaheed K. Ramazani considers this disjunction from a different angle: "[T]he most important principle of irony is not that it means something other than what it says, but rather that it does not mean what it says" (554). Ramazani's stance has the decided advantage of not advocating a single correct intended meaning. As we noted in chapter 1, considering irony as a process of simple decoding is reductive and impoverishing. The possibility of multiple meanings is crucial to irony. In fact, Ramazani is perhaps too quick to eliminate the apparent, surface meaning, thereby omitting an important dimension of the fundamental ambiguity and tension of all irony. Alain Berrendonner captures the reverberations between the two levels of meaning well when he describes verbal irony as "s'inscrire en faux contre sa propre énonciation, tout en l'accomplissant" (216). The negative quality that Ramazani associates with verbal irony, however—that it does *not* mean what it says—is significant in that it foregrounds the axiological stance typical of verbal irony, that is, a critical judgment. While verbal irony may be interpreted in a positive direction, using blame to indicate praise, for example, it is typically the case that positive statements convey a negative message. Berrendonner offers a cogent explanation for the negative predisposition of verbal irony: "[E]lle permet, tout simplement, d'argumenter sans avoir à en subir les conséquences" (237); "ce n'est pas que l'ironie serve fondamentalement à dire du mal, mais qu'elle a pour fonction de *déjouer une norme* qui, de manière générale, interdit de dire du mal" (239). Verbal irony's tendency to convey critical judgment holds for Corneille's theater as well as being true generally. Thus the hostility contained in Cliton's reaction to Dorante's comment is deflected or absorbed by the irony's indirection.

Signs

How do we know that what a speaker means may be different from what he or she says? By what signs does the disjunction make itself known to the receiver? Because we are dealing with the theater, to the extent that the verbal irony is to be associated with Corneille and not with a particular director and/or production of Corneille's plays, it must be rooted in the words spoken and not in the tone of voice or facial expression of the speaker. While in normal conversation such indicators may signal the presence of verbal irony, there are no stage directions in Corneille's theater dictating the physical manifestations of verbal irony. It might seem that the playwright is at a disadvantage by not having access to these nonverbal signs. Perrin, however, disagrees: "[C]'est…essentiellement à partir de la fausseté ouverte de ce qu'il exprime que le locuteur signale qu'il ne le prend pas réellement à son compte, et neutralise de ce fait la valeur argumentative intrinsèque de son énoncé" (199). For instance, when Pacorus gives his rival Suréna political advice, counseling him to obey Orode and marry Mandane, he says, "Recevez cet avis d'une amitié fidèle" (*Suréna*, l. 1373). The phrase "une amitié fidèle" can easily be understood to be ironic because Pacorus is Suréna's tenacious rival for Eurydice; his advice to Suréna thus becomes suspect. It is the falseness of his assertion of friendship that signals irony.

The signs of verbal irony may be obvious, such as a contradiction of some sort, whether it be between words and context or simply a logical inconsistency. Verbal irony need not be obvious, but in order for it to function as irony it must be perceptible. Signs of verbal irony, such as hyperbole, litotes, false reasoning, incompatibility, disproportion, change of register, etc., will be subject to variation in degree, from the obvious to the subtle. The stronger the signs and the greater the distance between ostensible and intended meanings, the more likely that the receiver will perceive irony. While we will focus in this chapter on those cases of verbal irony where there is little doubt, it is important to keep in mind that doubt and uncertainty are natural to the reception of verbal irony. What the ironist must do, in Schoentjes's words, is "oblige son public à s'arrêter et à s'interroger sur le sens de ses paroles" (171). As we examine the varieties of verbal irony that Corneille favors in his theater, doubt will temporarily take a back seat to certainty; in only a few cases, however, will it be banished entirely.

Types of Verbal Irony in Corneille's Theater

The simplest relationship between apparent and intended meaning is antiphrasis. Because it is based on an opposition, antiphrasis leaves little doubt concerning the ironic intentions of the speaker. In the last scene of *Rodogune*, the bride says to Antiochus, "Seigneur, c'est un moyen de vous être bien chère / Que pour don nuptial vous immoler un frère" (ll. 1759–60). It is perfectly obvious that Rodogune means the opposite of what she says. The interest of her statement lies in its insinuation that Antiochus would do well to interpret Cléopâtre's statements in a like manner. Similarly, in *Sertorius*, when Aufide says to Perpenna, "Ce maître si chéri [Sertorius] fait pour vous des merveilles" (l. 1529), it is not difficult to understand that he means that Sertorius is doing absolutely nothing for him. To limit verbal irony to antiphrasis is, however, overly restrictive, although the urge to do so is a common one, based on irony's profound ties to inversion in all of its manifestations (Couleau 151).

A second form of verbal irony involves what is best described by the French term *raillerie*. It involves taking a position different from one's own in order to mock the interlocutor. The position adopted need not be radically opposed as in the case of antiphrasis. Generally, such speech, or, more broadly, such an attitude, is found in Corneille's comedies, and is often associated with young women such as Cloris (*Mélite*), Doris (*La Veuve*), and Phylis (*La Place Royale*), whom Lemaître describes as "détachées et perpétuellement ironiques" (273). For example, in *La Veuve*, while Alcidon believes that Doris loves him, she in fact does not. Furthermore, she is perfectly aware that Alcidon is only feigning interest in her. Virtually everything she says to him has a second meaning quite different from the ostensible expression of her warm feelings:

> Quitte, mon cher souci, quitte ce faux soupçon,
> Tu douterais à tort d'une chose si claire,
> L'épreuve fera foi comme j'aime à te plaire,
> Je meurs d'impatience attendant l'heureux jour
> Qui te montre quel est envers toi mon amour.
>   (ll. 694–98)

It is rather more surprising to find *raillerie* in *Attila* as well, specifically in the tyrant's attitude towards the two kings. The verbal signs of respect he accords Valamir and Ardaric do not correspond to his actions; at times it is evident that he is mocking them. For instance, when neither king accepts Attila's demand to kill the other in order to win the hand of his own beloved (Honorie and Ildione, both betrothed to Attila), Attila exclaims,

> Quoi! l'amour, l'amitié, tout va d'un froid égal!
> Pas un ne m'aime assez pour haïr mon Rival!
> Pas un de son objet n'a l'âme assez ravie,
> Pour vouloir être heureux aux dépens d'une vie!
>   (ll. 1519–22)

The ingenuous attitude of surprise is unquestionably ironic.

The verbal irony of *raillerie* occurs in Corneille's prefatory material as well. The playwright thereby signals to his audience that he should not necessarily be taken at his word, but that a second meaning may be lurking. For example, Corneille mocks the prudishness of the theater in reference to Andromède's traditional nudity in the play's *Argument*:

> Les peintres, qui cherchent à faire paraître leur art dans
> les nudités, ne manquent jamais à nous représenter
> Andromède nue au pied du rocher où elle est attachée,
> quoiqu'Ovide n'en parle point. Ils me pardonneront si je
> ne les ai pas suivis en cette invention. (2:446)

Corneille takes the same teasing tone in discussing nudity in the *Examen*
to *Polyeucte* when explaining how he would treat the story of David and
Bethsheba: "[J]e ne décrirais pas comme il en devint amoureux en la voyant
se baigner dans une fontaine, de peur que l'image de cette nudité ne fît une
impression trop chatouilleuse dans l'esprit de l'Auditeur" (1:979). In the *Épitre*
preceding *Le Menteur* he playfully defends his use of Spanish sources despite
Spain's status as political enemy of France: "[J]'ai cru que nonobstant la guerre
des deux couronnes, il m'était permis de trafiquer en Espagne" (2:4).

Verbal irony is often described as a double entendre, which the Oxford
English dictionary defines as "a double meaning; a word or phrase having a
double sense."[35] A character says something that poses for the receiver the
quandary of undecidability. Unlike the case of authorial dramatic irony,
here the double meaning is ascribed to the speaker. Thus it is the intent of
the speaker to create ambiguity, an ambiguity that may arouse doubt and
the suspicion of irony in the receiver. Accused of overstepping his social
bounds by wanting to sit with the dukes, Don Sanche defends himself by
saying, "J'ai vu la place vide, et cru la bien remplir" (l. 192), playing on the
double meaning of *remplir*. The double entendre is doubtless obvious to
his interlocutors because the ostensible meaning is overly simple. Often, a
double entendre combines the possibility of a positive and a derisive meaning.
When Sophonisbe says to Syphax, "Je n'aime point Carthage à l'égal d'un
époux" (l. 330), he takes it strictly as reassurance, but the wording allows for
a quite different meaning: that she loves Carthage more than Syphax. Also in
Sophonisbe, where in fact there are quite a few such examples, Eryxe assures
Sophonisbe, "Votre félicité sera longtemps parfaite, / S'ils la laissent durer
autant que je souhaite" (ll. 933–34). Seeing as Sophonisbe has just stolen
Eryxe's fiancé, the length of time represented by "autant" is open to question.
Perhaps the most dramatic use of double entendre occurs in the last scene of
La Suite du Menteur when Philiste repeatedly tells Dorante, "Rentrez dans la
prison dont vous vouliez sortir" (ll. 1844, 1860, 1892). Given that Philiste
was responsible for Dorante's liberation from prison and that Philiste, unbeknownst to Dorante, is the latter's rival for Mélisse's affection, his meaning
seems both menacing and clear. In fact, Philiste is playing on the double
meaning of the word *prison*, referring not to jail but to Dorante's promise
to marry Mélisse.[36] It is ignorance of the double entendre that organizes the

suspense of this final scene; its revelation marks the resolution of the play's action. In *Héraclius*, the hero chooses to make a number of comments whose meaning shifts depending on whether the receiver believes him to be Héraclius or Martian. Here there is no onstage receiver who can grasp the second meaning, and therefore the irony. When in the first act Héraclius says, "Etant ce que je suis" (l. 275), Phocas, who believes the young man to be his son, cannot suspect another referent for these words. While Héraclius's double entendres function as retrospective dramatic irony, they are also verbal irony. Héraclius is choosing to speak in this double fashion, perhaps for his own pleasure. While verbal irony is deeply anchored in a communicative context, as we noted at the outset, auto-irony is a common feature of all of irony's varieties.[37] The fact that Héraclius's verbal irony has no onstage audience constitutes an acknowledgement of his situation of isolation.

Another possibility for verbal irony, one that Corneille employs often, is echoic mention. Dan Sperber and Deirdre Wilson argue that irony is a citational mode in which the words or thoughts of another are echoed in order to mark the speaker's distance from them ("Ironies" 407). Echoic mention thus operates by placing figurative quotation marks around the echoing statement. As Ramazani notes, the meaning of such echoic statements is "necessarily secondary to its illocutionary force (the act of repudiating the literal meaning)" (554).[38] The most well-known dramatic example from the period is the verbal joust between Arsinoé and Célimène in act 3, scene 4 of Molière's *Le Misanthrope*. Célimène echoes at great length the hypocritically polite phrases in which Arsinoé couched her verbal attack. Hamon recognizes that the notion of echoic mention as a source of irony provides a relatively stable context of substitution in which to establish irony, something that is of particular importance for literature, as the latter is inevitably more or less distant from its audience (152). Thus while one may well prefer not to go as far as Sperber and Wilson do—claiming that all irony can be conceived of in terms of echoic mention ("Ironies" 408)—it is nonetheless a useful concept, both for our discussion of verbal irony here and later when we examine Corneille's use of echoes across plays in chapter 5.

It is a significant feature of Corneille's theater, both comic and tragic, that characters verbally echo the exact words of a current or earlier interlocutor. While such echoes may have functions other than ironic—for example, Jean Boorsch notes that they serve to mark the rhythm/cadence of Cornelian dialogue (117)—it is rare that they are not also ironic in Corneille's theater. In most cases characters repeat the words of another in order to oppose them by casting them in a new light, a move that frequently entails hostility or mockery. As Paillet-Guth notes, echoes often indicate a power struggle: "Il s'agit d'un retournement de la propre parole de l'adversaire contre lui, qui vise une certaine inversion des rapports de force" (22). As such, it is almost always the case that the character who first speaks the words in question is on stage when they are repeated and made ironic. The words of one character thus become a weapon in the mouth of another and form the basis of a dramatic confrontation. Indeed, echoic mention is probably the most dramatic form of irony. The physical proximity of the original speaker of the words as well as the repetition itself function to countermand the distance so often associated with irony, distance that is in its essence undramatic.

The closer the repeated words are to their original utterance, the more intense will be the confrontation between the two characters, as the conflict between them is acted out through the repetition itself. With both the position of Roman emperor and Othon's hand in marriage still up in the air, the rivals Camille and Plautine confront each other in act 4 of *Othon*. "Si j'aimais toutefois, ou l'Empire, ou Pison" (l. 1351), says Camille, and Plautine immediately mimics her: "Et si j'aimais Madame, ou Pison, ou l'Empire" (l. 1353). Such brief, immediate echoes are typical in scenes of confrontation between female rivals. Near the end of a long such scene in *La Toison d'or*, Hypsipyle uses the polite phrase "Avec sincérité je dois vous avouer" (l. 1322), which Médée hurls back at her almost immediately: "Avec sincérité je dois aussi vous dire" (l. 1324). Sophonisbe says, "L'occasion qui plaît souvent fait succomber" (l. 920) to Eryxe, who counters, "L'occasion qui plaît semble toujours propice" (l. 922). Domitie asserts, "Je ne sais si je puis" (*Tite et Bérénice* l. 771), and Bérénice responds, "Et moi je ne sais s'il a droit…/ Mais je sais" (ll. 773–74). In each case, the ironic echoic mention serves to mark succinctly the rivalry, and even enmity, between characters.

When the distance between the original statement and the echo increases, the repetition often signals a power reversal, an elegant form of "gotcha!" The irony of the verbal echo remains evident provided that it is exact and highlighted in some fashion. Having gained the upper hand in the second act of *Pompée*, Cléopâtre throws back at her brother the same line he used with her in the first act: "Le temps de chaque chose ordonne et fait le prix" (ll. 256, 636). Similarly, in the last act of *Sertorius*, Perpenna threatens Aricie by boasting, "J'ai même entre mes mains un assez bon ôtage [Aricie], / Pour faire mes Traités avec grand avantage" (ll. 1737–38). When her estranged husband Pompée arrives and takes over, Aristie asserts Perpenna's loss of power by echoing his words with derision: "Avez-vous en vos mains un assez bon ôtage, / Pour faire vos Traités avec grand avantage?" (ll. 1817–18). Indeed, such echoes generally express mockery and derision. In *Agésilas*, Aglatide combines a distant and an immediate echo to mock her sister's compliant stance concerning the choice of a husband. Elpinice had claimed earlier, "Je ne sais aimer ni haïr" (l. 286) and now tells her father "Je ne sais qu'obéir" (l. 740). Aglatide echoes her sister's words ironically: "Vous ne savez que c'est d'aimer ou de haïr, / Mais vous seriez pour lui [Spitridate] fort aise d'obéir" (ll. 748–49). Obviously, the line between mockery and hostility is permeable. Attila is a master at combining the two; he attacks Honorie with her own line, "Les grands cœurs parlent avec franchise, / C'est une vérité que vous m'avez apprise" (ll. 1237–38; Honorie l. 1069), while turning Honorie's cruel suggestion to marry Ildione to Attila's captain of the guards against her.

The longer and more exact the echo, the more it will force itself on the audience's attention as ironic or potentially ironic. Even two words, however, can raise the possibility of irony when they are particularly charged, such as Sertorius's "heureux Sylla" (l. 809 echoing Pompée at l. 787) or Aspar's "sans feindre" (*Pulchérie* l. 1401 echoing Irène at l. 1399). Longer echoes sometimes have a playful, occasionally even comic, dimension. The mechanical rigidity that Henri Bergson ties so persuasively to the comic is manifest in echoic mention (Hamon 67). The following example, which is especially playful, involves mystification. Refusing to identify who exactly are the people unhappy at the prospect of Léon's becoming emperor, Aspar declaims arrogantly, "Le besoin de l'État est souvent un mystère / Dont la moitié se dit, et l'autre est bonne à taire" (*Pulchérie*, ll. 1289–90). Later in the same scene, Pulchérie informs Aspar that Martian has alerted her to be suspicious of someone; when he wants to know of whom, she responds, "Aspar, c'est un mystère / Dont la moitié se dit, et l'autre est bonne à taire" (ll. 1301–2). An additional element contributes to the comic possibilities of this interchange: the referent in both cases, which each refuses to name, are likely one and the same: Aspar himself. The victim of such irony, of course, is unlikely to perceive it as comic or playful. Clearly, directors and actors have considerable latitude in choosing the tone for echoic mentions, but their potentially playful dimension should not be discounted.

The final category of verbal irony that needs to be considered is sarcasm. Sarcasm shares with echoic mentions the presence on stage of the victim against whom it is directed; thus it too involves the inherently dramatic situation of confrontation. This is not a category of verbal irony like the others, however. First, all sarcasm entails some degree of hostility or cruelty: one cannot be lightly, sweetly, or gently sarcastic. *A Handbook of Literary Terms* describes sarcasm as "literally, flesh-tearing" (Yelland et al. 180). As Couton points out, Corneille uses the stylistic violence of sarcastic irony to mirror the violence of the action of *Médée*, in which Créuse, Créon, and Jason all die on stage (Corneille 1:1382). The fact that the aim of sarcasm is to be hurtful explains why its victim is normally on stage when it occurs: its hostility has ties to the *edge* that is a feature of all irony. The difference is that other forms of irony may or may not be hostile; sarcasm invariably is. Second, and markedly problematic, sarcasm must be obvious: "When one is speaking sarcastically…one also leaves absolutely no doubt—not even for the slightest moment—about what one means" (Stringfellow 17). It is the intent of the speaker of sarcasm that the victim understand the irony perfectly. For Perrin, however, it is precisely sarcasm's unequivocal nature that removes it from the domain of irony. He believes that the speaker of any ironic statement must feign to adopt the position that his words represent, thereby assuring that ironic discourse will be ambiguous, at least to some degree (144). Sarcasm is in no way ambiguous. While we include sarcasm as a type of verbal irony here, we need to acknowledge that it is indeed a borderline case.

The issue of the obviousness of sarcasm is linked to another problem, that of tone. We speak readily of a "sarcastic tone"; tone may even be used to define sarcasm (Kaufer 453). Indeed, both the hostility and the conspicuousness that characterize sarcasm may be conveyed entirely by tone. Tone, however, raises the obvious problem in theater that it is not generally indicated in the text, and certainly not in Corneille's plays as he wrote them. Of course, Corneille wrote numerous lines to which one could imagine giving a sarcastic tone. To the extent that tone is a matter of the actor's or the director's discretion, it lies outside of our study. What keeps sarcasm from slipping between the cracks of a literary analysis, however, is its obviousness, which allows it to be perceptible even in the absence of any indicator of tone. While certain lines may admit a range of possibilities of tone of delivery, other lines force one to recognize that sarcasm is the only reasonable option. Before we consider specific examples from Corneille's theater, we must acknowledge that not all sarcasm is ironic. In order for it to be ironic, sarcasm must employ the other forms and signs of verbal irony that we have already discussed, chief among them antiphrasis and exaggeration. Thus ironic sarcasm resembles other forms of verbal irony, with the added conditions that it be obvious and hostile. One might easily consider the example of echoic mention above from *Agésilas* ("Vous ne savez que c'est d'aimer ou de haïr, / Mais vous seriez pour lui fort aise d'obéir") to be an instance of ironic sarcasm: it is certainly obvious and the victim is on stage. The uncertainty lies in the realm of hostility: one could imagine Aglatide adopting a sarcastic tone or a lighter, more playful one. Thus the interpreter has a degree of latitude in perceiving such examples as sarcasm or simply as verbal irony.

Given that measure of interpretive leeway, we can locate abundant examples of potential sarcastic irony in Corneille's plays. In the context of this chapter, however, I would like to indicate a few that are unquestionably sarcastic. The first is based on antiphrasis: in *La Toison d'or*, Hypsipyle addresses her sarcasm directly at Jason after he has abandoned her and switched his attentions to Médée:

> Le ciel l'ordonne ainsi, ton change est légitime,
> Ton innocence est sûre au milieu de ton crime,
> Et quand tes trahisons pressent leur noir effet,
> Ta gloire, ton devoir, ton destin a tout fait.
> (ll. 1256–59)

What she says is the exact opposite of what she means; the irony is obvious, and the hostility patent. Similarly, sarcasm is the only interpretation possible for Médée's antiphrastic exclamation directed at Jason: "On ne m'a que bannie! ô bonté souveraine!" (*Médée* l. 845). Frequent as well are examples that involve exaggeration. Plautine rebuffs Martian in *Othon* by very obviously exaggerating his social standing relative to her (she is the daughter of the king's consul and he is a freed slave):

> Je viens de me connaître, et me vois à mon tour
> Indigne des honneurs qui suivent votre amour.
> Avoir brisé ses fers, fait un degré de gloire
> Au-dessus des Consuls, des Préfets du Prétoire,
> Et si de cet amour je n'ose être le prix,
> Le respect m'en empêche et non plus le mépris.
> (ll. 523–28)

What Plautine says is so evidently not what she believes and so clearly insulting to Martian in its obvious untruth and exaggeration that this passage cannot be read as anything other than sarcastic irony. Bérénice uses sarcasm in a like manner in conjunction with rank and ironic self-deprecation, saying to Domitian:

> Pour moi qui n'eus jamais l'honneur d'être Romaine,
> Et qu'un destin jaloux n'a fait naître que Reine,
> Sans qu'un de vous descende au rang que je remplis,
> Ce me doit être assez d'un de vos Affranchis [as a husband].
> (*Tite et Bérénice* ll. 727–30)

The victim of the sarcasm, Tite, is not on stage, however. Bérénice extends her hostility to Domitian, Tite's brother.

speciae: Nicomède
Pulchérie

Sarcasm may be rather global in nature: once it starts, it tends to continue. Act 5, scene 3 of *Attila* abounds with Attila's sarcasm. The first words of the scene, "Eh bien, mes illustres amis" (l. 1515), uttered in a context in which Attila clearly considers Valamir, Ardaric, and Honorie neither illustrious nor his friends, set the tone for much of what he says thereafter.[39] Because of its basically dramatic nature, Corneille makes widespread use of sarcasm and possible sarcasm, to the point where it is fair to say that it is a significant feature of the verbal jousting that extends throughout much of Cornelian dialogue. Having seen the broad variety of verbal irony present in Corneille's theater, we will turn now to a closer examination of how it operates within the context of two plays, *Nicomède* and *Pulchérie*.

C makes
widespread
use of sarcasm

– signif
feature of
verbal jousting

NICOMÈDE

Of all of Corneille's theater, irony is most readily associated with this play. Indeed, the widespread presence of verbal irony is one of its distinguishing features. Although most of the characters in this play employ verbal irony at one point or another, the lion's share belongs to the eponymous hero: irony is Nicomède's weapon off the battlefield. Nicomède's need for this rather unusual tool of intimidation is established in the first scene of the play, when Laodice insists that his power lies in his absence, when he is away at the head of the army, and that present in his father's court he is relatively powerless. Thus, as several critics have asserted, irony takes on a military cast as Nicomède's essential weapon in a civilian context. At the same time, irony is a "civil" weapon that allows the characters to avoid true violence (Merlin-Kajman 76). Nicomède's particular use of verbal irony is quite distinctive as well; it involves pointed politeness, aggressiveness, and distance.[40] While we will find a wide range of types of irony in *Nicomède*, it is this form of polite verbal attack that is of greatest interest and that gives "une couleur particulière à l'ouvrage" (Schlumberger 161).

Verbal Irony a
distinguishing
feature of
Nicomède

eo/o N's
weapon

as
"polite
verbal
attack"

A Cornelian hero so closely associated with irony has given some critics pause and has led to efforts at recuperation. Marc Fumaroli takes pains to justify Nicomède, arguing in exalted terms that the hero's ends—defending royal freedom—justify such unorthodox means ("Héroïsme" 341); André Stegmann calls Nicomède's irony "une forme nouvelle de la générosité" that functions to unmask "les faux généreux" (*Héroïsme* 614); and Lemaître offers a morally positive, even noble, interpretation of Nicomède's irony, which he finds to be anchored in self-possession and self-defense (312). Heroic irony is indeed an odd concept. Michel Prigent wonders, "Pourquoi l'ironie et l'admiration ont-elles partie liée dans *Nicomède*?" (283). I suspect that this may be precisely the challenge that Corneille set for himself with this play: the ironic hero.

nb. heroic
irony = odd
concept

The relationship between lies and verbal irony is problematic as well in this play, because the two are often associated and sometimes even confused with one another.[41] Verbal irony shares with lies a disjunction between ostensible and true meanings, but differs in that the ironist does not intend to deceive his listener, while the liar does. Kerbrat-Orecchioni describes the relationship between the two succinctly: in the case of the lie, "*L* dit *A*, pense *non-A* et veut faire entendre *A*," while in the case of verbal irony, "*L* dit *A*, pense *non-A* et veut faire entendre *non-A*" ("Problèmes" 13). We may see the basic constrast between ironist and liar reflected in that between two of Corneille's characters, Nicomède and *Le Menteur*'s Dorante. The former does not expect his interlocutor to accept his words at face value while the latter hopes that they will. It is, however, disquieting to note that in his first meeting with his father Nicomède leads off, not with irony, but with what can be called politically expedient lies. When Prusias asks him why he has returned, Nicomède responds:

> La seule ambition de pouvoir en personne
> Mettre à vos pieds, Seigneur, encore une Couronne,
> De jouir de l'honneur de vos embrassements,
> Et d'être le témoin de vos contentements.
> (ll. 463–66)

It is thus perhaps not surprising that Nicomède's heroic status requires some defending.

In examining Nicomède's particular brand of irony, it is important to consider its relationship to sarcasm. The two are closely related in that they are obvious to their onstage victims. Sarcasm differs from this type of irony, however, in the degree to which it displays hostility. Nicomède's irony is in part defined by polite distance, which makes the use of a sarcastic tone (itself one, but not the only, vehicle for both hostility and obviousness) unlikely. Because of the close ties between Nicomède's irony and sarcasm, however, it is not difficult to imagine a staging in which Nicomède would be blatantly sarcastic. In my own interpretation Nicomède covers his hostility with a screen of conventional politeness. An exception may make the distinction clearer: when Flaminius goes to great lengths to provoke Nicomède in front of his father, the prince eventually does display hostility, and thus, I would argue, sarcasm. He says: "Attale doit régner, Rome l'a résolu, / Et puisqu'elle a partout un pouvoir absolu, / C'est aux Rois d'obéir, alors qu'elle commande" (ll. 589–91). That note of anger seems absent from Nicomède's other ironic statements, although there is considerable room for differing interpretations. At the other end of the spectrum, Nicomède's form of irony is also related to *raillerie*, which is teasing rather than hostile.

At the heart of the polite attack of Nicomède's irony is what Paillet-Guth calls "une feinte adhésion à l'univers de croyance de l'autre" (24). The *autre* in question is normally on stage; Nicomède's irony is part of a dialogue. Thus his words are marked by distance from his true position, and often take the antiphrastic form of blame through praise or the more malleable form of exaggeration. This type of irony makes its appearance early in the play as Nicomède confronts Attale, while the latter is still unaware of the former's identity. In the older brother's long speech we find numerous jabs that may be said to contain an element of irony (italics mine in all of the examples):

> Et [Rome] vous [Attale] dégraderait peut-être dès demain
> Du titre *glorieux* de Citoyen Romain.
> (ll. 161–62)

> Et ne savez-vous [Attale] plus qu'il n'est Princes ni Rois,
> Qu'elle [Rome] daigne égaler à ses *moindres* Bourgeois?
> (ll. 165–66)

> Remplissez mieux un nom [that of Roman], sous qui
>   *nous tremblons tous.*
> (l. 170)

> Songez qu'il faut du moins, pour toucher votre cœur
> *La fille d'un Tribun, ou celle d'un Préteur:*
> Que Rome vous permet cette *haute alliance.*
> (ll. 173–75)

> *L'honneur souverain* de son [Rome's] adoption.
> (l. 177)

Elsewhere, Nicomède favors repetition as a clear signal of his ironic intent. Faced with Rome's demand that Attale be given a throne, Nicomède responds: "Attale a le cœur *grand*, l'esprit *grand*, l'âme *grande*, / Et toutes les *grandeurs* dont se fait un *grand* Roi" (ll. 592–93). He uses the same hyperbolic repetition to goad Flaminius into leaving the stage so that he may speak privately with Laodice:

> Vous avez dans son cœur [Laodice's] fait de *si grands*
>   progrès,
> Et vos discours pour elle ont de *si grands* attraits,

> Que sans de *grands* efforts je n'y pourrai détruire
> Ce que votre *harangue* y voulait introduire.
> (ll. 933–36)

According to Furetière, the word *harangue* is ambiguous: it can be used seriously or sarcastically. Paillet-Guth notes other signs typical of Nicomède's irony: "[L]'emploi paradoxal des comparatifs ou superlatifs *mieux, moindres, plus élevés*, ainsi qui des syntagmes qui impliquent une notion d'échelle: *égaler à, digne d'elle*, et l'opérateur argumentatif *du moins*, (signifiant 'au moins')" (24). The formal precision of such language hints at the deliberateness with which it is (over)constructed.

While Nicomède is the first to employ this particular brand of irony in the play, it quickly spreads to other characters, as though Nicomède were determining the weapon to be used in a duel. Laodice describes the advice Prusias has just given her as "une *si salutaire, et noble* Politique" (l. 752) and Flaminius rebukes Attale with "Vous êtes Souverain, et *tout vous est permis*" (l. 1462). The relative proportion of sarcasm and *raillerie* often seems open to interpretation. Because Arsinoé is the most acrimonious character, it is easy to imagine a sarcastic tone accompanying her parting shots as she leaves Prusias and Nicomède on stage in the fourth act:

> *Ce grand* Prince [Nicomède] vous sert, et vous servira
> mieux,
> Quand il n'aura plus rien qui lui blesse les yeux.
> Et n'appréhendez point Rome, ni sa vengeance;
> Contre tout son pouvoir *il a trop de vaillance*;
> Il sait *tous les secrets* du fameux Annibal,
> De ce héros à Rome *en tous lieux si fatal*,
> Que l'Asie et l'Afrique admirent l'avantage
> *Qu'en tire Antiochus, et qu'en reçut Carthage.*
> (ll. 1293–1300)

The fact that Arsinoé's sarcastically ironic attack occurs in the context of a trilogue, that is, an exchange between three onstage speakers, is not an accident. We have already discussed the ironic triangle made up of ironist, victim, and receiver for the irony. This configuration of characters on stage in fact favors and abets sarcasm in that it provides a protective shield for its hostility. Because there is no ambiguity concerning the intended meaning of a statement, the receiver may seem superfluous to the communication of the irony. However, the fact that the true meaning—hostile, obvious, and couched in polite discourse—is destined for the pleasure of the third party allows for the humiliating pretense that the victim is situated on the other channel, that of the sarcasm's ostensible meaning. The sarcasm is of course patently obvious to the victim, but he or she is structurally discouraged from acknowledging and responding to the true meaning by the presence of the third party. If there is no third party, the speaker of the sarcasm runs a far greater risk, in my opinion, that its victim will respond directly to the intended meaning. It is thus perhaps only natural that *Nicomède*, the play in which Corneille most heavily uses sarcasm, is also the site of numerous trilogues.[42]

Dramatic irony also plays a significant role in *Nicomède*. Because the history of this prince would have been little known to Corneille's audience, the playwright exploits dramatic irony in ways that do not depend upon such knowledge. The first involves Attale's ignorance of Nicomède's identity during their confrontation in the play's second scene: Laodice and the audience share the knowledge that Attale lacks. Elsewhere, Arsinoé engages in role-playing when she pretends, for Prusias's benefit, to take Nicomède's defense: "Grâce, grâce, Seigneur, à notre unique appui, / Grâce à tant de lauriers en sa main si fertiles, / Grâce à ce conquérant, à ce preneur de villes" (ll. 1150–52). Presumably, Prusias is taken in by her words, but both Nicomède on stage and the audience know that what she says is radically different from what she means. The repetition of "grâce" points antiphrastically to the damnation she wishes for her stepson. On two occasions, Arsinoé is unwittingly ironic: once when she hypocritically lectures Attale about how the truth concerning the supposed assassins, Zéon and Métrobate, will surely be revealed;[43] and again when she speaks to Attale about Laodice, "Qu'est-ce qu'en sa fureur une femme n'essaie?" (l. 1503). As I noted in chapter 2, the authorial dramatic irony in both of these cases allows one to read her words as ironically directed against herself, while at the same time establishing complicity between Corneille and the audience.

The play contains several varieties of verbal irony. Echoic mention is well suited to Nicomède's particular brand of irony. Arsinoé will not say what the two would-be assassins, Zénon and Métrobate, have revealed under interrogation, preferring insinuation: they have supposedly uttered "Deux mots de vérité qui vous [Nicomède] comblent de gloire" (l. 1056). The word "gloire" is clearly antiphrastic in this context. When Nicomède inquires about what those two words might be, Arsinoé answers, "Vous les saurez de lui [Prusias, the king]" (l. 1059). Nicomède immediately turns the situation around, using the same tactic of mystification and the identical words. Arsinoé asks what he means by "Mais…" (l. 1063), and he answers: "Deux mots de vérité qui font que je respire" (l. 1064), and follows, "Vous les saurez du Roi" (l. 1066). These "deux mots de vérité" (ll. 1056 and 1064) that Arsinoé and Nicomède sling at each other threaten radically different, and thus ironically distant, meanings despite their similarity. Another example involves Flaminius, who makes an elegantly ironic concession to Nicomède: "Le Pont sera pour vous, avec la Galatie, / Avec la Cappadoce, avec la Bithynie. / Ce bien de vos Aïeux, ces prix de votre sang" (ll. 699–701). The last line is a pointedly ironic echo of Nicomède's "Le bien de mes aïeux, ou le prix de mon sang" (l. 658) earlier in the same scene.

There is an element of ironic double entendre in the confrontation between Laodice and Arsinoé in the final act. Arsinoé opens scene 6 with "La cause de nos maux doit-elle être impunie?" (l. 1656). What may at first seem to be a quid pro quo—does "la cause de nos maux" refer to Arsinoé or Laodice?—almost immediately becomes a willful double entendre on the part of both women as they seek to cast each other in that unflattering role.

The oddest manifestation of verbal irony in this play involves a variant of antiphrasis. Throughout an entire scene, Araspe, the king's captain of the guards, uses contradictory language to evaluate Nicomède's actions for Prusias's benefit. The opening of the scene is a model of what follows. When Prusias declares himself shocked by Nicomède's unbidden return to the city, Araspe replies,

> Sire, vous auriez tort d'en prendre aucun souci,
> Et la haute vertu du prince Nicomède
> Pour ce qu'on peut en craindre est un puissant remède.
> Mais tout autre que lui devrait être suspect:
> Un retour si soudain manque un peu de respect,
> Et donne lieu d'entrer en quelque défiance
> Des secrètes raisons de tant d'impatience.
>   (ll. 366–72)

Araspe continues in this vein throughout the scene, ostensibly defending Nicomède while at the same time repeatedly insinuating, if not asserting outright, that Nicomède is guilty for having returned to Nicomédie. By arguing both for and against Nicomède simultaneously and insistently, Araspe creates an untenable tension between the two positions, thereby compelling the receiver to choose which of the two will be interpreted as serious and which will be rejected as ironic. Maintaining both positions simultaneously, Araspe deftly avoids taking responsibility himself for accusations directed against the prince. If, as it seems, he is subtly urging Prusias to blame his son for his unbidden return, then what are we to make of his statement "Le Prince est vertueux et vous êtes bon père" (l. 400)? If we read the first half of the line as antiphrasis, are we not compelled to do the same with the second half? Could Araspe be ironically attacking Prusias as well? This is one of the strangest scenes in all of Corneille's theater: not only is the dilemma never entirely resolved, but the reiteration of attack and defense itself borders on the comic.[44] It is only at the end of the play, when Araspe is killed by Attale and his men, that one feels confident in interpreting his words. Araspe's discourse, while it does contribute to the general atmosphere of irony that pervades the play, stands in direct opposition to Nicomède's irony of polite attack. It is manipulative through its ambiguity, whereas Nicomède is far more obviously ironic. Instead of offering a game of substitution, Araspe creates undecidability, of a kind that we find nowhere else in Corneille's theater. It sets itself apart from other examples of undecidability by being so clearly intended as such by the onstage speaker.

With so much irony running through *Nicomède*, it is legitimate to be concerned about contagion. In order for the audience to believe that Nicomède is sincerely magnanimous, particularly at the play's dénouement, it is crucial that we not wonder at that point whether he is once again being ironic. I believe that Corneille uses Laodice and, more specifically, the couple Laodice and Nicomède, to ensure the presence of the unironic and the audience's clear perception thereof. He opens the play with Nicomède and Laodice alone together on stage (a very unusual configuration of two main characters as the curtain rises),[45] and they speak without irony in this scene. When Laodice calls Nicomède "un si grand conquérant" (l. 4) here, it would occur to no one to think she is being in any way ironic. The same words later in Arsinoé's mouth, for example, or in Laodice's referring to Attale, would immediately signal irony. Here, however, what is said provides the benchmark of non-irony from which each will deviate in later scenes, but never with one another. It is also the place to which both will return in the final scene, guaranteeing the sincerity of Nicomède's generosity towards Attale, Arsinoé, and Prusias. Corneille thus successfully contains irony's danger of contagion.

One might have reason, however, to wonder about Arsinoé's sincerity when she bows to Nicomède's magnanimity in the last scene. Petit de Julleville goes even further: "Arsinoé ment encore, nous n'en doutons guère; mais peu importe; le spectateur satisfait la voit réduite à l'impuissance de nuire" (937). A comparison to the dénouement of *Cinna* is instructive. Napoleon famously doubted the sincerity of Auguste's pardon of the conspirators, but, interestingly, everyone seems ready to accept the sincerity of Émilie's *conversion*. Like Arsinoé's malice, Émilie's hatred melts before the grandeur of the (male) heroic gesture. In both cases, the woman, who is also the individual with the greatest enmity, concedes first, followed by the males (Cinna, Maxime, Prusias). Is it really that simple? Perhaps in the dénouements of both *Cinna* and *Nicomède* Corneille affirms noble heroic values, while still leaving room for their subversion. After all, the matter of Annibal's death has not been satisfactorily dealt with. A plot that fails, like Arsinoé's plot against Nicomède or Cinna and Émilie's against Auguste, may be forgiven. A plot that succeeds—Arsinoé's against Annibal—is quite a different matter. Thus Arsinoé may be acting out of fear of Nicomède and in the politically expedient hopes of foreclosing any more discussion of the betrayal she orchestrated that led to Annibal's death.[46]

For Paillet-Guth, irony in *Nicomède* serves in large measure to discredit Roman political values (23). In my opinion, irony's role is far greater here. Verbal irony provides the weapon with which the central conflict of the familial power struggle is played out. Furthermore, verbal irony works together with the lies and slander in which many of the characters deal to create an environment of verbal instability, one that is only resolved in the last scene where stability is reestablished through familial reconciliation. Irony is seemingly banished from this scene, but the unresolved issue of Annibal's death leaves us entitled to wonder whether things are what they seem.

PULCHÉRIE: DUPLICITY AND IRONY

Corneille's penultimate play, *Pulchérie*, which deals with the choice of an emperor and a husband, provides a completely different example of the interplay of ironies, particularly verbal irony. As we noted in the discussion of *Nicomède*, lies and verbal irony both involve a disjunction between the ostensible and true meanings of the words spoken, with the crucial difference that the liar seeks to deceive his audience, while the ironist does not. In *Pulchérie* we find an unexpected relationship between the two: when one character is habitually less than honest with the others, they, perceiving the duplicity, react with irony and even sarcasm. Thus, while the ambitious general Aspar seeks to deceive, the others use verbal irony to indicate that they are not taken in.

Most of the irony in this play is verbal, but two significant examples of situational irony provide the larger context in which the verbal irony operates. First, Léon formally proposes to the Senate that it name Pulchérie empress and allow her to choose a spouse who would be emperor (rather than the Senate naming an emperor who would then be expected to marry Pulchérie). While Pulchérie had fervently hoped that the Senate would choose her beloved Léon as emperor, when the choice and the responsibility become her own—through the very success of Léon's proposal—she cannot bring herself to do so. Thus, ironically, Léon's own suggestion to the Senate forecloses all possibility of marriage between himself and Pulchérie. Second, Aspar argues that Pulchérie should eliminate several of his fellow generals from consideration as possible husbands (and emperors) because they already

have made romantic commitments to other women (5.4). Pulchérie imme- *[margin: situational irony.]*
diately and pointedly rejects Aspar as a suitor on precisely the grounds of
his own argument: he is betrothed to Irène, Léon's sister. In both cases, the *[margin: plots backfire against 2 men who want to marry Pulchérie]*
tactics of the men seeking to marry Pulchérie, whether for love or advantage,
backfire against them. Clearly, Corneille employs situational irony in this
play to accentuate the fact that the choice of spouse and emperor belongs
to Pulchérie alone.

Verbal irony in *Pulchérie* appears primarily as a reaction to the basic
duplicity of Aspar. Aspar does not hesitate to prevaricate and misrepresent *[margin: verbal irony = reaction to Aspar's duplicity]*
in order to further his own chances of occupying the throne.[47] In fact, much
of Aspar's duplicity is a result of his efforts to occupy two incompatible positions simultaneously: Irène's betrothed and an avid if undeclared seeker of
Pulchérie's hand. He attempts to convince Léon to share the throne with
him (1.4), while insinuating that his own name might garner more support
from the Senate than Léon's (ll. 265–66). He then maintains to Irène that
he loves her ("Je vous aime, et jamais une ardeur plus sincère…" l. 313) and
that his own ambition to occupy the throne will benefit her as his wife. He
tries to convince Martian that there will be objections to Léon being named
emperor, while completely distancing himself from their source: "[J]'apprends
qu'on murmure" (l. 539); he later makes the same assertion to Pulchérie ("un
murmure infaillible," l. 1270). Pretending to support Martian for the position of emperor, Aspar immediately suggests a power-sharing relationship
and even implies that he would be willing to sacrifice his love for Irène in
order to become Martian's son-in-law (ll. 567–70, 581–83, 587–90). Aspar's
duplicity is transparent enough that none but the young and innocent are *[margin: only young + innocent taken in by him —]*
taken in by him. Even that realm of potential influence is cut off early in
the play, however, as Irène warns her brother Léon and Martian alerts his *[margin: but they're warned]*
daughter Justine about Aspar's deceptive nature (1.3 and 2.3). Corneille
makes certain that Aspar's duplicity is evident to the audience as well. In a
brief monologue, Irène tells us that his love for her is but an "illusion" (l. *[margin: audience knows, also]*
367) and Martian lets us know that Aspar "roule des projets qu'il ne dit pas
à tous" (l. 628).

One form of duplicitous discourse calls forth another in this play.
Because Aspar is dishonest in his dealings with the other characters, they
adopt forms of double discourse in their responses to him. Léon, immediately
after his sister has made him aware of Aspar's motives, responds ironically
to Aspar's suggestion that they share the throne by saying, "Je craindrais de
tout autre un dangereux partage, / Mais de vous, je n'ai pas, Seigneur, le
moindre ombrage" (ll. 269–70). It is far from certain that Aspar perceives
Léon's irony here; Irène on stage and the audience off stage, however, do.
Most other examples are more obviously interpretable as verbal irony, even

for Aspar. In fact, most could be classified as *raillerie* or even sarcasm. Martian responds to Aspar's suggestion that the former share the burden of the throne with a son-in-law, were he to become emperor: "Il faudrait que ce gendre eût les vertus d'Aspar, / Mais vous aimez ailleurs, et ce serait un crime / Que de rendre infidèle un cœur si magnanime" (ll. 584–86). The *raillerie* becomes a bit more pointed when Martian suggests that Aspar address his suggestions directly to Pulchérie, closing with "La vérité lui plaît, et vous pourrez lui plaire" (l. 614). The conversation between Martian and Aspar even elicits an ironic reaction from the innocent Justine, although only after Aspar leaves the stage:

> Il [Aspar] n'a pour but, Seigneur [Martian], que le bien
>   de l'Empire.
> Détrônez la Princesse, et faites-vous élire,
> C'est un amant pour moi que je n'attendais pas,
> Qui vous soulagera du poids de tant d'États.
>   (ll. 629–32)[48]

Pulchérie is most obviously ironic in dealing with Aspar. As we saw earlier, she uses verbal echo to playful effect when she throws Aspar's words ("un mystère / Dont la moitié se dit, et l'autre est bonne à taire," ll. 1289–90 and 1301–2) back at him. In the same scene, Pulchérie pointedly refers to Aspar's love for Irène: "Je la [Irène] laisse avec vous, afin que votre zèle / S'allume à ce beau feu que vous avez pour elle" (ll. 1313–14). The words "beau feu" are obviously ironic. The irony in the characters' reactions to Aspar serves to signal to him, without having to say so directly, that his duplicity is obvious. Their irony thereby allows for the prolongation of double discourse, while undermining Aspar.

Thus unique to *Pulchérie*, we find the repeated structure of duplicity eliciting various responses of verbal irony from all of the characters. The duplicitous Aspar is more or less conscious of being the victim of the others' ironic statements.[49] He eventually adopts the same technique as the others: he too employs verbal irony, specifically in his conversation with Irène when he echoes her plea ("Vous la [Irène's hand] voudrez peut-être, et la voudrez trop tard. / Ne vous exposez point, Seigneur, à ce hasard," ll. 1395–96) with "Vous le voudrez peut-être, et le voudrez trop tard. / Ne laissez point longtemps nos destins au hasard" (ll. 1431–32), referring not to her hand in marriage but to a power-sharing arrangement with whomever is chosen to be Pulchérie's husband. Verbal irony has therefore come full circle, embraced even by its chief victim.

While the back-and-forth movement between duplicity and verbal irony seems straightforward, it is complicated by two issues pertaining to Aspar. First, is Aspar capable of sincerity or does his duplicity preclude sincerity? And second, how politically powerful is Aspar? Does he pose a potential danger to the other characters? Our answer to this second question will influence how we interpret both his duplicity and the verbal irony thrown at him.

The problem of sincerity centers on Aspar and Irène. While it is eminently clear that Aspar is motivated by selfish ambition, when it comes to his feelings for Irène we are left in a quandary. Does the fact that he is willing to sacrifice her to his ambition necessarily mean that he does not love her? After all, doesn't Pulchérie make precisely that sacrifice, all the while declaiming her presumably sincere love for Léon? Does the fact that everyone (including Irène) ironically belabors the questionable nature of Aspar's love for Irène eliminate the possibility that he has true feelings for her? Aspar assures Irène that he does have such feelings: "J'ai pour vous un amour à ne jamais s'éteindre" (l. 1402). When he says to her, "Votre main qui m'attend fera ma sûreté, / Et contre le courroux le plus inexorable / Elle me servira d'asile inviolable" (ll. 1392–94), do we see only selfishness? Is there not a note of tenderness as well, or can we dismiss these lines as empty verbiage? Once a character embarks on a path of double discourse, of whatever variety, the move to sincerity is problematic. Léon's greatest protection from the suspicion of similar duplicity is the fact that Corneille has him appear onstage at length before Aspar does. Aspar alone introduces the issues of ambition and dishonesty. Thus Léon benefits from a presumption of sincerity.

Aspar is a problematic character, and indeed critics vary significantly in their reading of him.[50] Such widely varying interpretations are a function, in my opinion, of the difficulty we have in determining the degree to which Aspar constitutes a danger. On the one hand, he borders on the ridiculous. He is incapable of fooling any but the most naive. In his bluster and in the ironic reaction he elicits in others, Aspar is reminiscent of Matamore in *L'Illusion comique*. While Aspar thinks his duplicity is opaque, as does Matamore, everyone else finds it to be transparent. In sharp contrast to Aspar, one thinks of Attila, who poses a serious threat to those around him. While an occasional note of irony or sarcasm is uttered in response to Attila, that is hardly the only or even the dominant reaction. Because of latter's power, Ardaric, Valamir, Honorie, and Ildione are concerned primarily with swaying or placating him. Irony is a very poor persuasive tool. Thus the presence of irony and sarcasm directed at Aspar suggest that he is not perceived as dangerous. At the same time, in his capacity as general, in his dealings with the Senate, Aspar does seem to wield some power. We never learn whether his more or less veiled threats that a revolt would ensue if Léon were named emperor are serious or completely empty. Aspar therefore remains suspended between two poles, a threat because of his stature and ridiculous because he elicits irony and sarcasm from those around him. Resolution is elusive because Aspar never acts: he takes no decisive step either to incite insurrection or to marry either Pulchérie or Irène. He does no more than unsuccessfully attempt to convince others to share the throne with him. One thing is certain: no one much likes or respects Aspar. It is curious therefore to find that he resembles Pulchérie in a number of significant respects. Structurally they are both isolated, Pulchérie because of her elevated position and Aspar because of the lack of trust he inspires and the ironic tone others adopt when addressing him. Unlike the four other characters, neither Aspar nor Pulchérie shares the stage with a family member, both are politically ambitious, and, most significant, both are willing to sacrifice love for political power.

In the final analysis, Aspar remains undecidable, never resolving neatly into a stable entity. The last word on Aspar belongs to Pulchérie, who calls him "cet esprit flottant" (l. 1756). He is excluded from the stage at the dénouement, in part because the play's resolution does not extend to him: we know only that he has two days to decide whether or not to marry Irène. More importantly, he must be kept off stage in the final scenes because the language of resolution cannot be double. Indeed, irony, sarcasm, and duplicity disappear once Aspar has left the stage for good after act 5, scene 4.

The dénouement of *Pulchérie* shares with *Nicomède* a strong sense of resolution and hope for the future. Both happy conclusions, however, are open to ironic reversal. We noted in the case of *Nicomède* that the unresolved issue of Annibal's death may lead one to doubt the universal reconciliation in the last scene. Here the issue is age. While Aspar shows himself to have certain drawbacks in terms of personality, as we have seen, it is nonetheless noteworthy that of the three male characters he alone is of appropriate age and stature to be emperor. Léon is very young and inexperienced while Martian talks of dying in short order due to the responsibility of the throne.[51] While Pulchérie's motivations (to rule) and aspirations (to see the man she loves on the throne) are clearly set out, the exclusion of Aspar—both from the stage and from the throne—may be read to undermine the dénouement ironically. The use of verbal irony in *Pulchérie* is quite unusual in Corneille's theater because of the extent to which it is woven into the central issue of the play and especially because of the degree of doubt it introduces. While Pulchérie's search for the appropriate emperor is resolved, the doubt surrounding Aspar and the verbal irony he occasions never is.

*

Verbal irony in a theater of language is obviously central; indeed, it is widespread and evident throughout Corneille's theater. The clearly ironic intent of speaking characters indicates the wide range of active ironists that people the playwright's stage. While such verbal irony is only rarely the dominant note in a character's voice, it is one that echoes throughout the plays. Ranging from *raillerie* to judgmental distance to hostility, verbal irony provides nuance, layering of meanings, and undecidability. Echoic mentions, perhaps the most common form that verbal irony takes in Corneille's theater, allow for a particularly dramatic confrontation, wherein irony parries and attacks, itself a verbal weapon. We will examine verbal irony further in part 2, focusing on less evident cases, where the ironic intent is more open to doubt.

Notes

[35]The definition continues, indicating that the term is often, but by no means exclusively, used to "convey an indelicate meaning." Needless to say, sexual innuendo is not common in Corneille's theater. We may, however, if we so desire, credit Corneille with a sexually based double entendre when Paulin describes how Didyme managed to be the first in the lupanar, where Théodore is to be ravished by countless soldiers, by saying: "Il entre sans obstacle" (*Théodore*, l. 1267).

[36]Verhœff points out that the seeming reversal of meaning from negative to positive in this instance may in fact signal the inverse: "Le jeu de mots, en effet, pourrait être interprété aussi comme un *lapsus*. Chez Corneille en général et pour Dorante en particulier, le mariage est loin d'avoir la valeur d'une garantie ou même d'une promesse de bonheur. La prison d'autre part, on l'a vu, n'était pas pour le héros une réalité néfaste, mais un abri" (*Comédies* 146).

[37]Schoentjes notes that, "comme façon de se mettre soi-même en question, l'auto-ironie renoue avec le caractère antique de l'*eirôn*…Nous apprécions plus volontiers l'ironie chez quelqu'un qui ne la dirige pas de façon systématique contre les autres mais se l'applique à l'occasion à lui-même" (186).

[38]Perrin has been quite critical of Sperber and Wilson, saying that what is specific to irony is not the fact of mentioning a statement that one seeks to discredit, but the paradox that results. "L'approche de Sperber et Wilson exclut d'emblée la possibilité de rendre compte non seulement de l'antiphrase mais de tout ce qui a trait au paradoxe, au double jeu énonciatif contradictoire qui caractérise l'ironie" (125).

[39]Lyons calls "Attila's last stage entry in Act V…one of the most remarkable examples of sarcastic humor in seventeenth-century French theater" (*Tragedy* 169).

[40]Prigent focuses on the issue of distance and notes: "*Nicomède* inaugure une nouvelle forme de tragédie politique qui évite la catastrophe en créant une distance entre le héros et ses adversaires. L'instrument de cette distance est l'ironie" (302).

[41]Hutcheon notes that the similarities between verbal irony and lies have long been responsible for the suspect moral character often attributed to irony (*Edge* 118).

[42]*Nicomède* contains eleven trilogue scenes, the largest number in all of Corneille's theater.

[43]"Qu'en présence des Rois les vérités sont fortes! / Que pour sortir d'un cœur elles trouvent de portes! / Qu'on en voit le mensonge aisément confondu!" (ll. 1075-77).

[44]Araspe:

> Pour tout autre que lui je sais comme s'explique
> La règle de la vraie, et saine Politique.
>
> . . . .
>
> C'est un crime d'État, que d'en pouvoir commettre,
> Et qui sait bien régner l'empêche prudemment
>
> . . . .
>
> Et prévient par un ordre à tous deux salutaire
> Ou les maux qu'il prépare, ou ceux qu'il pourrait faire.
> Mais, Seigneur, pour le Prince, il a trop de vertu,
> Je vous l'ai déjà dit.
>
> (ll. 431–42)

[45]Elsewhere, in Corneille's serious theater, such a configuration is found in the opening scene only in the case of *Pulchérie* (Pulchérie and Léon) and arguably *Œdipe* (Dircé and Thésée).

[46]Annibal's centrality to the play should not be underestimated. Fumaroli judges Nicomède to be but an ironic reflection of the great Carthaginian general ("Rhétorique" 318).

[47]I hesitate to call Aspar a "liar" because he bears no resemblance to the Dorante of *Le Menteur*: he does not invent fictions out of whole cloth, but rather hides his base self-interest under a pretense of loyalty, devotion, even love.

[48]Interestingly, Stegmann thought it necessary to add a footnote: "Ces quatre vers sont évidemment ironiques" (*OC* 786).

[49]Dorante, in both *Le Menteur* and *La Suite du Menteur*, elicits a similar reaction but, generally speaking, only from Cliton.

[50]Stegmann sees him first as "un pur machiavélique" (*Héroïsme* 644) and then a few pages later seemingly changes his mind: "Plutôt qu'un ambitieux machiavélique, Aspar est un grand de Cour insoumis" (647); Rathé finds him to be "la caricature du politicien calculateur, de l'obsédé ridicule de la comédie, semblable au détective moderne qui rôde sur scène muni d'une loupe et de lunettes de soleil" ("Distribution" 101); Zimmermann calls him "difficile à saisir" (101) and finds that he ought to be played by an actor with a great deal of sex appeal (102). Curiously enough, Couton makes no mention of him whatsoever in his "Notice" to the play (Corneille 3:1654–64).

[51]Zimmermann notes astutely that the three male characters embody the three ages of man:

> Si on juxtapose ces trois hommes on comprend qu'à un certain niveau ils ne font qu'un. Ils incarnent les trois stades de l'homme: jeune et idéaliste (Léon); adulte, orgueilleux, cherchant à s'établir dans le monde (Aspar); et vieux, ayant renoncé aux ambitions, doué d'une certaine sagesse désabusée, paternel et essentiellement observateur d'un monde qu'il s'apprête à quitter (Martian). (102)

CHAPTER 4
SITUATIONAL IRONY

Situational irony entails a contradiction, opposition, or contrast between two contiguous elements or events. For instance, at the very moment when Chimène and Rodrigue's betrothal is to be finalized, circumstances force Rodrigue to fight her father in a duel. The contiguity in question may be spatial or temporal; in this example, it is temporal. The union and happiness of the young couple is reversed from one moment to the next. The incongruous juxtaposition characteristic of spatial contiguity often involves temporal contiguity as well. Thus, it is ironic that in the final act of *Don Sanche* Don Raymond arrives at Isabelle's court at just the moment that a letter, kept secret under the most romanesque circumstances for twenty years, reveals Carlos's identity. The physical juxtaposition of the letter and Don Raymond, both necessary for the positive identification of the long-lost heir to the throne of Aragon, is incongruous, to say the least.

Situational irony differs radically from verbal irony in that its source is not a character on stage. At issue is not the opposition between verbal and nonverbal, because much situational irony is conveyed by language, but rather, ironic intent. In the case of situational irony, ironic intent cannot be localized on stage. Our understanding of intent in terms of situational irony will hover between two poles. On the one hand, a focus on reception rather than intention dispenses with the need for an intending ironist: "Interpreters are active agents in making all irony happen, but ironists as intentional actants are necessary and functional only in *certain* ironies" (Hutcheon, *Edge* 122). The other alternative is to credit the irony to a superior or superhuman source, whether it be a god or fate. The basic and problematic uncertainty of whether there exists an intending source for situational irony can be sidestepped to some degree in the context of Corneille's theater because, while the presence of a superhuman order is open to question in our world, and may vary from one dramatic universe to the next (*Œdipe* and *Polyeucte* unquestionably present superior orders, but does, for instance, *Sophonisbe?*), in the domain of literature there is always a superhuman source: the author. While reception may suffice, as Hutcheon contends, no one would argue with the assertion that irony works best when there is both reception and intention. Thus in identifying situational irony in Corneille's theater our task is made easier by the presence of a readily available intending source to

55

which it can be ascribed: the playwright.

There are other complications, however. For instance, how may we distinguish between coincidence and irony? Situational irony often entails coincidence, as in the above example taken from the dénouement of *Don Sanche*. Literary plots in general revolve around or at least make extensive use of coincidence. Corneille provides numerous such examples: Auguste summons Cinna at just the moment the latter is discussing the conspiracy with Émilie (*Cinna* 1.4); Pertharite reappears just as Grimoald is trying to force Rodelinde to marry him (*Pertharite* 3.4); Sertorius is killed just as the news arrives that Sylla has abdicated (*Sertorius* 5.2–3). In order for the coincidence to be considered irony, there must be an edge, a constructible critical viewpoint on the coincidence that we may credit to our intending source, Corneille. The example from *Don Sanche* illustrates the difficulty perfectly. Of course, the playwright orchestrated the simultaneity of the two events, but is he making an ironic statement thereby? One could easily answer "no," that he was merely using the coincidence as a means of removing any conceivable doubt concerning Sanche's identity in order to end the play. Or one can ascribe ironic intent to Corneille: the coincidence in question is so heavy-handed that we may speculate that the playwright is using it to mock the standard resolution of a tragicomic plot. The ambiguity in the case of *Don Sanche*'s dénouement provides a sense of the limitations of the author's control over irony. The spectator can perceive irony in that coincidence even if Corneille had no such intent.

The other three coincidences mentioned above are more evidently ironic because they contain another characteristic of situational irony: a logically ordered relation between events, generally along the lines of symmetry or inversion. In the first two, a reversal results from the coincidence. Cinna moves abruptly from bravura to apprehension and Grimoald abandons his cruel courtship of Rodelinde. In the case of Sertorius, the irony is considerably greater because the general's murder, though a perfect reversal of fortune, is not causally linked to Sylla's abdication.

Incongruity is also a characteristic of situational irony, and is clearly related to coincidence:

> Another way of explaining why it is ironic for a robber to be robbed or a swimming instructor drowned is to point to the unlikelihood of this, that is, to the disparity between what might be expected and what actually happens. The wider the disparity, the greater the irony. (Muecke, *Irony* 53)

All four of the examples above could be said to juxtapose two incongruous elements, although the one taken from *Cinna* does this decidedly less. Given Cinna's function as an advisor to the emperor, it does not seem particularly surprising that the latter should summon him. The revelation of the letter coupled with Raymond's arrival, Grimoald's desire to marry Rodelinde paired with the sudden appearance of the latter's husband, and Sylla's abdication juxtaposed with Sertorius's assassination, on the other hand, are quite startling.

There is a striking connection between the issues of order and incongruity, both typical of situational irony, and certain of Corneille's abiding preoccupations. The incongruity characteristic of situational irony fosters surprise while also running the risk of *invraisemblance*. The tension between surprise and *vraisemblance*, as is well known, is a recurring feature of Corneille's theater and was the source of considerable friction with his contemporary critics. The playwright's profound affection for surprise would suggest an affinity for situational irony. Furthermore, throughout his career, Corneille demonstrated an abiding taste for logical order of all sorts, perhaps especially for antithesis and symmetry.[52] Thus in certain respects it would appear likely that the playwright found situational irony to be a natural terrain. However, the suggestion of a superior order (other than that of his own status as the author), which is typical of much situational irony, is basically alien to Corneille.

Situational irony is no doubt the broadest category of irony, and perhaps the most ambiguous as well. In this chapter we will focus on the most evidently ironic varieties and conclude with an analysis of a particular form of situational irony that Corneille employs in several of his plays, the oracle. The less clear-cut varieties of situational irony will be taken up in part 2.

TYPES OF SITUATIONAL IRONY IN CORNEILLE'S THEATER

Reversal of fortune is a common form of situational irony, and one of the most problematic. First, the notion of reversal is a basic literary structure: like coincidence, it is found everywhere in literature, at every level. Aristotle, for example, considered a reversal of fortune basic to the plot of tragedy (72–73). There is no doubt that Corneille was very fond of reversals, but surprising turnabouts are not in themselves ironic. Rather, reversal is a necessary but not sufficient condition for one type of situational irony. An example will illustrate the problem. It is clear that in *Horace* the eponymous hero suffers a radical reversal of fortune in the space of the fourth act. He goes from being the savior of Rome to killing his sister, from glory to ignominy. To call his situation ironic, while certainly possible, is not the obvious choice for the simple reason that to do so is to posit a superior order to which he has fallen victim.[53] Horace's fall would thus no longer be his own responsibility and the

(margin notes:) risk of invraisemblance · Corneille liked surprise · "seems to have had affinity for sit'l irony · also liked order, esp antithesis, symmetry · ? of superior order & nC · TYPES · 1) reversal of fortune · nb not all reversals are ironic

notion of heroism, so central to the tetralogy, would be compromised.

A completely different problem posed by reversal of fortune concerns the direction of the reversal. Theoretically, the shift could be in either direction, from fortune to misfortune, or vice-versa. After all, both reversal of fortune and the *trompeur trompé* are tied to the notion of justice. The Gospels famously refer to such a justice-based reversal of fortune: "[T]he last will be first, and the first will be last" (Matthew 20:16). In practice, however, just as verbal irony more typically uses praise in order to blame rather than vice-versa, ameliorative reversals are not often perceived as ironic, particularly in the context of tragedy. Consider the transformation that Auguste undergoes in *Cinna*, one that can easily be read as a reversal of fortune. The emperor goes from being the object of multiple assassination conspiracies to being the focus of public veneration and is given assurance of no further threats to his life. An ironic reading of this reversal seems problematic, in part, as in the case of Horace, because Auguste's own role in the reversal would thereby be eliminated, and in part because the "edge" that Hutcheon describes as essential to irony is absent. So while a reversal of fortune upward remains a theoretical possibility, in practice the association with a downward shift prevails.

The notion of *trompeur trompé* is closely related to reversal of fortune because it too is based on a structure of reversal. It is far less problematic, however, because of its tight, economical structure. By foregrounding order, symmetry, and simple justice, the suggestion of a superior order is forceful, and the conclusion of irony is inescapable (see Schoentjes 69). The tighter the structure, the more powerful the irony. The seriousness of the subject matter does not seem to matter; Corneille uses this construction in both his comedies and his serious plays. The subtitle of *La Veuve*, *Le Traître trahi*, for example, is an explicit formulation. Alcidon, the *traître* in question, tries to steal Clarice from Philiste, and eventually kidnaps her with the help of his friend Célidan. When Célidan comes to understand the treachery that motivated the kidnapping, he turns the tables and betrays Alcidon by freeing Clarice. Alidor frees himself in *La Place Royale* from his relationship with Angélique, rejecting her on two occasions; at the end of the play she rejects his overtures by choosing a convent over reconciliation. In *Le Menteur*, Dorante lectures Alcippe, "[D]onnez moins de croyance / Aux premiers mouvements de votre défiance, / Jusqu'à mieux savoir tout, sachez vous retenir" (ll. 769–71). The plot of the entire play, however, is based on the fact that Dorante himself has jumped to a mistaken conclusion concerning the identity of Lucrèce.[54] In *La Suite du Menteur*, Cliton, the manservant who has reproached Dorante throughout both plays for lying, is himself forced to prevaricate in order to coax Philiste away from Mélisse's window (4.5), a fact that he underlines and laments. More seriously, *Rodogune*'s Cléopâtre is to some extent a figure of *trompeur trompé* in that her plans to destroy Rodogune and her sons lead instead to her own death. Arsinoé's scheme to ruin Nicomède is articulated using this same ironic structure: "Tous deux [Zénon and Métrobate] voulaient me perdre et tous deux l' [Nicomède] ont perdu" (*Nicomède* l. 1078). In both *Pertharite* and *Attila* a character's own words are turned against him- or herself. In the former, Éduïge accuses Grimoald of defending himself poorly against her accusations of unfaithfulness. She goes on to detail a number of better excuses he might have employed. He responds, "J'embrasse un bon avis de quelque part qu'il vienne" (l. 367) and uses Éduïge's sound reasoning to try to convince Éduïge's rival, Rodelinde, to marry him. When, in *Attila*, Honorie haughtily suggests that Ildione should be forced to marry a commoner as a punishment (ll. 1227–28), Attila immediately proposes the same option for Honorie as well: "Agréez cependant pour vous même justice, / Et s'il faut un Sujet à qui dédaigne un Roi, / Choisissez dans une heure, ou d'Octar, ou de moi" (ll. 1234–36). In *Cinna*, Auguste at one point sees cruel justice in casting himself as a *trompeur trompé*; speaking to himself, he says, "Rends un sang infidèle à l'infidélité / Et souffre des ingrats après l'avoir été" (ll. 1147–48). It is clear from these examples that Corneille employs the ironic figure of *trompeur trompé* quite widely in his theater.

Juxtaposition and incongruity provide a more spatially oriented way of considering situational irony. Two elements or events are placed in close proximity; their juxtaposition suggests irony because of some contradiction between them. Forestier points out the ironic paradox at the root of Suréna's fate: "[Q]u'un roi veuille perdre celui qui a sauvé son royaume, sans autre motif que celui précisément d'avoir sauvé son royaume" (*Génétique* 40). In a similar vein, it is ironic that *Rodogune*'s Cléopâtre seeks to do away with her sons rather than cede the throne, while they insist that they would be perfectly happy to allow her to continue to reign. When they tell her—"Nous pouvons sans régner vivre tous deux contents, / C'est le fruit de vos soins, jouissez-en longtemps, / Il tombera sur nous quand vous en serez lasse" (ll. 601–3)—she simply refuses to believe them.

To the extent that the juxtaposition involves an opposition of some sort, there will be no disagreement about calling it ironic. Créon says to his dying daughter, "Et pour lit nuptial il te faut un tombeau" (*Médée*, l. 1420). The clash of "lit nuptial" and "tombeau" forms the basis of the irony. In fact, Corneille creates an atmosphere of both irony and pathos in this scene by multiplying such *pointes* based on ironic opposition. Recognizing that her desire to possess Médée's dress is responsible for her father's death as well as her own, Créuse says, "Je ne puis excuser mon indiscrète envie / Qui donne le trépas à qui je dois la vie" (ll. 1401–2). Similarly, Amarante, the eponymous character of *La Suivante*, comments: "Puisqu'un jeune amant suit les lois de l'avarice, / Il faut bien qu'un vieillard suive celles d'amour" (ll. 1683–84). *Être* and *paraître* are opposed in the ironic situation of Œdipe: he seems to be the illegitimate ruler of Thèbes, a point which Dircé belabors, while in reality his legitimacy is guaranteed by his birth, which remains hidden until the play's dénouement.[55] However, if the juxtaposition is a matter of incongruity rather than opposition, questions may easily arise about whether it is ironic or not, because what one person perceives as incongruous may not necessarily seem so to another. For example, is the discordance between the violence described in the opening scene of *Cinna* and the subtitle of the play, *La Clémence d'Auguste*, ironic, as Christophe Triau suggests (86)?

The ironic possibilities for juxtaposition extend to Corneille's plays themselves. Corneille was quick to point out that *Pompée* and *Le Menteur* had been composed concurrently. Seemingly taking pleasure in calling attention to the discordance caused by the juxtaposition of the two, he opens his *Épître* to *Le Menteur* with "Je vous présente une pièce de théâtre d'un style si éloigné de ma dernière [*Pompée*], qu'on aura de la peine à croire qu'elles soient parties toutes deux de la même main, dans le même hiver" (2:3). He develops the contrast at great length, revelling in the antitheses: with *Pompée* he sought to explore the possibilities of "la majesté du raisonnement et la force des vers dénués de l'agrément du sujet," and with *Le Menteur*, "l'agrément du sujet dénué de la force des vers" (2:3). Reading the two plays in tandem is indeed disconcerting, and insofar as the two are opposites of one another in certain respects—genre, level of rhetoric—as they were written simultaneously, their juxtaposition may indeed be considered ironic.

Situational irony offers less assurance of intention and relies more on reception than dramatic or verbal irony, in part because it may be less localized on stage than the other two, and in part because incongruity is a matter of degree. As such, situational irony is more apt to be categorized as possible, rather than evident. We will return to these possible situational ironies in part 2. One variety of situational irony, however, is far less susceptible to uncertainty: the irony of fate.

IRONY OF FATE

Irony of fate is probably the most well known form of situational irony, and certainly the one most readily associated with tragedy. Here the superior order is unquestionably understood to be the intending source of the irony. Furthermore, "God, or destiny, or the universal process, is represented as though deliberately manipulating events to frustrate and mock the protagonist" (Abrams 83). Thus, it is no longer a matter of the simple suggestion of a superior order; in irony of fate a superior order clearly exists, it has deliberate intentions, and those intentions are malevolent. Furthermore, the irony of fate is intrinsically linked to dramatic irony, as we noted earlier: in order for the audience to experience its force, we must know in advance what awaits the characters.

It is fascinating how little use overall Corneille makes of the irony of fate. The primary example, of course, is *Œdipe*, but even here, Corneille demonstrates his ambivalence about the subject by including elements that undermine the presence of a superior order. Specifically, Corneille gives Thésée a speech concerning free will (ll. 1149–70) and he emphasizes that Œdipe takes responsibility for his situation. At the same time, however, Corneille underscores the irony of fate in this play through incongruity: he describes the motivations behind Iphicrate's actions and decisions as "pitié" (l. 1703), Phorbas's as "compassion" (l. 1724), and Polybe's as "une amitié fort tendre" (l. 1697), thereby marking the distance between the three men's generous intentions and the far more powerful and nefarious intent of the gods. A second play which can be said to employ irony of fate is *Attila*. The notion of a superior order is carefully set up at the beginning of the play by the prophecies concerning the future of Méroüee in Gaul (soothsayers predict he will found a magnificent empire, ll. 89–96) and Valamir in Rome (another diviner has predicted that Valamir's offspring will sit on the Roman throne, ll. 310–12). While the audience is most likely not familiar with the plot of the play in advance, the universally known future of Gaul works to caution all predictions by seers and thus to assure the existence of a superior power in this dramatic universe. At the end of the play, we move from the bright futures awaiting Gaul and Valamir to the dark irony of the fate awaiting Attila. Honorie suggests, "Lorsque par les Tyrans il [God] punit les Mortels, / Il réserve sa foudre à ces grands criminels / Qu'il donne pour supplice à toute la Nature" (ll. 1583–85). Like Œdipe, Attila is ignorant of his fate. He believes himself to be the scourge of God ("On me craint, on me hait, on me nomme en tout lieu / La terreur des Mortels et le fléau de Dieu," ll. 883–84), and that it is his role to bring a deluge of blood to mankind as a divine punishment, but he is unaware that the flood will be of his own blood and that the final punishment (a massive hemorrhage) is reserved for him alone. A looser variant of irony of fate can be said to be at work in *Suréna*. There is no specific superior force, as in the other examples, but rather an atmosphere of inevitable doom. In most of Corneille's plays, not only is the end at least in part positive, but the characters engage in active struggle. Here, Suréna and Eurydice seem cognizant from the first act of the inevitability of separation and its consequences for both of them: "Toujours aimer, toujours souffrir, toujours mourir" (l. 268).

In the religious plays, *Polyeucte* and *Théodore*, God is explicitly taken to be an acting and intending force, but irony of fate is out of the question

[margin notes:]
irony of fate ⇒ we know their fate in advance

C uses little of this; the exception = Œdipe

yet – undermines presence of superior order even here.
+ free will

men's intentions vs intentions of gods

or: Attila

where ∃ superior power

or: Suréna – no superior force, but doom

because in both we find a benevolent Christian God, not the mockingly cruel gods of ancient Greek tragedy. Even in the three other plays (besides *Œdipe*) based on Greek mythology, it is not appropriate to speak in terms of the irony of fate. In both *Médée* and *La Toison d'or*, the focus is on Médée's own choices and power, rather than those of the gods. In *Andromède*, while the gods are both present and active, the frustration they mete out to humans leads to a happy fate, except for Phinée, who is despoiled of his fiancée.

A particular variety of situational irony linked to the irony of fate involves words spoken lightly that later come devastatingly true. The irony here is grounded in the possibility that the words may somehow conjure that reality, a possibility that suggests the presence of a malevolent superior force. For example, as part of his argument for delaying any decision concerning marriage, Sertorius tells Perpenna, "Et ma tête abattue ébranlerait la vôtre" (l. 1422). Indeed, Sertorius's statement is prophetic, although Perpenna does not heed it: he has Sertorius killed and is in response slain by the crowd. In the play-within-a-play in the fifth act of *L'Illusion comique*, the character Clindor plays changes his mind about being unfaithful to his wife. Burdened with guilt, he tells Rosine, "Faites sortir vos gens destinés à ma perte, / N'épargnez point ma tête, elle vous est offerte" (ll. 1605–6). The terrible irony of his words is that Rosine's husband's men will indeed kill him in the following scene (5.5), although she does not summon them. While this kind of irony has ties to dramatic irony based on rereading or reviewing, the focus remains on the inscription of a horrible fate. Ian R. Morrison notes a lighter variant of this mechanism in *Cinna*. Cinna's words to Auguste in the second act suggesting a propitious reign for the emperor if he does not abdicate prove to be true despite Cinna's actual intentions to assassinate him. Livie's prophecy in the final scene of the play coupled with audience knowledge of Roman history confirm that Cinna was inadvertently and ironically correct (190).

The central question remains: why would an author of tragedies who so closely identifies himself with Aristotle in his critical writings largely reject this core element of the theater Aristotle describes? There are many possible and partial answers, but taken together, I believe they go to the heart of Corneille's specificity as an author. From a biographical perspective, one can perceive a basic incompatibility between a cruel, ironic God and the religious faith ascribed to Corneille. Indeed, there is little or no sign in his theater of fear and awe of a malevolent superior power. In another realm, we find a profound dissimilarity between Ancient and Cornelian tragedy (see Matzat 164); Serge Doubrovsky goes so far as to suggest that Corneille does not understand the nature of Greek tragedy (337). Furthermore, Corneille's fondness for surprise in his plots runs directly counter to irony of fate, because the latter is based on the implacable unfolding of the inevitable and

Margin notes:

In religious plays, God = benevolent Christian God, ∴ no irony

In mytho'l plays, focus = on chars' power, not gods

Interesting case: words spoken lightly come true

↳ horrible fate

NB –
C identifies w/ Aristotle, yet rejects (mostly) this core ell

why?

his faith ≠> malevolent higher power

or

C doesn't really understand Ancient tragedy
or

or · fondness for surprise

thus, at least for the audience, the foreseeable. Finally, Corneille's characters typically demonstrate a desire to take control of their situations, a stance that does not admit or respect a higher power. Auguste's act of clemency in *Cinna*, for example, is traditionally presented as an expression of his own will.[56] Corneille's characters are typically faced with and make choices; the notion of choice is not congruent with that of fate.

While it is clear that irony of fate is not central to tragedy as Corneille envisioned it, such a position did not leave Corneille himself immune to being its victim. One might argue that a malevolent superior force made Corneille's own words cruelly prophetic. In his *Examen* to *Pertharite*, a play which was a devastating failure, the playwright discusses the future of the theater: "[I]l en viendra de plus heureux après nous qui le [theater] mettront à sa perfection, et achèveront de l'épurer. Je le souhaite de tout mon cœur" (2:715). Racine would begin to fulfill Corneille's words not long after he wrote that *Examen* in 1660. We can only imagine how much Corneille suffered on account of that particular irony of fate.

ORACLES

Despite the relative paucity of irony of fate, it has one privileged manifestation in Corneille's theater: the oracle. *The New Shorter Oxford English Dictionary* defines *oracle* as "a frequently ambiguous or obscure response or message...supposedly from a god and usually delivered by a priest or priestess." Oracles thus share with the irony of fate its basic precondition: the existence of some superior order, without which oracular discourse can be no more than a sham. Oracles normally pertain to the future, thus the need for the divine in order to provide the necessary assurance of veracity. It is only when that future becomes the present, however, that the full meaning of an oracle reveals itself. Oracles are thus the verbal extension of the irony of fate. We discuss them here, rather than in the chapter dealing with verbal irony, for two reasons: first, because they are so closely tied to the irony of fate, and second, because the articulation of oracles in Corneille's plays is often second-hand—reported divine discourse rather than direct speech—and thus functions at a remove from the stage that is the locus of verbal irony. Whereas Corneille shies away from most forms of tragic irony, as we noted earlier, he seems to be quite comfortable with oracles, employing them in fact more frequently than any other French seventeenth-century playwright (Louvat-Molozay, "Oracle" 397).

It is a customary feature of oracles to be in some fashion obscure, ambiguous, and/or enigmatic. The oracle's fundamental difference from human discourse is thus manifested through the interpretive problems it poses. It is, according to Bernard Magné, "un discours piégé" (250). Corneille calls attention to these issues when he has Camille say,

> Un Oracle jamais ne se laisse comprendre,
> On l'entend d'autant moins que plus on croit
>   l'entendre,
> Et loin de s'assurer sur un pareil Arrêt,
> Qui n'y voit rien d'obscur doit croire que tout l'est.
>   (*Horace* ll. 851–54)[57]

Indeed, the playwright admits that he prefers that oracles appear clear at first, the better to accentuate the reversal:

> Il [the oracle in *Horace*] semble clair d'abord, et porte l'imagination à un sens contraire, et je les aimerais mieux de cette sorte sur nos Théâtres, que ceux qu'on fait entièrement obscurs, parce que la surprise de leur véritable effet en est plus belle. (*Examen* to *Horace* 1:842)

Reversal constitutes the source of the irony.

For Corneille, oracles are clearly distinguished from dreams and prophesies, despite the fact that they all share the capacity to announce the future in some fashion. The playwright states his position concerning dreams in the *Examen* to *Horace*: "Je voudrais qu'ils eussent l'idée de la fin véritable de la Pièce, mais avec quelque confusion, qui n'en permît pas l'intelligence entière" (*Examen* 1:842). Unlike oracles, then, dreams do not even give the appearance or illusion of clarity. In *Horace*, Corneille takes pains to place the two in opposition to one another: "Un Oracle m'assure, un songe me travaille" (l. 1211), laments Camille. Dreams in Corneille's theater, found only in *Horace* and *Polyeucte*, are emotionally fraught visions that resist comprehension until later in the play. Whereas oracles shift radically from apparent to real meaning, dreams move from the incomprehensible to the comprehensible and they are thus less likely to give rise to irony. Premonitions and *la voix du sang* are similarly imprecise and become intelligible only in retrospect.[58] The potential for irony is even smaller in the case of prophecies because they contain no hint of ambiguity. While the receiver may choose to give credence to the prophecy or not, if the discourse is indeed prophetic, it is true and straightforwardly so.[59] Oracles are clearer than dreams, premonitions, or *la voix du sang*, but less transparent than prophecies. They lend themselves to irony because of the balanced tension between clarity and lack of clarity.

Corneille first employs an oracle in *Horace*. When Camille hears the oracular pronouncement,

*I like this part —
addresses an elt
that niggled at me for
years!
though Louvat / Molozay
did work on in 2002*

Albe et Rome demain prendront une autre face,
Tes vœux sont exaucés, elles auront la Paix,
Et tu seras unie avec ton Curiace,
Sans qu'aucun mauvais sort t'en sépare jamais
(ll. 195–98)

*C's first
oracle =
Horace*

she interprets it to mean that there will be peace between the two cities and that she will marry Curiace. The seeming clarity of the oracle is placed in direct opposition to Camille's "mille songes affreux" (l. 216), which she characterizes as "confusion" (l. 222). The clarity of the oracle is illusory, of course, and its irony comes from the fact that the word *unie* refers to being joined in death, not in wedlock. This oracle is of Corneille's invention; the source material for the play—taken from Livy—contains no mention of any oracle. In the editions prior to 1660, Corneille took pains to underline the irony of reversal in this oracle by having Julie end the play with a short monologue that makes the point explicitly.[60] Bénédicte Louvat-Molozay argues that Corneille's use of the oracle in this play indicates that he believes that such passages should appear in the exposition and then reappear in the dénouement and be subject to two antithetical interpretations ("Oracle" 400). Whether the decision to drop Julie's final monologue in 1660 was wise or ill-advised is open to some debate.[61] One consequence of its elimination is a significant reduction in the foregrounding of the tragic irony at play in the oracle. Indeed, we may speculate that Corneille chose to remove that final passage because he wanted the focus to be on the choices made by the individual characters, especially Horace, Camille, and Tulle, and not on the control exercised by fate.

*(takes out
ref to oracle
in dénouement —*

*(more focus on
chars' choices,
not fate?)*

In *Andromède*, Corneille alters and multiplies the single oracle provided by the play's source, Ovid's *Metamorphoses*. Whereas the oracle of Jupiter Ammon in the latter demanded that Andromède be given over for sacrifice to the monster, Corneille imagines that the oracle calls for a young woman, chosen by lot and thus not necessarily Andromède, to be sacrificed to the monster every month:

Andromède

Pour apaiser Neptune, exposez tous les mois
Au Monstre qui le venge, une fille à son choix,
Jusqu'à ce que le calme à l'orage succède:
    Le sort vous montrera
    Celle qu'il agréera;
Différez cependant les noces d'Andromède.
(ll. 176–81)

Corneille's oracle contains a second point—about delaying Andromède's wedding—that is absent from the Ovidian source. Corneille has obviously increased the level of ambiguity in his oracle, leaving everyone with questions. Are the two parts of the oracle related? If so, how? Is Andromède supposed to put off her wedding because she is to be sacrificed?

Corneille then invents a second oracle which contrasts strikingly with the first. Furthermore, it is an oracle uttered by Venus directly on stage:[62]

> On va jeter le Sort pour la dernière fois,
>   Et le Ciel ne veut plus d'un choix,
>   Pour apaiser de tout point sa colère:
> Andromède ce soir aura l'illustre époux,
> Qui seul est digne d'elle, et dont seule elle est digne.
>
>   (ll. 355–59)

Like the first oracle, this one has two parts, again dealing first with the sacrifice of young women and second with Andromède's wedding. And while the second oracle seems to follow seamlessly from the first—from monthly sacrifice to final sacrifice, from the wedding suspended to the wedding scheduled for that very evening, from ominous to propitious—it replicates the interior disjunction of the first oracle. What does the final sacrifice have to do with Andromède's wedding? Is one (which one?) a celebration of the other? The ambiguity of this oracle is concentrated in the unknown identity of two of the three individuals implied by it. We know that Andromède will be wed, but the oracle does not specify to whom. Vénus does not reveal the identity of the final sacrificial victim either. Corneille waits an entire act to provide that additional piece of information, from 1.3 to 2.3, when the king pulls Andromède's name out of the vase three times. At that point the two parts of the oracle seem to be in contradiction to each other: Andromède is to be sacrificed and Andromède is to be married. The entire remainder of the play is encapsulated in that seeming paradox as Persée, by saving Andromède from the monster, earns the right to displace her fiancé Phinée and marry her. Vénus's oracle is ironic in that it seems at first to mean one thing but in fact means something radically different. Through its centrality and the frequent references that are made to it, Vénus's oracle is far more dramatically successful than is the oracle in *Horace* (Louvat-Molozay, "Oracle" 411).

There is even a third oracle in *Andromède*, again of Corneille's invention, and it in turn appears to contradict Vénus's pronouncement. Neptune announces, "Et j'ai su du Destin, qui se ligue avec nous, / Qu'Andromède ici-bas n'aura jamais d'époux" (ll. 1048–49). The key to reconciling this oracle and Vénus's is contained in the words "ici-bas." Indeed, Neptune's oracle proves true: Andromède's wedding and presumably her married life will not take place *ici-bas*, but in the heavens. Corneille develops multiple lines of tension between the oracles in *Andromède*. He seems to take pleasure in the paradoxes he constructs. Irony is woven throughout, as all three oracles shift and reverse their meaning.

In *Œdipe* as well, Corneille relies on oracles taken from his source material, but he makes extensive and significant alterations. The inherited myth of *Œdipe* is based entirely on oracles and the attempts to circumvent what they predict. In the *Au lecteur*, Corneille proudly claims, "[J]'ai retranché le nombre des oracles qui pouvait être importun, et donner trop de jour à Œdipe pour se connaître" (3:19). Indeed, of the three oracles in Sophocles' version—that a pollution, specifically Laïus's murderer, must be driven from the land in order to rid the country of the plague, that Laïus and Jocaste's son was destined to kill his father, and that Œdipe was told that he would marry his mother and kill his father—Corneille simply eliminates the third, leaving Œdipe completely ignorant of his own fate. The role of oracles in the play is not thereby reduced, however. Rather, Corneille alters, complicates, and disperses the remaining two oracles in order to attempt something quite different from what Sophocles accomplished.

In the case of the first oracle, Corneille surprises his audience by a radical shift. Dymas returns from Delphi, not with the response the audience expected, but with nothing: "Aucune [response]." /... "Ils [the Gods] sont muets, et sourds" (ll. 358–59). Corneille ingeniously has Œdipe explain the silence of the gods as a function of their anger at being shown to be wrong in their earlier oracle concerning Jocaste and Laïus's infant son.[63] Most of the information contained in Sophocles' first oracle is transferred to Laïus's shade, who speaks to Tirésie in what we will call the second oracle:

> Un grand crime impuni cause votre misère;
> Par le sang de ma Race il se doit effacer,
>   Mais à moins que de le verser,
>   Le Ciel ne se peut satisfaire,
> Et la fin de vos maux ne se fera point voir,
>   Que mon sang n'ait fait son devoir.
>   (ll. 605–10)[64]

The dead Laïus is not, of course, a proper oracle, but both he and Tirésie ("le devin Tirésie," l. 1026) are closely allied with the power of oracular discourse. As in the case of *Andromède*, it is not clear how to reconcile the two parts of Laïus's pronouncement. Is the "sang de ma Race" responsible for the "grand crime impuni" or only for removing it?[65] Corneille provides a highly inventive embellishment to this second oracle by having the king killed while journeying to visit the oracle once again to learn what the gods held in store for his second child, the newborn Dircé.

In contrast to Sophocles, Corneille makes several moves to attenuate the force and authority of the oracles and thus, I would argue, their irony. Œdipe is not satisfied with the ambiguity of the oracular pronouncement conveyed by Laïus and demands more clarity: "[I]l faut un second ordre, et plus exprès, des Dieux" (l. 952). The people of Thebes take issue with the oracle as well, suspecting Œdipe of having bribed Tirésie to invent Laïus's speech in order to eliminate the troublesome Dircé (ll. 1613–16). Similarly, the oracle that Laïus and Jocaste received years earlier about their son is called into question. Thésée suggests that it may have been false: "Delphes a pu vous faire une fausse réponse, / L'argent put inspirer la voix qui les prononce, / Cet organe des Dieux put se laisser gagner" (ll. 1173–75). What could be more subversive of an oracle than the suggestion that it has been bought? While Corneille does not go so far as to introduce actual corruption into the oracles of this play, its mere suggestion, attached to each of the two oracles in turn, adds a curiously untragic note. While it was ingenious of Corneille to have characters question the validity of oracles in a world where they (specifically here, Laïus and Jocaste, but not Œdipe) imagine that they can outsmart them, accusations of corruption leveled against the gods do not lend themselves well to the structure of situational irony. Jocaste attacks the oracle as well, accusing the gods not of corruption but of being too timid to saddle one person with both parricide and incest (ll. 1537–44). In the case of Jocaste's allegation, we find situational irony based on a structure of inversion: the gods have indeed done what she accuses them of being too timid to do. This is compounded by dramatic irony, as we noted in the last chapter: the audience knows full well that a single individual is responsible for both the incest and the parricide. Finally, at the play's dénouement the characters await another oracular pronouncement scheduled for the following day. Indeed, Œdipe's soul is said to "Attend l'ordre des Dieux pour sortir tout à fait" (l. 1980). By suggesting the possibility of another oracle, one not grounded in the mythic material, Corneille opens the dénouement to new contingencies, and thereby undermines the tragic finality of Œdipe's discovery of his own identity and, with it, his crimes.

The Œdipus myth contains material that is inherently and profoundly ironic and whose irony is rooted in the oracles. In Corneille's version, we still find the fundamental dramatic irony of the play described in chapter 2. There is also situational irony in the tension we find repeated between the double and the one. How does one reconcile the two roles in the second oracle, the criminal and the member of Laïus's family who must pay for the

crime? How does one reconcile this oracle with the earlier one Laïus and
Jocaste received about their son? Corneille is original in creating an ironic
tension within the second oracle, but he sacrifices the ironic coincidence of
the oracles delivered in Sophocles' version first to Laïus and Jocaste and later
to Œdipe. Furthermore, Dircé and Thésée, whose speaking roles constitute
forty-three percent of the play, remain, despite Corneille's best efforts to
implicate them in the oracular discourse, completely outside of the tragically
ironic mechanism of the basic myth.

Oracles appear elsewhere in Corneille's theater as well, but play less
significant roles. In *L'Illusion comique*, *oracle* refers to a character rather than
the discourse. Upon meeting Alcandre, Pridamant calls him an "oracle" (l.
109), which is precisely how he will function. Pridamant looks to him as a
magical and thus supernatural source of truth about his son, but he is unable
to interpret correctly much of what Alcandre tells him. The double meaning of the parade of Dorante's elegant clothes, the "splendeur" (l. 135) and
the "grandeur" (l. 136) of the young man's position in the world, as well as
the nature of his apparent death in the last act all work to make the father
a victim of situational irony. Interestingly, Alcandre's oracular discourse
pertains to the past and present rather than the future. The disjunction is
more spatial than temporal.

We mentioned the prophecies in *Attila* earlier in conjunction with
the irony of fate. Prophesies foretell the future in a straightforward fashion,
while oracles are obscure and ambiguous. Corneille seems to play with the
distinction between the two in *Attila*, calling the first, which foretells the
rising power of Méroüée and the eventual world domination of the Franks,
an *oracle*:

> Mais si de nos devins l'oracle n'est pas faux,
> Sa grandeur [Méroüée's] doit atteindre aux degrés les
>   plus hauts,
> Et de ses successeurs l'Empire inébranlable
> Sera de siècle en siècle enfin si redoutable,
> Qu'un jour toute la Terre en recevra des lois,
> Ou tremblera du moins au nom de leurs François.
>   (ll. 91–96)

The source of this oracle is "nos devins" (l. 91), a term that appears in only
one other of Corneille's plays, *Œdipe*, where it twice refers to Tirésie.[66] In
Attila, the *devins* are the sole link to divine will. Valamir reports that they have
also revealed that "un Théodoric qui doit sortir de moi / Commandera dans
Rome et s'en fera le Roi" (ll. 311–12). Neither of the pronouncements by

the *devins* is ambiguous or obscure and no second meaning is ever revealed. The spectator, however, may well be misled by the use of the word *oracle* because of the norm Corneille has established in his other plays, where an oracle always means something different than it appears to mean. Corneille may be playing with our expectation of irony in conjunction with oracles by destabilizing these passages in *Attila* in other ways as well. Valamir raises the possibility that one might doubt the word of the *devins* by asserting the contrary ("Vous [Ardaric] qui n'avez jamais douté de leurs oracles," l. 146), that one could somehow abet them ("D'un si bel avenir avouez vos Devins, / Avancez les succès, et hâtez les destins," ll. 151–52), or even impede them:

> Mais s'il est glorieux, Seigneur, de le hâter,
> Il l'est, et plus encor, de si bien l'arrêter,
> Que la France en dépit d'un infaillible augure
> N'aille qu'à pas traînants vers sa grandeur future.
>   (ll. 155–58)

The two oracles in *Attila*, however, are in fact simple prophecies, completely devoid of all irony.

    The final example of oracles in Corneille's theater comes from *Psyché*, for which Corneille's role was limited to the versification of over half of the lines of the play.[67] The presence of an oracle in the play is thus not of Corneille's choosing, but it is worth noting that he employs the same strategies that we have seen elsewhere. As in *Horace*, *Andromède*, and *Œdipe*, the oracle is ironic, albeit amelioratively. It seems to promise an unspeakable monster as Psyché's husband; in fact, its meaning shifts and she is led to a happy union with the god of love.

    Oracles are privileged sites for irony in Corneille's theater, on the one hand seemingly clear and on the other, by convention, apt to mean something quite different than first thought. The presence of an oracle, or even its vocabulary (e.g., *devin*), signals the existence of a superior order, and thus the possibility of ironic intent. With the exception of *L'Illusion comique*, oracles are anchored in time, speaking misleadingly in the present about a moment in the future. The temporal element is crucial, because the shift of meaning of the oracle, marking a before and an after, is precisely what ties oracles to the tragic. The irony of oracles also has ties to dramatic irony because in certain plays—*Andromède* and *Œdipe*—the spectator may already be aware of the future; furthermore, the domain of oracles is, if not ignorance and knowledge, then misapprehended knowledge and correct knowledge. In terms of the ironic potential of oracles, the model of Sophocles' *Œdipus Rex* weighs heavily on Corneille and his contemporaries.

*

We have not exhausted the subject of situational irony in this chapter. Because ironic intent cannot be localized in the same way it can be when an onstage speaker is its source, situational irony is inherently open to a higher degree of doubt than either verbal or dramatic irony. To localize that intent in the person of Corneille, the playwright, begs the question, because one must accept a general proclivity for irony on his part in order credit him with ironic intent in a particular setting. Given that I am writing this study to demonstrate that very proclivity, I can hardly assume it to be true. Situational irony entails doubt as well because a number of its characteristic signals—reversal, coincidence—may appear in unironic as well as ironic environments. Thus, a significant portion of what we might term *situational irony* is subject to a substantial degree of doubt, and will be considered in part 2 where we will focus on possible, as opposed to evident, irony. Nonetheless, along with the widespread presence of evident dramatic and verbal irony in Corneille's theater, evident situational irony is far from absent. While Corneille does not often employ the irony of fate, he favors the ironic structure of the *trompeur trompé*, shows a strong proclivity for the logically ordered relations characteristic of situational irony, and, in a number of plays, explores the ironic potential of oracular discourse.

Notes

[52]See Greenberg's *Corneille, Classicism and the Ruses of Symmetry*; also Ekstein ("Metaphors") on the subject of mathematical relationships in Corneille's theater.

[53]One could venture that the superior order is Horace's subconscious, that he himself undoes his own heroic status without being aware of doing so. While such a reading is indeed possible, a psychologizing approach to Corneille's theater has not, in general, proven to be particularly fruitful and I will not pursue it.

[54]Sweetser put it well when she said that in *Le Menteur* "le trompeur trompé devient en fait le trompeur qui se trompe, de nom et de femme" (*Dramaturgie* 131).

[55]Forestier notes how this "jeu ironique d'opposition entre le paraître et l'être" superimposes itself over the traditional irony of Œdipe blindly investigating himself as he searches for the source of the plague (*Génétique* 335).

[56]Defaux would disagree; he reads *Cinna* as a Christian play and Auguste's actions as divinely inspired.

[57]Dircé echoes this stance in *Œdipe*: "Souvent on l'entend mal, quand on le croit entendre, / L'Oracle le plus clair se fait le moins comprendre" (ll. 917–18).

[58]Curiace feels a premonition of defeat (*Horace* ll. 366–68); Émilie endures foreboding when Cinna is summoned by Auguste at the end of the first act (*Cinna*, ll. 288–92); when all appears to be going well in *Othon*, Plautine says, "Je me trouble, et ne sais par quel pressentiment / Mon cœur n'ose goûter ce bonheur pleinement" (ll. 1751–52). Discussing *la voix du sang* in *Don Sanche* and *Héraclius*, Lyons notes, "Like any oracular device this murmur of instinct takes its meaning from what follows" (*Disguise* 128).

[59]Corneille uses prophecy on a number of occasions: Livie prophesizes Auguste's glorious future at the end of *Cinna* (ll. 1753–74); Polyeucte foretells the emperor Décie's death (*Polyeucte*, ll. 1127–34); in *Pompée*, Cornélie predicts Ptolomée's death (ll. 1584–86) as well as the terrible consequences of César's desire to marry Cléopâtre (ll. 1751–52); Jupiter uses this method to outline the destinies of Médée, Jason, Hypsipyle, and Aète in *La Toison d'or* (ll. 2194–2215).

[60]   Camille, ainsi le Ciel t'avait bien avertie
          Des tragiques succès qu'il t'avait préparés;
          Mais toujours du secret il cache une partie
          Aux esprits les plus nets et les mieux éclairés.
          Il semblait nous parler de ton proche hyménée,
          Il semblait tout promettre à tes vœux innocents;
          Et nous cachant ainsi ta mort inopinée,
          Sa voix n'est que trop vraie en trompant notre sens:
          Albe et Rome aujourd'hui prennent une autre face;
          Tes vœux sont exaucés, elles goûtent la paix;
          Et tu vas être unie avec ton Curiace,
          Sans qu'aucun mauvais sort t'en sépare jamais.
                                        (Corneille 1:1572–73)

[61]D'Aubignac favored dropping it (2:126–27), while Stegmann calls the passage "fâcheusement retranchée" (*OC* 267). Louvat-Molozay, in her excellent article on Corneille's oracles, opts for the first position when she concludes that the oracle in *Horace* does not rise beyond the status of rhetorical ornament ("Oracle" 404–5).

[62]Well, almost on stage: Vénus hovers in the air as she speaks. Louvat-Molozay notes that "L'oracle prononcé par Vénus constitue une parole spectaculaire, pour la mise en scène de laquelle le talent du machiniste est nécessaire; c'est même cette mise en scène qui confère à l'énoncé oraculaire son caractère 'imposant'" ("Oracle" 408).

[63]   Les Dieux, qui tôt, ou tard savent se ressentir,
          Dédaignent de répondre à qui les fait mentir.
          Ce fils, dont ils avaient prédit les aventures,
          Exposé par votre ordre, a trompé leurs augures,
          Et ce sang innocent, et ces Dieux irrités
          Se vengent maintenant de vos impiétés.
                                        (ll. 371–76)

[64]Tirésie himself never appears on stage; Laïus's words are conveyed by Nérine, thus compounding the distance between oracular discourse and the stage.

[65]Louvat-Molozay speaks of Corneille's oracles in this play as polyvalent and duplicitous, making specific reference to this example ("Oracle" 413).

[66]None of these "devins" ever appears on stage. As in the case of *Œdipe*, this distance enhances their privileged relationship with the supernatural.

[67]The introduction, entitled *Le Libraire au lecteur*, states: "Ainsi il n'y a que le prologue, le premier acte, la première scène du second, et la première du troisième, dont les vers soient de lui [Molière]. M. Corneille a employé une quinzaine au reste" (Corneille 3:1079).

Part II: Signals of Possible Irony

Introduction

In part 1 we established the substantial presence of different forms of irony in Corneille's theater. Using the presence of evident irony as a foundation, in part 2 we move on to an exploration of the limits of Corneille's use of irony. Evident and possible ironies can be understood to exist on a kind of continuum along which doubt plays an ever-increasing role. Doubt does not undercut the possibility of irony; it is itself a defining trait of irony. Thus possible irony should not be considered peripheral to an examination of irony, but rather both central and necessary.

Doubt is relevant to both reception and intention. We have seen the consequences of reception for evident irony. As ironic intent becomes more difficult to ascertain, reception requires even closer attention. In the balance between intent and reception, the scales tip towards the latter in part 2. Indeed, the term "possible" implies the perspective of the receiver, not the intender. The foregrounding of reception here brings to light certain potential problems: specifically, not perceiving irony where it is intended or espying it where it is not intended. As Freud notes, "[L]'ironie risque très facilement de demeurer incomprise" (267). Kerbrat-Orecchioni enjoins,

> Freud a raison, lorsqu'il signale l'ambiguïté fréquente du procédé dont le statut est bien paradoxal: l'ironie est faite pour être perçue mais sur un mode toujours dubitatif; elle se doit d'utiliser certains indices, mais qui restent seulement présomptifs et toujours incertains—sinon, à quoi bon utiliser ce procédé sophistiqué? L'ambiguïté est proprement constitutive de l'ironie. ("Problèmes" 15)

The second tendency is just as troubling: reading irony anywhere and everywhere, completely independently of what one understands the author's intentions to have been. While reception is of necessity foregrounded in the case of possible ironies, intent is by no means banished, in part in order to preclude such unrestrained ironic interpretation. It is "impossible d'être indifférent à ce que l'on suppose être l'intention signifiante de l'émetteur" (Kerbrat-Orecchioni, "Trope" 113). For every instance of possible irony there must be some attempt to theorize or construct a plausible claim for ironic intent, conscious or unconscious. In the absence of such a claim we may only entertain the idea of irony of fate at Corneille's expense, as we do

75

in the case of Racine's rise to fame mentioned in chapter 4.

In order to make claims of ironic intent I will rely on a range of signals of irony, textual indicators that, by being typical of irony, will compensate for the relative paucity of more explicit intent. Part 2 is therefore organized by such signals as repetition, symmetry, exaggeration, incongruity, and gaps. Exaggeration in particular, because it is defined as a deviation from a norm, and because it can appear in combination with other signals, may be the most basic signal of possible irony. It will be the focus of its own chapter, but appears throughout part 2 as an enhancing factor for other forms of irony. Signals are crucial to alerting the receiver to the possibility of irony.

While we can agree that such signals may indicate the presence of irony, significant uncertainty arises when we ask whether such signals *must* be interpreted ironically. Søren Kierkegaard provides an interesting analogy to the problem faced in reading signs of irony:

> There is a work that represents Napoleon's grave. Two tall trees shade the grave. There is nothing else to see in the work, and the unsophisticated observer sees nothing else. Between the two trees there is an empty space; as the eye follows the outline, suddenly Napoleon himself emerges from this nothing, and now it is impossible to have him disappear again. Once the eye has seen him, it goes on seeing him with an almost alarming necessity. (19)

Certain readers of Corneille, needless to say myself included, have had a similar experience: we have seen irony materialize in the space between two elements, and once it materializes it never disappears.

Clearly, while signals of irony will provide the foundation, we will be dealing with considerable interpretive speculation in part 2. In a domain defined by doubt, this is as it should be. Furthermore, irony is complex and subtle; it is not black or white, but has numerous gradations (e.g., a hint or a touch of irony); it is but one strand, whether evident or veiled, in the complex structures that are Corneille's plays. The integration of irony is finally more important than its isolation and identification. Part 2 is divided into four chapters. The first two focus on signals based on reduplication and excess where there should be singularity, and the second two concentrate on signals that indicate gaps where there should normally be continuity.

CHAPTER 5
POSSIBLE IRONY I: REDUPLICATION

In this chapter we will focus on irony that may be signaled by the reduplication of words or events in situations where the normal expectation would be singularity: specifically, the signals of repetition, symmetry, and coincidence. While the signals may be relatively clear in this domain, the choice to read a given situation ironically on the basis of that signal may be open to question and will, in the final analysis, depend on the choice of the interpreter.

REPETITION

Repetition is an often-used signal of irony. Hamon notes, "[T]oute forme de répétition formelle…[a] certainement des connivences avec l'ironie et avec sa dualité-duplicité structurelle" (48). The duplication of the same words, clearly not particularly supportive of a communicative function, suggests the possibility of some other purpose or effect. Repetition and its ironic potential need not be limited to the verbal, but may be extended to encompass other elements or events. Its relationship to irony operates on a continuum: a single repetition may or may not suffice to bring the possibility of irony into play; two or more repetitions likely would, depending on the context. Too much repetition, however, can undermine irony. Discussing Mark Antony's repetition of "Brutus is an honourable man" in Shakespeare's *Julius Caesar*, Beda Allemann points out that after several iterations irony gives way completely to scorn (391).[68] The element of doubt so characteristic of irony disappears because of insistent repetition. Repetition may thus simultaneously serve as a signal of irony and yet work to undo the very irony it has helped to construct. This is perhaps less surprising when one considers the breadth and complexity of the phenomenon of repetition and its relation to meaning, to time, even to the operation of the unconscious.[69]

Corneille demonstrates a decided penchant for formal repetition. McFarlane describes Corneille's "tendency to repetition…as an outstanding characteristic of the rhetoric as a whole, so much so that one may see in it a characteristic of Corneille's imagination" ("Notes" 185). Here our focus is primarily on the repetition of motifs, rather than the repetition of language to which McFarlane refers, but the same holds true in both domains. The central issue in terms of irony and repetition in Corneille's theater involves

77

determining the point at which such repetition might reasonably be viewed as ironic. Auguste consults several times in *Cinna*, first with Cinna and Maxime, then with Livie, and finally with Cinna again as he invites the latter to name his own punishment. Yet one would be hard pressed to make an argument for irony in this case. Thus repetition alone may not suffice. Generally speaking, the possibility for irony increases to the extent that the element repeated is *normally* considered unique.[70] For example, a king is understood to be a sole and supreme ruler. The two kings in Attila's court, through their hollow duplication of Attila's position as well as their similarity to each other, clearly suggest the possibility of irony. Sophonisbe has two husbands; Aricie (*Sertorius*) and even Rodelinde (*Pertharite*) almost find themselves in the same position. There are two kings where there should be only one in *Pertharite* and two incarnations of Héraclius where the expected number was zero, as he had supposedly been put to death twenty years earlier. Corneille even repeats what is legendarily unique: in *Médée*, Jason independently contemplates killing his children (ll. 1561–68) at a moment when Médée is in fact doing so. Repetition involving children in *Héraclius* suggests the possibility of irony as well: not only does Léontine switch babies twice, but a comment made by Pulchérie to Phocas suggests the possibility that four other such switches may have occurred as well.[71] Such proliferation is certainly a distraction from the serious tone of these plays; it is possibly also a playfully ironic commentary on the action. More risky would be to assign some particular function to these repetitions: for instance, is Corneille in his duplication of kings engaging in a subversive commentary on the legitimacy of throne and its occupants? Perhaps, but there remains a significant measure of doubt. The multiplication of what ought to be singular is a potential signal of possible irony, one that Corneille employs fairly often.

While marriage is by no means inherently unique, the multiplication of new unions in a single play may open the door to irony simply because weddings are perceived customarily as once-in-a-lifetime events. Thus multiple weddings signal both coincidence and repetition at once. Marriage is of course a generic norm for seventeenth-century comedy and two simultaneous unions are common in that context. While Corneille does not actually exceed that limit in his comedies, he knowingly and playfully raises the possibility. At the end of *La Galerie du Palais*, the suggestion is made that in addition to the unions of the two young couples, the mother of one of the heroines should marry the father of the other. The mother, Chrysante, demurs, ending the play with "Outre l'âge en tous deux un peu trop refroidie, / Cela sentirait trop sa fin de comédie" (ll. 1825–26). The original ending of *La Suite du Menteur*, Corneille's final comedy, finds Cliton complaining that only a single marriage has been settled upon; Dorante immediately responds with three other possible couples.[72] Forestier discusses these two examples, noting Corneille's ironic stance; he is careful, however, to draw a distinction in order to preserve the sanctity of the marriage of the main couple: "[O]n remarquera que dans les deux cas l'ironie de Corneille ne porte que sur les mariages des personnages secondaires, en aucun cas sur l'union du couple principal" ("Structure" 244).[73] Forestier's somewhat defensive reaction suggests that the possibility of irony carries with it some danger of destabilizing the dramatic universe. Certainly the juxtaposition of the central union or unions with the suggestion of others that are little more than quasi-mathematical pairings of available males and females does little to affirm the seriousness of those central marriages. In the 1660 *Examens*, Corneille himself points to the peculiar unions of Éraste and Cloris at the end of *Mélite* (1:7) and especially that of Clitandre and Dorise in *Clitandre* (1:102), both secondary couples. The playwright thus mocks his own proclivity for *invraisemblable* multiple unions and in the process opens the door to the possibility of an ironic stance towards marriage itself.

This possibility for irony is further supported by Corneille's use of multiple marriages in his tragedies and other serious plays. While two marriages may be almost conventional in comedy, tragedy does not usually involve any such union. Corneille himself does not make any comment about the subject outside of the realm of comedy, but on three occasions he ends serious plays with the possibility or likelihood of three simultaneous unions. In *Agésilas*, after numerous complications, Cotys is joined with Mandane, Spitridate with Elpinice, and Aglatide with Agésilas. Once the eponymous tyrant has died in *Attila*, the path is clear for Valamir and Honorie, Ardaric and Ildione, and even the two confidants, Octar and Flavie, to marry. Finally, at the dénouement of *Pulchérie*, Martian is to marry the empress, Léon marries Martian's daughter Justine, and Pulchérie gives Aspar two days to make up his mind about marrying Irène. Can we construct some plausible intent of irony in these three plays? We might suggest that Corneille may be mocking the requirement that all loose ends be resolved at the end of a play. While the initial repetition, or doubling, of some element may or may not open the door to irony, depending how far it is from the norm, the third iteration seems to be a strong signal of potential irony. Three simultaneous marriages, even in the absence of identifiable intent, certainly run the risk of being perceived ironically.

COINCIDENCE

We discussed the relationship of coincidence and irony in the preceding chapter as a means of understanding more clearly the notion of situational irony. We return to it here, because it is indeed a signal of possible irony.

Webster's *New World Dictionary* defines coincidence as "an accidental and remarkable occurrence of events or ideas at the same time, suggesting but lacking a causal relationship." What is required to move from coincidence to irony is to furnish that causality through the construction of plausible ironic intent.

Many coincidences avoid the suspicion of irony because of generic expectations. Coincidences in tragicomedy, where they are the norm, do not function in the same fashion in tragedy, where they are not. Thus when Corneille underlines the coincidence of two simultaneous assassination attempts in *Clitandre* ("Qu'en deux dessins divers pareille jalousie, / Même lieu contre vous, et même heure a choisie," ll. 753–54), the play's generic designation as a *tragi-comédie* weakens the likelihood of there being an ironic edge to the situation. Similarly, plot construction typically relies on coincidence, all the more so in a theater governed by the unities of time and space. Thus, that Albe and Rome declared war on precisely the day that Camille and Curiace became engaged, while certainly a highly visible coincidence, seems conventional rather than potentially ironic in that it ties the political plot to the sentimental one. Certainly one might choose to read this situation in *Horace* as irony of fate. Corneille's theater contains numerous such examples, as does almost all literature that is based on plot.

While all coincidence is structurally open to an ironic reading, coincidence will not likely invite such a reading unless it calls attention to itself in some fashion, generally speaking, along the lines of exaggeration or incongruity, themselves independent signs of possible irony. *Agésilas* offers several examples of coincidence sufficiently incongruous that one might indeed wonder whether Corneille was ironically mocking the conventions within which he worked. That Spitridate should suddenly declare his love for Elpinice (1.3) immediately after Elpinice has suggested an exchange of fiancés with her sister that would make Spitridate her husband (1.1) is awkward and heavy-handed. It would seem that Corneille may be ironically calling attention to the artificiality of the dance of potential marriage partners that undergirds so many of his plays, and perhaps *Agésilas* most of all. Coincidence takes on a spatial character in this play as well. When Agésilas has been reduced to pleading with Spitridate, "Sauvez-moi du chagrin de montrer que je l' [Mandane] aime" (l. 1799), the young woman he does not want to see magically appears, as though it were normal for an outsider just to pop into the king's chamber! Similarly, in *Tite et Bérénice*, Flavian's advice to Tite not to see Bérénice is immediately followed by her arrival on stage (5.3–4). The coincidences of the onstage appearance of these two women suggest the possibility that Corneille may be mocking the artificially conventional nature of most onstage arrivals and exits. In both *Agésilas* and *Tite et*

Bérénice the ironic potential of the coincidences works to gently undermine the ostensibly serious tone of the two plays.[74]

SYMMETRY

Symmetry is closely allied with repetition, and numerous scholars have noted Corneille's affinity for formal symmetry. McFarlane discusses "the extraordinary extent to which Corneille's mind sees things not in isolation, but in pairs, or presents the single feature in binary form" ("Notes" 197) and Jean Rousset asserts, "Corneille, plus que tout autre, a pratiqué les symétries" (*Forme* 7). Symmetry, perhaps even more than repetition, provides the logical order characteristic of situational irony. The same issues of degree and visibility as in the case of repetition need to be considered. Is the symmetry of two rivals sufficient to provoke a perception of irony in the receiver? Probably not. When the symmetry is accentuated by reduplication, the chances increase that the possibility for irony exists. Three of Corneille's plays are particularly noteworthy for their elaborate symmetries: *Horace*, *Attila*, and *Rodogune*.

Horace is constructed upon the binary opposition of Rome and Albe. On each side are arrayed three undifferentiated brothers, the three Curiaces and the three Horaces. Onstage, the three are reduced to one representative for each side, each of whom is coupled with a woman who is the sister of the warrior representative of the opposite side. Both women feel painfully torn by familial and affective ties.[75] In *Attila*, the symmetry surrounds the central figure of Attila. Balanced on either side of the central tyrant are two powerless kings, Valamir and Ardaric, who differ little from one another in personality. Superimposed on that symmetry are Attila's two fiancées, Honorie and Ildione, who, while far more differentiated than their male counterparts, occupy identical positions. Symmetrical too are the two possible couples formed by the pairings of fiancée and powerless king. The balanced composition extends to onstage dialogue, as Valamir and Ardaric spend a good part of the first act arguing that each other's beloved should marry Attila. The accumulated symmetries may well be seen to function ironically to diminish the stature of the two kings. Curiously, that accumulation suggests the possibility of a further symmetry between the playwright, who is responsible for it, and Attila, who is understood to have orchestrated the presence of the two fiancées and two kings within the universe of the play, and who, like the playwright, belongs to no evident symmetrical pattern. The artificial nature of the symmetry in both of these plays undermines the *vraisemblance* of the worlds they depict and makes the audience question the meaning of their overconstruction. Is Corneille possibly mocking the norms of the theater?

Symmetry, along with repetition and coincidence, are widespread in

Rodogune, to such an extent that it is impossible to avoid the question of possible irony. Jacques Scherer notes that "Le sujet tout entier s'inscrit…dans un principe de symétrie" (85). We find symmetry everywhere in the play. There are two princes in the place of a single heir, both in love with the same woman. Cléopâtre, in a curious move that enhances symmetry, doubles herself metaphorically by referring to her hatred as if it were another person: "Éclatez, il est temps, et voici notre jour. / Montrons-nous toutes deux, non plus comme Sujettes, / Mais telle que je suis, et telle que vous êtes" (ll. 406–8). Both Antiochus and Séleucus independently devise identical plans to cede the throne to the other in exchange for the right to marry Rodogune. Rodogune's reluctance to identify which of the two brothers she prefers parallels Cléopâtre's veil of secrecy concerning the identity of the firstborn. When Nicanor, long before the play's action begins, learned that Cléopâtre had married another, he decided to do the same ("Que piqué jusqu'au vif contre son Hyménée / Son âme à l'imiter s'était déterminée," ll. 231–32). Both Cléopâtre and Rodogune, at similar points in two successive acts, demand that one of the twins kill the other woman in order to win their favor. Cléopâtre appeals to her sons to take her own act of murder as a model: "Ce n'est qu'en m'imitant que l'on me justifie" (l. 668). Rodogune, on the other hand, urges the two brothers to resemble their father: "J'aime les fils du Roi, je hais ceux de la Reine" (l. 1024). Rodogune thus appeals to a genetic resemblance between son and father; the symmetry of her feelings for both brings with it a slight suggestion of incest.[76] Horrified at the thought of complying with either of these demands, Antiochus attempts parallel arguments to persuade each woman to set aside her homicidal designs. Rodogune and Cléopâtre both yield to his impassioned pleas, at least seemingly. Talking to his mother, Antiochus frames his position in symmetrical terms: "Nous périrons tous deux, s'il faut périr pour vous; / Mais aussi…/ Nous périrons tous deux, s'il faut périr pour elle" (ll. 1330–32). Cléopâtre's response, "Périssez, périssez" (l. 1333) is symmetrical, repetitive, and strikes me as playfully ironic. At first glance it seems to be nothing more than a rhetorically insistent rejoinder; only later can we see it as an indicator of Cléopâtre's project to kill both of her sons. This is thus an instance of dramatic irony apparent only upon rereading or reviewing the play. In the final act, Cléopâtre and Rodogune's positions as suspects in Séleucus' murder are identical (ll. 1665–67) and Corneille underlines the symmetry through their language: Cléopâtre: "Quoi, vous me soupçonnez!"; Rodogune: "Quoi, je vous suis suspecte!" (l. 1671). Scherer notes that Antiochus in this scene is "jusqu'à la fin victime de la symétrie" (86). Rodogune distinguishes herself from Cléopâtre by twice saving Antiochus from the poisoned *coupe* (ll. 1689 and 1805–8). Corneille thus has her deviate from the symmetry only to create a new repetition.

Quite evidently, the entire play is riddled with symmetry and doubles, and at every level. One consequence of the insistent nature of this feature is the loss of *vraisemblance*, as the artificiality of a given situation is compounded with each additional symmetry, many of which are quite implausible. Co-incidence, another marker of possible irony, functions as well to challenge *vraisemblance* here. The final scene of Rodogune involves two blatant coin-cidences. First, the mere mention of Séleucus ("mon frère," l. 1599) leads almost immediately to Timagène's arrival on stage to talk about Séleucus's whereabouts. Second, as we learn from Timagène, Séleucus expired just as he was about to name his assailant. Corneille gives an ironic twist to this glaring coincidence by having Timagène ascribe the timing to supernatural forces: "La Parque à ce mot lui coupe la parole" (l. 1647). The suggestion of supernatural forces brings with it the possibility of the irony of fate. Indeed, there is frequent reference in *Rodogune* to a variety of such superior forces (e.g., "dieux," "sort," "destin," "ciel"); however, none of them seems very active. Until the final act, the gods seem to be nothing more than figures of empty rhetoric; instead it is Cléopâtre who appears to be the driving force orchestrating events. It is odd, however, that Cléopâtre does not do a better job of killing her son: she uses a knife ("Le fer m'a bien servie," l. 1508), a weapon requiring close contact with the victim, and yet she does not make certain that he is dead before leaving. Thus *La Parque* may indeed be credited with determining the moment of Séleucus's death.

The combination of evident and possible ironies in *Rodogune* focuses attention on the highly structured nature of this dramatic universe. The question remains, however, what precisely Corneille might be critiquing or calling into question with the excessive use of symmetry and doubles, and by blatant coincidences. One possibility concerns theater itself. Could Corneille be critiquing the well-made play, calling into question the rules governing dramatic production? The plot is overly constructed, as though Corneille were parodying the complication and balance that were expected of a tragedy in the middle of the seventeenth-century. Scherer notes that the *récits*—more numerous and developed in this play than in any of Corneille's others—are almost superfluous (86). Corneille opens with a dialogue between two secondary characters, a virtually unheard-of combination, and there are seven monologues in the play, a strikingly elevated number. *Rodogune* abounds in multiple and reiterated signs of possible irony. The possibility exists that Corneille uses irony here to mock the norms of the theater.

ECHOIC MENTION

Echoic mention is another signal of possible irony based on reduplica-tion. An echoic mention is not merely an echo, that is, an exact or almost exact repetition of words; it is also a mention. Thus it refers to some earlier statement as well as or instead of simply referring to the real world (see Berrendonner 197). It is this attribute as a mention that contributes to its difference from the original, and thus to its potential for irony. We discussed echoic mentions earlier in chapter 3 as a form of evident verbal irony. There, we limited our discussion to those echoic mentions that occur in close proximity to one another or that are both highlighted and exact, and that typically operate as a feature of a confrontation between two characters. Here we will take up examples of echoic mention with considerable distance of some sort between the original statement and its repetition. With this distance comes greater uncertainty; thus we may only speak of possible, rather than evident, irony, and ironic intent is plausibly claimed rather than presumed. This distance may be within one play, or it may extend beyond its borders to another of Corneille's plays or to some other text. If the scope remains within a given play, the source of the possible irony can be attributed to the character who voices the echo or to Corneille, depending on such features as whether the character repeating the statement was present on stage when it was first uttered. However, if an echoic mention reaches beyond the single play, the source of the possible irony can only be Corneille.

　　Certainly echoic mention is impossible without repetition. François Rostand studied Corneille's verbal echoes within his theater and found 169 repetitions of a line or more in length and 41 instances where a given line is repeated two or more times (7–8). Extending his count to include hemistiches and phrases, he reaches the figure 750 (8). Obviously, such repetition is widely perceived as a feature of Corneille's theater; Claude Abraham calls it a "prédilection cornélienne" ("Envers" 372). Critics rarely discuss the possibility of irony, however;[77] rather, such self-citation receives a number of other explanations. One possibility is simple laziness. Rostand suggests that Corneille simply couldn't be bothered to always vary certain conventional or transitional turns of phrase (12). Perhaps Corneille merely forgot that he had already employed a line that occurred to him spontaneously as he was writing (Rostand 12). Along these lines, echoes from one of Corneille's plays to another may be viewed as a kind of verbal tic which may reveal something about the workings of his mind. Harriet Allentuch notes that the line "voilà quelle je suis et quelle je veux être" appears in four of his plays with a close variant in a fifth (99).[78] It requires little effort to interpret this line as an expression of Corneille's preoccupation with *volonté*. Another explanation for echoes is opportunism. Rostand notes that Corneille extracted and reused fragments of plays that were unsuccessful on stage (11–12), as though he were loathe to let such fine alexandrines go to waste. A crueler hypothesis concerning the playwright's extensive self-citation is sterility.[79] Rostand notes

[margin notes:]
repeats words while also referring to some earlier statement

can occur w/ considerable distance btwn

--even another play! (=> source = C)

C. echoes self frequently ("self-citation")

laziness?

forgetfulness?

verbal tic revealing important theme?

opportunism?

sterility?

that Corneille reuses his own lines more and more as his career advances (20): "Ne serait-ce pas la marque d'un affaiblissement de l'inspiration, d'une diminution de la confiance en soi? Corneille préférerait recourir à des vers déjà éprouvés. Il s'imiterait pour ne pas se montrer inférieur à lui-même" (14). Rostand wonders whether Corneille was conscious of his self-citation (12), an important consideration, as such consciousness is a precondition for ironic intent. Opportunism implies self-conscious repetition; the other explanations offer less assurance that Corneille was cognizant of what he was doing. Correspondingly, one might ask whether Corneille thought that his audience would recognize the echoes. For whatever the intent, without audience (or reader) perception of the echo, there can be no possibility of irony.

It is thus clear that irony is far from the only possible explanation for the reuse of lines in Corneille's plays. Given the numerous options, how do we go about establishing the possibility that Corneille may have at times been ironic when he repeats certain lines? Repetition is an obvious given, but above and beyond that lies the need for some form of opposition or inversion that itself signals possible irony. The repeated statement must also imply some sort of value judgment concerning the original (Schoentjes 227), essentially a critical judgment which functions to mark the difference between the original and the echo.[80] Unfortunately, this last criterion is considerably less reliable than the preceding one: the value judgment is almost always implicit rather than explicit, so that to posit the presence of a critical judgment is in fact to do nothing more than postulate ironic intent on the part of the speaker or Corneille. As we have seen, intent can only be argued for, not demonstrated.

Despite such limitations, we may point to several possibly ironic echoic mentions featuring distance between the two occurences of a given statement. Within the domain of a single play, we will begin by considering two examples of echoic mention, one almost certainly ironic and the other much more open to question. In *Le Menteur*, when Cliton discovers that Dorante has lied to him about having killed Alcippe in a duel, he reacts by throwing Dorante's words back at him, words that Dorante had already spoken twice to Cliton, once much earlier in the play and once relatively recently. When Cliton first witnesses one of Dorante's lies, he requests that his master provide some sign in the future to alert him that he is lying. Dorante assures Cliton that "Tu seras de mon cœur l'unique Secrétaire, / Et de tous mes secrets le grand dépositaire" (ll. 701–2). Later, Dorante prefaces his colorful narrative of his duel against Alcippe with the same assurance of sincerity, saying to Cliton, "Mais à toi, de mon cœur l'unique secrétaire, / À toi, de mes secrets le grand dépositaire / Je ne célerai rien" (ll. 1129–31). Having discovered the truth to be radically different than what Dorante asserts, Cliton echoes the latter's words, "À moi, de votre cœur l'unique secrétaire! / À moi, de vos secrets le grand dépositaire!" (ll. 1169–70). Here the inversion involves truth value: the exclamation marks obviously call into question the veracity of Dorante's statement. Indeed this is sarcasm, and there is nothing subtle about the irony of this example. Cliton doubles the echoic mention by following with "Avec ces qualités [being the trusted guardian of Dorante's secrets] j'avais lieu d'espérer / Qu'assez malaisément je pourrai m'en parer [with ridicule, due to taking Dorante's lies for truth]" (ll. 1171–72), echoing the way he himself had responded to Dorante's first statement concerning his privileged role as confidant: "Avec ces qualités j'ose bien espérer / Qu'assez malaisément je pourrai m'en parer" (ll. 703–4). Again what was uttered seriously the first time is now turned on its head because of the change of context in which it is spoken. The echoic mentions, while fairly distant, are sufficiently underscored—through length, repetition, and inversion—to leave little doubt concerning ironic intent.

< Horace

The second example comes from *Horace*. In the last act, Tulle responds to Valère's request for justice with "je ferai justice. / J'aime à la rendre à tous, à toute heure, en tout lieu, / C'est par elle qu'un Roi se fait un demi-Dieu" (ll. 1476–78). Later in the same scene, Horace uses similar language to discuss the lofty expectations placed on a hero by the people: "Il veut qu'on soit égal en tout temps, en tous lieux" (l. 1565). The juxtaposition of a form of time and place, each accompanied by the adjectif *tout*, is fairly rare in Corneille's theater, appearing in only four other plays, and never more than once.[81] While Horace's statement contains no hint of sarcasm, it nonetheless offers the possibility for reversal: where Tulle aspires to mete out justice any time and anywhere, and seems to succeed, Horace is not able to meet the high standards of heroism at all times, in all places. Thus Horace may be

(cant resolve this one!)

understood to recognize the difference between himself and Tulle (unironic), or to criticize Tulle's assertion of unfailing adherence to his role (ironic), or even to mock the king's pretension to dispense justice (ironic). The play does not provide enough information to resolve the issue; after the speech from which Horace's line is taken, he says nothing further.

< Sophonisbe

Sophonisbe contains a complex example of echoic mention within a single play, one that raises the possibility of irony in a different fashion. In the second act, Sophonisbe assures her rival Eryxe, "Ce n'est pas mon dessein de vous le [Massinisse] dérober" (l. 589). One act later, after Sophonisbe has in fact married Massinisse, Eryxe asks her, "Vous n'aviez pas dessein de me le dérober?" (l. 919). While it is entirely reasonable to assume that Eryxe asks this question ironically or even sarcastically, given the context of reversal, it is less certain that the spectator would remember Sophonisbe's line across the span of an entire act. Interestingly, however, this echoic mention occurs in the context of another repetition. Both of the scenes in which the above lines appear are opened by very similar statements made by Eryxe. In the first, she says, "Tout a changé de face, / Madame, et les Destins vous ont mise en ma place" (ll. 575–76). By this she means that whereas earlier Sophonisbe was free and Eryxe a prisoner, their positions have now been reversed because of Syphax's defeat at the hands of the Romans.[82] Act 3, scene 3 opens in an almost identical fashion with Eryxe saying, "Une seconde fois tout a changé de face, / Madame, et c'est à moi de vous quitter la place" (ll. 917–18). Sophonisbe, now married to Massinisse, is no longer a prisoner, while Eryxe, having lost her fiancé and defender, is once more in a vulnerable position. Unlike the two lines containing "dérober," this echo would very likely attract the audience's attention. The privileged position as the first lines of scenes, buttressed by the repetition of "tout a changé de face" and the word "place," ensures perceptibility. The second of the two lines spoken by Eryxe is not, however, an echoic mention in the same sense as the examples considered above. First, both lines are spoken by the same character. Thus the echo cannot function as a vehicle for conflict as it usually does. Second, the repetition is in no way a critical judgment of the initial statement. Both simply make reference to reality: in the space of the act separating the two, circumstances have changed radically. The same words refer to two different shifts. This example is more a matter of situational irony, specifically involving reversal of fortune, than of ironic echoic mention. What is ironic is that the shifts referenced move in opposite directions. Echoic mention still has a role here, however, in that Eryxe's choice to employ identical terms signals self-deprecation. The same language appears a third time, much later in the play. Sophonisbe opens act 5, scene 4 with "Une troisième fois mon sort change de face, / Madame et c'est mon tour de vous quitter la place" (ll. 1643–44). Indeed, the situation has been transformed once again so that Sophonisbe has been separated from Massinisse and is once more a prisoner of the Romans. In all three scenes, both women are present, a situation that might lead one to expect that Sophonisbe is turning Eryxe's words against her in this third iteration. In fact, such is not the case: like that of Eryxe, Sophonisbe's repetition signals situational irony and self-deprecation. In fact, Sophonisbe's echo could be called an "anti-gotcha" moment: instead of directing hostility toward her rival, Sophonisbe, like Eryxe before her, directs it against herself. The result is a bitter self-deprecating irony shared by both women that points to the irony of fate because of the reversals in content.

The echoes of lines from one of Corneille's plays to another are numerous, as many have noted. The issue of irony readily comes to the fore in the case of well-known lines. Two in particular seem to reverberate through a number of plays: "S'attacher au combat contre un autre soi-même" (*Horace*

l. 444) and "Il est beau de mourir maître de l'Univers" (*Cinna* ll. 440 and 496). "Un autre soi-même" varies to include "un autre lui-même" or "moi-même" as it appears in six other plays.[83] The expression is used to denote either closeness between two individuals or a romantic substitution. Only once is it presented as anything less than completely serious: in *Nicomède*, Laodice flippantly suggests that Attale continue his unwelcome courting of her with Nicomède, whom she calls "un autre moi-même" (l. 1000), so close that he could answer in her place. She thereby amusingly conflates the two meanings of the expression. "Il est beau de mourir maître de l'Univers" is echoed on five occasions in Corneille's theater.[84] Because both of these lines are well-known to the audience as rhetorical high-points taken from plays that enjoyed enormous success, the audience is likely to recognize the echo immediately. The spectator hears the onstage character speak the words within his or her immediate context, while at the same time one hears Corneille's voice reminding us of the well-known earlier context in which these same words were spoken. It does not seem plausible that Corneille would have been unaware of the echo.[85] Thus several conditions for irony have been met: along with the repetition, we find consciousness of its presence on the part of both Corneille and the audience. Irony is not, however, the only explanation for these echoes: opportunism on Corneille's part—the desire to take advantage of past success in order to build present good fortune—seems at least as, if not more, plausible. The point I would like to make is that Corneille sets up the conditions for the possibility of an ironic reading of these echoic mentions. All that is needed is some inversion or opposition between the two contexts in which the virtually identical lines appear. One would be hard pressed to construct a forceful opposition between Cinna's line and Agésilas's moment of self-sacrifice: "Mais enfin il est beau de triompher de soi" (l. 1982). In the case of Dorante telling Mélisse to love Philiste—"Aimez en ma faveur un ami qui vous aime, / Et possédez Dorante en un autre lui-même" (ll. 1785–86)—while the words are spoken most seriously, the context of the comic theme of selecting marriage partners contrasts sharply with the tragic glory of killing a brother-in-law and a friend in *Horace*. The shift in context thus permits, but does not insist upon, an ironic reading. In all cases, Corneille's use of echoic mention to advance the heroic pretensions of the character doing the repeating runs the risk of irony and ridicule simply because the echo references two contexts simultaneously.

A very similar process is at work when Corneille echoes well-known lines from outside of his own theater. The pleasure of recognition couples with a momentary loss of mimetic illusion as the echo reverberates between two inevitably dissimilar contexts. To the extent that these are well-known lines, and thus recognizable to the audience, as well as plausibly deliberate echoes

[margin note: but seems to be more opportunistic here than ironic]

[margin note: C also echoes plays not his own]

on the part of Corneille, the real possibility for irony exists. For example, upon learning that Émilie was part of the conspiracy against him, Auguste cries out, "Et toi, ma fille, aussi!" (l. 1564). While Corneille thereby implicitly compares the sense of betrayal Caesar felt at finding Brutus among his assas- sins to Auguste's shock at learning that his beloved Émilie seeks his death, the radical difference between the two situations—for one thing, Auguste discovered the betrayal in time whereas Caesar obviously did not—opens the door to possible irony on Corneille's part. We find an odd variant of this intertextual echoing in *Œdipe* when Thésée responds to Œdipe's inquiry about his amorous interests:

> Seigneur, il est tout vrai, j'aime en votre Palais,
> Chez vous est la beauté qui fait tous mes souhaits,
> Vous l'aimez à l'égal d'Antigone, et d'Ismène;
> Elle tient même rang chez vous, et chez la Reine.
>
> (ll. 151–54)

This passage sounds remarkably like a riddle; all that is needed is the addition of "Qui est-ce?" The allusion to the Sphinx's riddle that Œdipus was called upon to solve seems quite apparent. The radical shift in context provides an opposition between the two: whereas Œdipus's life depended on the answer he gave to the Sphinx, here there are no significant stakes and Thésée's choice of formulation is perfectly gratuitous. The possibility of playful irony on Corneille's part thus seems not only plausible but likely.

Corneille himself has been the victim of precisely this sort of playfully ironic echoic mention. Racine, for instance, parodies the description of Don Gomès in *Le Cid* ("Ses rides sur son front ont gravé ses exploits," l. 21) by changing the meaning of the word *exploits* in L'Intimé's description of his own lawsuit-obsessed father ("Il gagnait en un jour plus qu'un autre en six mois: / Ses rides sur son front gravaient tous ses exploits," *Les Plaideurs* ll. 153–54). Molière famously parodies Pompée's "Je suis maître, je parle, allez, obéissez" (*Sertorius*, l. 1868) by putting it in Arnolphe's mouth in *L'École des femmes* (l. 642).

The reduplication of language—echoic mention—signals the possibil- ity of irony as well as numerous other interpretations. The conditions for irony have been met in the cases we describe, thus grounding ironic reception. We will turn now to an extended examination of a complex case of possible irony based primarily on reduplication within a single play.

Sabine in *Horace*

The character of Sabine, sister to Curiace and wife to Horace, is the source of considerable possible irony. There are essentially three aspects to the question here. First, does Sabine employ verbal irony in her speech to Curiace and Horace when she proposes that one of them kill her first in order to legitimize a battle between them (2.6)? Second, is she ironic when she requests being put to death a second and a third time (4.7 and 5.3)? Finally, how does Sabine's possibly ironic intent relate to possibly ironic intent on Corneille's part? Interpretations of Sabine as a character are extraordinarily diverse, a function no doubt at least in part of the fact that Corneille completely fabricated her, yet placed her within the context of a series of events that he did not invent, but rather adopted closely from Livy.[86] She has been called weak yet bloodthirsty (Tiefenbrun, "Blood" 624 and 626), steadfast (Reiss 42), "a sheep in wolf's clothing" (Woshinsky 43), and overly emotional (Toczyski 223). She has been dismissed for being superfluous to the action (Pavel 49), for being "useless and somewhat ridiculous" (Lancaster 2,1:311), and for having no character (Petit de Julleville 299). She has been compared to l'Infante in *Le Cid* (Verhœff, *Tragédies* 125), and like the latter, at times has been simply omitted from performances of the play.

To suggest that Sabine's speech in 2.6 may be ironic is hardly a maverick stance; a number of others have used the term "irony" in this context.[87] The subject has not found common agreement, however, perhaps because of the consequences entailed by an ironic reading, as we shall see. It is worth considering in detail the signs of verbal irony in this speech (ll. 613–66) as well as signs of (unironic) seriousness in order to gauge the ambiguities. Sabine's opening sounds perfectly earnest:

> Non, non, mon frère, non, je ne viens en ce lieu
> Que pour vous embrasser et pour vous dire Adieu.
> Votre sang est trop bon, n'en craignez rien de lâche,
> Rien dont la fermeté de ces grands cœurs se fâche.
> (ll. 613–16)

It will soon become clear, however, that she means the opposite of what she says. Peter Newmark notes the juxtaposition of opposites in lines 615 ("bon" and "lâche") and 616 ("fermeté" and "se fâche") as a telltale sign (6). Sabine's subsequent entreaty to be allowed to speak sounds even more innocent, but here the language is ambiguous, allowing for very different interpretations: "Pourrai-je toutefois vous faire une prière / Digne d'un tel époux, et digne d'un tel frère?" (ll. 619–20). The terms "digne" and "tel" are decidedly equivocal. As Sabine begins to frame her proposition, she again places words in opposition to one another, here at the end of lines 621 and 622 ("impiété" and "pureté") and lines 623 and 624 ("crimes" and "légitimes"). This antithetical movement pervades Sabine's speech in 2.6, as Newmark notes (6–7). While it appears perfectly clear that Sabine is ironic in declaiming the innocence of her proposition, the proposition itself—that either Curiace or Horace kill her and that the other avenge her death, thereby somehow normalizing the combat between the two brothers-in-law and friends—poses a different set of problems.

The offer contains a number of classic signs of possible irony, several of which we will return to in later chapters. Sabine juxtaposes her murder with the men's combat, a juxtaposition with a sharp edge—so sharp in fact that Peter Nurse calls it Sabine's "bombshell" (30). The second sign of possible irony is the exaggerated degree of violence she proposes:

> Il lui faut, et sans haine, immoler un beau-frère.
> Ne différez donc plus ce que vous devez faire,
> Commencez par sa sœur à répandre son sang,
> Commencez par sa femme à lui percer le flanc,
> Commencez par Sabine à faire de vos vies
> Un digne sacrifice à vos chères Patries.
>
> (ll. 639–44)

In essence she argues that if it is a sign of honor to have the mettle to kill one's brother-in-law for one's country, then is it not also so to kill one's sister or one's wife for the same cause? The willful extension or exaggeration of heroic values that Sabine expresses here is abetted by the repetition of "Commencez par" and by the possibility for sarcasm suggested by the two adjectives in the last line ("digne," "chères"). Sabine's line of argumentation is problematic as well, which might in itself constitute a sign of irony. Her initial assertion—"Du saint nœud qui vous (Horace and Curiace) joint je suis le seul lien" (l. 625)—is highly questionable. What of the friendship between Curiace and Horace or the love between Camille and Curiace? Even if one accepts Sabine's premise, it is a rather breathtaking leap to conclude that her death will break the ties between them (Newmark 6) or that her murder will somehow make the combatants less culpable. The excessive claims of her proposal make one suspect irony.

At the same time, Sabine's speech retains a fundamental ambiguity, leaving the receiver uncertain whether she is in fact sincere or ironic. Throughout her speech, Sabine seems to move back and forth between the two poles:

> Qu'un de vous deux me tue, et que l'autre me venge;
> Alors votre combat n'aura plus rien d'étrange,

Et du moins l'un des deux sera juste agresseur.

(ll. 631–33)

"Rien d'étrange" invites an ironic interpretation by being both counterin-
tuitive and categorical, while the last line above seems earnest in its modest
qualification of her assertion. This back-and-forth movement between possible irony, possible sarcasm even, and absolute seriousness persists throughout
the speech. The instability is reflected in critical reaction: Knight and Nurse
find Sabine's proposal to be ironic;[88] Han Verhœff, on the other hand, takes
Sabine at her word, crediting her with the desire "à compenser, à justifier au
fond, les méfaits de la guerre, et non pas, comme chez Camille, à les mettre
en cause" (*Tragédies* 125).

    Uncertainty concerning Sabine's intent in making the proposal
obviously complicates its interpretation. Does she seek merely to prevent
the combat? In support of that position Newmark points to Curiace's and
Horace's reactions to her speech and Camille's support, asserting that "she no
more intends to die than does Rodrigue when he tries to weaken Chimène's
resolution by begging her to kill him" (5–6). Or is her goal more broadly
an attack on the heroic values underlying the combat, as Nurse (30) and
Lagarde (197) propose?

    I have always suspected that a different kind of motivation might
explain Sabine's proposal in this scene: torn between competing loyalties,
she is also completely marginalized and isolated as a woman. No one has
consulted her or even consoled her. Her proposal forges a central role for
herself in the conflict between Rome and Albe, moving her from the pe-
riphery to the center. She even displaces the men, at least to some extent,
by assigning them a new motivation for their combat, replacing honor and
patriotism with personal revenge. Her proposal is thus quite literally a self-
centered one. She seeks thereby to become an active part of the events that
have such a profound impact on her life. She even creates a concrete image
of that self-centeredness when she threatens to throw herself between the
combatants if they refuse her request:

Vous ne les [hands] aurez point au combat occupées
Que ce corps [her own] au milieu n'arrête vos épées,
Et malgré vos refus il faudra que leurs coups
Se fassent jour ici pour aller jusqu'à vous.

(ll. 659–62)[89]

To call Sabine self-centered undermines an ironic reading. Either Sabine
is focused entirely on her own needs and suffering, a reading supported by
Sabine's inability to recognize the similarity of Camille's devastation to her

own (3.5) as well as by her assertion that she is the only tie between the men, or else she is focused on undermining the logic leading the men to fight each other. The two are not perfectly incompatible, but they are difficult to reconcile because of the blindness implicit in self-centeredness and the perceptive acuity required for aggressive irony.

In the final analysis, Sabine's request can only be taken seriously, that is to say unironically, if we are prepared to accept that she seeks in this scene to legitimize, rather than prevent, the threatened combat between the men. That is a difficult proposition to defend. Sabine's focus on the deleterious effect of her speech on the men is evident in Camille's aside to her, "Courage, ils s'amollissent" (l. 663), which Sabine follows with a further statement directed at the men: "Quelle peur vous saisit? sont-ce là ces grands cœurs, / Ces Héros qu'Albe et Rome ont pris pour défenseurs?" (ll. 665-66), lines that lend themselves without hesitation to an ironic interpretation.[90]

To go beyond the confines of this particular scene supports our perception of possible irony in Sabine's offer. Both she and Camille employ decidedly ironic epithets in other contexts. Camille prepares to assault her brother by saying, "Dégénérons mon cœur, d'un *si vertueux* père, / Soyons indigne sœur d'un *si généreux* frère" (ll. 1239-40, italics mine), and Sabine accosts Horace in act 4, antiphrastically highlighting his "illustre colère" (l. 1335) and the "spectacle si doux" (l. 1337) of Camille dying as a result of his "généreux coups" (l. 1338). While the evidence is hardly copious, the fact that Sabine as well as Camille use verbal irony elsewhere confirms the likelihood of irony in 2.6 and even suggests that irony may be a significant weapon for women in a world of male violence.

The possible irony of Sabine's speech in 2.6 centers largely on her proposal that she be killed by either Horace or Curiace. That request belongs to a larger context as well because Sabine twice again asks to be killed. The possibility for irony in the two later pleas is relevant to our interpretation of the first; the three can hardly be read in isolation from each other. If the petition for death in 2.6 is read as ironic, does it follow that the other two she makes must be ironic as well? Or conversely, if the last two requests are unironic, does that necessarily call into question an interpretation of the first request as ironic?

Sabine's second request comes as she confronts Horace immediately after he has killed Camille:

> Immole au cher pays des vertueux Horaces
> Ce reste malheureux du sang des Curiaces.
> Si prodigue du tien n'épargne pas le leur,
> Joins Sabine à Camille, et ta femme à ta sœur.
>
> (ll. 1339–42)

She claims to deserve death at his hand even more than Camille, for she weeps for three of the fallen, as opposed to only one, and persists despite the example of Camille's punishment. The only sign of irony, and it is slight, is the possibility for antiphrasis and sarcasm in the words "lâches" and "vertu" when she says: "Quoi? ces lâches discours / N'arment point ta vertu contre mes tristes jours /…?" (ll. 1377–79). Her final plea in this scene, however, does not contain any hint of irony:

> Cher époux, cher auteur du tourment qui me presse,
> Écoute la pitié, si ta colère cesse,
> Exerce l'une ou l'autre après de tels malheurs
> A punir ma foiblesse, ou finir mes douleurs.
> Je demande la mort pour grâce ou pour supplice,
> Qu'elle soit un effet d'amour, ou de justice.
>
>   (ll. 1383–88)

[margin note: H. does feel threatened by #2]

It is noteworthy that Horace's reaction to this second plea is very similar to his and Curiace's response to the first. "À quel point ma vertu devient-elle réduite!" (l. 1395), he exclaims as he openly flees his wife. In both cases, Horace feels threatened by Sabine's words. Whether that threat is occasioned by the caustic assault of irony remains open to interpretation.

Sabine's third request to become a sacrificial victim comes in the final scene of the play, as Horace is being judged by the king. She addresses Tulle directly: "Et punissez en moi ce noble criminel; / De mon sang malheureux expiez tout son crime" (ll. 1602–3). As in the last example, this passage contains no obvious signs of irony unless one is prepared to read "noble" as antiphrastic. Reaction to this final offer has varied widely. Doubrovsky rejects all hint of irony and speaks of her "sincérité impuissante et pathétique" (157). Others dismiss her offer as absurd (Lancaster 2,1:310), extravagant (Herland, *Horace* 196), and even insincere, in that Sabine knows full well that no one is likely to do as she asks (Bouvet 129). The fact that her offer is ignored by all suggests its lack of significance (Verhœff, *Tragédies* 125). My reading of Sabine as completely self-centered fits comfortably with this third request: Sabine bursts on stage and immediately places herself front and center: "Sire, écoutez Sabine, et voyez dans son âme / Les douleurs d'une sœur, celles d'une femme" (ll. 1595–96). She substitutes her form of justice for that of the king, while depicting herself as more important to Horace than he is to himself ("Les nœuds de l'Hyménée et son amour extrême / Font qu'il vit plus en moi, qu'il ne vit en lui-même," ll. 1607–8), an assertion for which we have seen little evidence.

[margin note: 3rd-bursts in yet again]

The only critic I have encountered who finds all three of Sabine's re-

[bottom margin note: EKSKIN. S = self-centred!]

quests for death to be ironic is Alphonse Bouvet.[91] His interpretation points
to a central problem raised by Sabine's reiterated requests: consistency of character in relation to irony. Can a character be serious after having been ironic,
particularly in parallel or similar circumstances? Is there not some effect of
contagion inherent to ironic discourse? The discomfort one feels in following
Bouvet's interpretation of a consistently ironic Sabine coupled with the solid
logic of his argument may be responsible for the general dearth of comment
on the relationship of Sabine's second and third requests to her first.

A second issue raised by Sabine's repeated requests to be killed involves
a central concern of this chapter: repetition. As we stated at the outset,
the possibility for irony increases to the extent that the element repeated
is *normally* considered singular. Certainly a request to be killed meets that
standard. Sabine is dismissed by many in part because the repetition of her
plea raises the disquieting possibility that she may mean something other than
what she says, and this possibility for irony jars with the pity she ostensibly
seeks to arouse.

While approaching Corneille through an interrogation of his characters'
psychology is not generally a very fruitful line of approach, it has some interesting ramifications here. One is struck by Sabine's death wish, an aspiration
tied to her inability to accept the situation she confronts. Not only does she
make a plea to be killed on three occasions, but four times she threatens suicide
as well, albeit at considerably less length than she devotes to asking others
to kill her.[92] While it is more common for a character to threaten suicide in
the universe of classical theater than to request death from another's hand,
the same mechanism of potential irony through repetition is at work here.
Because of the multiple iterations of a desire to die unaccompanied by any
concrete action, Sabine's death wish must reasonably be called into question,
thus allowing for the possibility that she is ironic. Indeed, how can she mean
what she says and still be alive at the end of the play?[93]

In the final analysis Sabine is tied to two very distinct types of possible
irony: the possible verbal irony of 2.6, which includes her first request to be
killed, and the possible irony of repetition. One might argue that two kinds
of merely possible irony make the presence of some irony all the more likely.
More interesting to consider, however, is the question of the source of the
possible irony and how it might differ in these two types. We saw in chapter
3 that while Corneille is obviously the final source of everything that is said
in a play, verbal irony is to be credited to the character speaking. Thus the
potential for irony in Sabine's speech in 2.6 belongs to her. The situation
is more ambiguous in the case of her repeated pleas to be killed. The most
compelling reason to have recourse to Corneille as a source for the possible
irony of repetition in *Horace*, as distinct from Sabine, is the disjunction in

the latter's conduct, which in turn gives rise to incongruity (itself a signal of possible irony, one we will discuss at length in chapter 7). Whereas Sabine may be making pleas to be killed in order to shock her auditors (ironic) or as earnest, if perhaps unconvincing, entreaties (unironic), Corneille may himself be using them for ironic or unironic ends. Unironically, the pleas work to surprise and even shock the audience. The outrageousness of the demand as well as its repetition fit within the norms of Corneille's dramatic practice. Sabine's request is not dissimilar from Rodogune's demand that whoever will marry her must first kill Cléopâtre. Furthermore, there are three other occasions in Corneille's theater where the possibility of death is raised three times. In *Le Cid*, Rodrigue thrice puts his life in jeopardy; in *Rodogune*, Antiochus on three occasions offers to die in order to satisfy either Cléopâtre or Rodogune; finally, in its most concentrated manifestation, Phocas threatens Martian with death three times in a single scene (*Héraclius* 5.3). Considering Sabine's three requests for death from this perspective undermines the possibility for irony, but gives Corneille a motivation for the repetition that is independent from his character's. On the other hand, the possibility remains that Corneille is ironically mocking Sabine by means of her reiterated offers to die or that he seeks to undermine the concept of heroism.

A debate arose in the 1950s about whether Sabine's character (particularly in 2.6) might in fact be voicing Corneille's opposition to Roman values of heroism. Newmark argued that by having Sabine voice the Roman ideal ironically, Corneille himself is attacking that ideal. While certainly provocative, the idea of Corneille assailing heroic values through the mouthpiece of Sabine seems somehow unlikely. As J. W. Scott notes, "Why, if Corneille's approach to 'l'éthique de la gloire' was indeed ironic, have generations of his countrymen failed to realize the fact?" (16). I would like to suggest that a more complex arrangement of Sabine and Corneille as intending sources may be at work, one that would provide a possible answer to Scott's question. First, we noted a disjunction between the three pleas that Sabine makes to be killed in terms of the presence and absence of signs of irony. Second, the possibility of irony from Corneille's perspective does not line up comfortably with the possibility of irony from Sabine's. Corneille may be using either the initial offer or its repetition seriously or ironically. The same may be said for Sabine, but her motivations are unrelated to Corneille's, so that one might imagine an earnest Corneille, eager to shock his audience, combined with either an ironic Sabine, attacking her husband and brother with irony, or a pathetic and desperate Sabine, who makes her requests most seriously. The opposite is possible as well. One might envision Corneille attacking Sabine's earnest pleas for death with the irony of repetition as a means of attenuating and even camouflaging Sabine's ironic attack on Roman values in 2.6. This would explain how both Newmark and Scott could both be correct in their debate, and leave Corneille in a perfectly double and antithetical position, itself open to ironic interpretation. However one chooses to understand Sabine's speech in II,6 and her repeated pleas for death, it is difficult to avoid an incongruous disjunction between Sabine's stance and Corneille's.[94]

Sabine provides an excellent example of the difficulties one may encounter in attempting to label words and actions as ironic. The sheer accumulation of relatively codified signs of irony—repetition, antiphrasis, and incongruous disjunction—point to the possibility of irony, but do not assure it. The receiver is left with the final interpretive choice. Does her extensive speech in the play signal impotent self-pity, or is it a sign of her crucial role? Does Sabine use irony as a weapon in a situation, much like Nicomède's, in which other arms are denied her? Or does Corneille employ her as a vehicle for his own ironic denigration of heroism? These are choices with consequences for our understanding of Sabine's role in *Horace* and perhaps for our reading of the entire play. I have always perceived Sabine as an outsized and ill-fitting component of this hyperconstructed tragedy that ostensibly champions the heroic establishment of the Roman state. The possibility of irony provides a place for Sabine that disrupts the traditional structure of symmetries and the values that undergird it. An ironic Sabine pulls the play towards her and creates a second perspective, undermining the primary theme of patriarchal heroism. Clamoring for death in front of and from the men works to cast an ironic light on their power and violence.

*

Reduplication in its various forms is a feature of all literature; its scope greatly exceeds irony. At the same time, reduplication lends itself well to irony. Repetition, symmetry, coincidence, and echoic mention all function as signals of ironic intent, suggesting, but not offering final assurance, of its presence. These signals open the door to an exploration of the possibility of irony that, as we have seen in this chapter, has rich implications for our understanding of Corneille's theater.

NOTES

[68]He suggests that "le degré de l'effet ironique obtenu par un texte est inversement proportionnel à la dépense de signaux nécessitée par l'obtention de cet effet" (Allemann 393).

[69]Rimmon-Kenan, in her article on the subject, frames repetition in terms of a series of paradoxes, a particularly apt stance in light of our discussion of irony. See also Kawin.

[70]Pascal describes how the repetition of the unique can engender a reaction: "Deux visages semblables, dont aucun ne fait rire en particulier, font rire ensemble par leur

ressemblance" (58). The relationship between irony and laughter is clearly a complex one, one that I will not deal with here, because Corneille's theater has few overtly comic moments. Suffice it to say that irony may at times elicit laughter, particularly from someone who is not its victim, such as a spectator.

71   Si l'on t'a bien donné Léonce pour mon frère,
        Les quatre autres peut-être, à tes yeux abusés,
        Ont été, comme lui, des Césars supposés.
        L'État qui dans leur mort voyait trop sa ruine
        Avait des généreux, autres que Léontine,
        Ils trompaient d'un Barbare aisément la fureur,
        Qui n'avait jamais vu la Cour, ni l'Empereur.
        Crains, Tyran, crains encor, tous les quatre peut-être
        L'un après l'autre enfin se vont faire paraître.
                                                    (ll. 1036–44)

72   L'Auteur y peut mettre ordre avec fort peu de peine,
        Cléandre en même temps épousera Climène,
        Et pour Philiste, il n'a qu'à me faire une sœur
        Dont il recevra l'offre avec joie et douceur,
        Il te pourra toi-même assortir avec Lyse.
                                                    (Corneille 2:1262)

I discuss the issue of multiple unions in "Women and Marriage in Corneille's Theater."

73 He goes to some lengths to stress the distinction:
        Pour quelle raison l'ironie ne porte-t-elle pas aussi sur le mariage du couple
        principal, s'il est vrai qu'il s'agit de la forme la plus traditionnelle du dé-
        nouement de la comédie moderne? N'est-ce pas parce que le mariage de
        Dorante et de Mélisse [*La Suite du Menteur*] est lié à l'organisation même de
        l'intrigue, parce que l'intrigue est construite de façon à aboutir au mariage
        des héros? ("Structure" 244)
Forestier's argument is not terribly convincing, especially if one considers that the union of the main couples in both of the plays he discusses is the result of problematic courtships.

74 Corneille's decision to call *Agésilas* a tragedy, so inexplicable and inapt, may itself be open to an ironic interpretation.

75 Greenberg examines the symmetries and dissymmetries of this play, showing how the former are modeled on the division of the sexes ("Horace" 272).

76 Bénichou notes the confusion, if not precisely the incest: "Rodogune l' [Nicanor] appelle 'chère ombre,' par un mouvement inattendu, comme si son *moi,* en quête d'une issue glorieuse dans le présent, pouvait se laisser aller à un sentiment d'autrefois, et revivre l'amour du père alors que le fils est tendrement aimé" (97).

77 Indeed, Rostand's entire book on the subject, *L'Imitation de soi chez Corneille*, makes no mention of irony.

78 *Théodore* l. 407; *Héraclius* l. 149; *Pertharite* l. 7; *Sophonisbe* l. 695. In *Attila* Ildione says: "Voilà quelle je suis, voilà ce que je pense" (l. 705).

79 Baker discusses the reappearance of earlier lines in *Tite et Bérénice* in such terms ("Sounds" 224).

80 "The attitude expressed by an ironical utterance is invariably of the rejecting or disapproving kind. The speaker dissociates herself from the opinion echoed and indicates that she does not hold it herself" (Sperber and Wilson, *Relevance* 239).

81*Le Cid* ("À toute heure, en tous lieux, dans une nuit si sombre," l. 1023), *Le Menteur* ("Mais vous en contez tant, à toute heure, en tous lieux," l. 1175), *Œdipe* ("Je l'entends murmurer à toute heure, en tous lieux," l. 384), *Pulchérie* ("J'en ai l'âme à toute heure, en tous lieux obsédée," l. 850).

82There is a secondary meaning as well: while Massinisse was once Eryxe's betrothed, he now seems to have transferred his romantic interest to his ex-fiancée Sophonisbe.

83This includes two plays written prior to *Horace*, *La Veuve*, and *La Place Royale*, as well as, far more significantly, four after: *La Suite du Menteur* (Dorante: "Aimez en ma faveur un ami qui vous aime, / Et possédez Dorante en un autre lui-même," ll. 1785–86); *Héraclius* (Martian: "Épousez Martian, comme un autre moi-même," l. 867); *Nicomède* (Laodice: "Votre importunité, que j'ose dire extrême, / Me peut entretenir en un autre moi-même," ll. 999–1000); and *Attila* (Attila: "J'ai lieu de vous aimer comme une autre moi-même," ll. 986).

84Limiting the echo to the combination of "il est" and a heroic aspiration, often involving death, we find examples in *Rodogune* (Cléopâtre: "Il est doux de périr après ses ennemis," l. 1534); *Œdipe* (Dircé: "Il est beau de mourir pour en [of honor] suivre les lois," l. 806); *Agésilas* (Agésilas: "Il est beau de triompher de soi," l. 1982); *Attila* (Ildione: "Il est beau que ma main venge tout l'Univers," l. 704 and Ardaric: "Il est beau de périr pour éviter un crime," l. 1409). All of these examples come from the latter part of Corneille's career.

85Rostand discusses what he calls "des imitations *significatives*" and notes "elles sont très probablement conscientes, car Corneille ne pouvait avoir à ce point oublié ce qu'il avait écrit" (12).

86"*Horace*, notons-le bien, est l'une des rares pièces dans lesquelles Corneille s'est astreint à suivre pas à pas le schéma diégétique de sa source historique, Tite-Live" (Forestier, *Génétique* 83).

87 Indeed, Newmark has written an entire article about Sabine's irony in this scene. Others who find Sabine to be ironic here include Bouvet (122–23), Abraham (*Corneille* 64), Harvey (91), Lagarde (197), and Tiefenbrun ("Blood" 626).

88"Ironique, la proposition de Sabine: 'Qu'un de vous deux me tue et que l'autre me venge,' puisque ce n'est qu'une protestation contre une situation intolérable" (Knight, "*Andromaque*" 21); "Not for a moment does Sabine doubt the monstrosity of this suggestion and her purpose is achieved when the two warriors recoil in horror" (Nurse 30). Petit de Julleville agrees that her offer could not possibly be serious, but asserts that because it is not, it is nothing more than cold rhetoric (299).

89Clarke notes that Corneille takes pains to anchor Sabine's project in Plutarch's narrative of the Sabine wives throwing themselves between their fathers and their husbands through his choice of name for his invented character ("Plutarch" 47).

90One can easily imagine these lines spoken with a sarcastic tone as well. That Sabine is capable of sarcasm is supported by her later comment to Horace *père*:

> N'appréhendez rien d'eux [Horace and Curiace], ils sont dignes de vous,
> Malgré tous nos efforts vous en devez attendre
> Ce que vous souhaitez, et d'un fils, et d'un gendre,
> Et si notre foiblesse ébranlait leur honneur,
> Nous vous laissons ici pour leur rendre du cœur.
> (ll. 686–90)

91Bouvet calls Sabine's second offer "dérision," and insists, "Si l'actrice tient absolument à mettre dans les deux derniers vers ["N'importe: tous ses traits n'auront rien que de doux / Si je les vois partir de la main d'un époux," ll. 1390–91] autre chose que l'horreur, le mépris et le dégoût de l'époux en question, nous lui laissons l'entière responsabilité de cette interprétation" (127). He uses similar terms for the third request: "Le même affreux persiflage qui stupéfiait Curiace et Horace à l'acte II, Horace, son père, le roi Tulle et Valère sont contraints de l'entendre encore en ce moment," and he makes particular note of Sabine's description of her husband as Rome's "si bon défenseur" (l. 1630; Bouvet 128).

[92] "Le refus de vos mains y condamne la mienne" (l. 656); "Nous avons en nos mains la fin de nos douleurs, / Et qui veut bien mourir peut braver les malheurs" (ll. 937–38); "Et n'employons après que nous à notre mort" (l. 1402); and finally, "Ma main peut me donner ce que je vous demande" (l. 1624).

[93] Lockert seems to be commenting on this problematic gap between words and action in Sabine when he proposes an alternate ending: she should kill herself at the end as a punishment for Horace and thus a validation that he has done something wrong. "Many critics have found Sabina's role, with her often reiterated eagerness to die, monotonous and ineffectual. As the consummation of her recurrent desire and a pivotal feature of the denouement, her suicide would greatly lessen the force of that reproach. It would be a very hard blow to Horatius" (42).

[94] Merlin-Kajman suggests another possibility for irony on Corneille's part here, one that is situated on a different level entirely. She reads Sabine's position at the play's dénouement—that is, married to her brothers' killer—as Corneille's ironic rejoinder to the criticism of Chimène in *Le Cid*: "Subtile ironie cornélienne: Chimène n'aurait pas dû *consentir* à épouser Rodrigue. Mais que peut faire Sabine?" (90).

CHAPTER 6
POSSIBLE IRONY II: EXAGGERATION

As we noted at the beginning of part 2, exaggeration is a basic signal of irony, "souvent l'indice privilégié" even (Paillet-Guth 24). It is perfectly adapted to possible irony in that it functions by degree and relies on perception. When used in conjunction with other signals exaggeration reinforces the likelihood of irony; when used alone, it raises the possibility of its presence. In Kerbrat-Orecchioni's terms, "[L]'outrance dans la formulation peut dénoncer une séquence comme ironique" ("Problèmes" 34). Sabine's reiterated expressions of a desire to die, whether by her own hand or by someone else's, can easily be interpreted as an exaggerated response. Certain of Corneille's characters—Médée, Matamore, Dorante, Cléopâtre, Attila—are figures of exaggeration because of their outsized ambitions, powers, or pretensions, and we may legitimately wonder just how far they are meant to be taken seriously. Because exaggeration is widespread and takes many forms, this chapter will focus primarily on those cases where it is the primary or sole signal of irony. Irony based on exaggeration may be verbal (anchored in the words of a character) or it may be situational. In the former case, the intending source of the irony may be either the speaking character or Corneille, and in the latter it is Corneille alone. This chapter will be quite eclectic in its examination of the relationship between exaggeration and irony in Corneille's theater, ranging from character to theme to stylistic technique, as well as dealing with its manifestations in the prefatory material that Corneille published with his plays.

Irony based on exaggeration is clearly more difficult to identify with any certainty than irony based on antiphrasis, which is why it fits squarely under the heading of possible irony. First, it is much less obvious than antiphrastic irony, in large part because it is a matter of degree rather than of simple reversal. Doubt concerning the speaker's or author's intent is inherent to exaggeration, and persists even if the receiver decides that the intent is ironic, because the exact position of the speaker remains elusive. On the other hand, exaggeration offers significant compensations in both breadth and depth of ironic effect: "Lorsqu'elle est fondée sur une exagération, l'ironie est donc parfois moins sensible mais elle est par ailleurs beaucoup plus productive, plus féconde" (Perrin 190). Exaggeration, like other forms of irony, involves doubling, but the double in question is not a discrete element, as in the cases

101

of repetition or symmetry, but is rather a norm. The gap between what is considered normal and the exaggerated element allows one to entertain the possibility of irony.

Some use the terms "exaggeration" and "hyperbole" interchangeably, but we will follow Perrin in making a distinction between exaggeration as a form of irony and hyperbole, which, while structurally identical to exaggeration, does not have any ironic intent (192). It is worth considering this distinction in some detail because Corneille has a decided affinity for unironic hyperbole, as we shall see. Perrin describes hyperbole as obvious, conspicuous, and yet at the same time somehow appropriate to what is being represented, and gives the example of Cyrano de Bergerac's nose.[95] A problem may arise, however, if the hyperbole is too hyperbolic or if the object of the hyperbole is too ordinary. Perrin quotes Quintilien: "[D]ans l'emploi de l'hyperbole, il faut observer une certaine mesure. En effet, si toute hyperbole sort de la vraisemblance, il ne faut pas qu'elle sorte de la mesure" (79–80). Perrin also cites Longinus's *Traité du sublime*:

> Les hyperboles de cette qualité sont risibles…C'est pourquoi il faut savoir, pour chaque cas, jusqu'où l'on peut reculer la limite; car il arrive qu'à pousser trop loin les limites de l'hyperbole, on la détruise; et une tension excessive de ces sortes de choses amène le relâchement, et il se peut faire qu'on arrive au résultat tout à fait contraire. (79)

Thus, going too far will result in a failed or infelicitous hyperbole. The salient point here is that an infelicitous hyperbole is impossible to distinguish from an ironic exaggeration, except by intent. Perrin gives an example which is open to either interpretation and notes that consensus about whether it is intended irony or infelicitous hyperbole is unattainable.[96] The interpreter of Corneille's theater is at times confronted with the same quandary, as the example of Sabine makes clear: is Corneille overreaching or being ironic? Perrin's discussion of hyperbole points to the degree of uncertainty that inevitably accompanies the assessment of irony based on exaggeration.

Indeed, a specific point of friction lies between Corneille's unironic dramaturgical preoccupations and ironic exaggeration. That point is Corneille's fondness for going beyond the norms prescribed by *vraisemblance*. In his *Discours de l'utilité et des parties du poème dramatique*, the playwright says, "Mais les grands sujets qui remuent fortement les passions, et en opposent l'impétuosité aux lois du devoir ou aux tendresses du sang, doivent toujours aller au-delà du vraisemblable" (3:118). It is reasonable to posit that what is exaggerated is generally *invraisemblable*. In fact, in his *Discours de la tragédie*

Corneille discusses the *invraisemblable* in terms that seem to describe exaggeration: "Pour plaire il [the playwright] a besoin quelquefois de rehausser l'éclat des belles actions, et d'exténuer l'horreur des funestes. Ce sont des nécessités d'embellissement, où il peut bien choquer la vraisemblance particulière" (3:171). One may conclude that a measure of exaggeration is thus inherent to Corneille's dramaturgy and some account must be taken of his tendency to use exaggeration for reasons that likely have little to do with irony. Indeed, it would seem to be his desire to attain the sublime that may lead him into dangerous exaggerations that in turn open the door to interpretations of irony.[97] The *invraisemblable* and the sublime both occupy territory that may be difficult to differentiate from ironic exaggeration.

That exaggeration may suggest irony can be illustrated by specific examples in Corneille's theater. Attila opens the second scene of the play by addressing Valamir and Ardaric as follows:

> Rois amis d'Attila, soutiens de ma puissance,
> Qui rangez tant d'États sous mon obéissance,
> Et de qui les conseils, le grand cœur, et la main,
> Me rendent formidable à tout le genre humain.
> (*Attila* ll. 73–76)

The praise and lofty position Attila accords the two kings clashes with their obvious powerlessness. Attila's choice to use exaggeration functions perhaps unironically to flatter the two, or, more plausibly, to mock them ironically. This arouses in the audience a doubt that will extend to much of what Attila says to the four characters who are his prisoners as well as his guests. We saw in chapter 3 how exaggeration is clearly used as a form of verbal irony when Plautine inflates Martian's social status in order to mock him (*Othon*, ll. 523–28) or when Nicomède grossly overstates Attale's qualifications for the throne (*Nicomède*, ll. 592–93). Chimène can be interpreted as a figure of excess, both in her language (e.g., when she addresses Don Sanche, "Tu me parles encore, / Exécrable assassin d'un Héros que j'adore?" *Le Cid*, ll. 1723–34) and in her persistent pursuit of retribution for her father's death. In her case, however, no ironic intent can be ascribed to the character. If the possibility for ironic intent exists in relation to Chimène, it must belong to the playwright. While it is perhaps not the most obvious reading, there exists the possibility that Corneille is mocking his heroine through exaggeration, thereby containing the danger her demands represent to the interests of the state.

Several of Corneille's characters, both comic and serious, are unquestionably figures of excess. In each case, exaggeration is at play; what is unclear is whether irony is as well. The tipping point between infelicitous hyperbole and ironic exaggeration depends on individual standards and judgment. Among Corneille's serious characters, three stand out in this regard: the Médée of 1639, Cléopâtre (*Rodogune*), and Attila. Médée has manifest supernatural powers; Attila believes himself to be the scourge of God. The incorporation of the supernatural motivates and naturalizes the excesses of these two characters and thus makes irony somewhat less likely. Cléopâtre, excessive in her ambition and the violence she is happy to place in its service, provides a decidedly different case. Despite frequent reference to "ciel" and "dieux," as we noted in the previous chapter, there is little sign that any higher realm exists in the world of *Rodogune*. The absence of a supernatural realm makes Cléopâtre more open to an ironic reading because of the gap it reveals between her language and her situation. Indeed, one might describe the entire play as hyperbolic with its excessive heroine, its multiple doubles, the presence of coincidence, and the persistent symmetry (see chapter 5), as well as the immoderate use of both monologue and *récits*. The question is whether the hyperbole of Cléopâtre's words and actions, and more broadly the hyperbole of the entire play, are felicitous or infelicitous. The line between the two is neither clear nor stable. It is always a matter of individual judgment, but at one extreme we may note that Cléopâtre not only personifies her hatred and addresses it as her double (ll. 406–8), but in the following scene presents it as marriageable: "On ne montera point au rang dont je dévale, / Qu'en épousant ma haine, au lieu de ma rivale" (ll. 499–500). The overall result is a mixed sensation of thrill and discomfort for the spectator: the thrill comes from the hyperbole, and the discomfort comes from the potential for irony.

In the case of excessive characters from comedy, the situation is far easier to reconcile with irony. Dorante and Matamore both use language to create the reality in which they would like to operate. Matamore employs exaggeration in his outrageous narrative flights in support of his dual role as military giant and irresistible lover. In his case exaggeration crosses over into pure fiction. The supernatural is very much a part of his fabulation but is entirely absent from the world of the characters he addresses. The disjunction between Matamore's universe and theirs is so extreme that it is easy to imagine a stance of mocking irony on Corneille's part towards his character. The Dorante of *Le Menteur* is similar, yet the reduced degree of exaggeration in his language—he makes up elaborate and melodramatic lies, but his lies remain just shy of the line dividing the credible from the incredible—theoretically brings with it a commensurate reduction in the likelihood that the playwright is ironically mocking him. It remains a strong possibility, however:

the tall tales that Dorante's fellow characters may swallow, such as the *festin sur l'eau* or the account of his forced marriage to a young woman in Poitiers, are palpably fictional to the play's audience. In both comic examples, the conclusion of mocking irony through exaggeration on Corneille's part is entirely plausible.

Exaggeration is a frequent feature of Corneille's theater, one that attaches itself to different aspects of a play and that may signal irony or something quite different, specifically the playwright's affinity for the *invraisemblable*. We will turn now to several areas where exaggeration seems particularly tied to the possibility of irony.

Parody

Parody links repetition and exaggeration. It is based on the former, as we shall see, but it often takes the latter as a signal. Jean Schlumberger links exaggeration and parody explicitly when he says of *Pompée*, "[C]onstamment la mesure est dépassée et la surcharge confine à la parodie" (102). Exaggeration is central to parody, first as a signal and a means of distinguishing it from pastiche, and second because for Corneille parody is above all self-parody, a notion that can itself be called excessive.

Parody is a form of repetition. It is similar to echoic mention in many respects, but differs first and foremost in terms of scale. The language of an author, or even of a character, may be parodied, but hardly a single line. Parody refers to larger features of a text than does echoic mention: ideas, situations, characters, style. Such features must be recognized by the audience in order for their repetition to function as parody. The same is true of echoic mention, but here the breadth of such features increases the likelihood that they will be recalled. Hutcheon, on whose seminal work, *A Theory of Parody*, I will base the discussion that follows, defines parody as "repetition with critical distance, which marks difference rather than similarity" (6). She immediately links parody to irony, stating that "parody...is a form of imitation, but imitation characterized by ironic inversion" (*Theory* 6), a definition very similar to the criteria we set out in the last chapter for echoic mention. Parody implies some form of ridicule, often involving criticism of what is parodied.[98] This "ridiculing ethos" (*Theory* 60) is what sets parody apart. Subtlety, ambiguity, and undecidability are not the domain of parody, which explains Vladimir Jankélévitch's opinion that parody is "la forme la plus voyante de l'ironie" ([1936] 53). The ridicule that characterizes parody can, however, range widely, from the scornful to the playful. Parody is similar to echoic mention in presupposing intent on the part of the author, here the intent to ridicule. One cannot call Corneille's *Œdipe* a parody of Sophocles' *Œdipus Rex* or Seneca's *Œdipus*, despite the obvious presence of repetition with difference, unless one is prepared to believe that the seventeenth-century playwright intended to ridicule the earlier texts. Whatever one may think of Corneille's *Œdipe*, no one, to my knowledge, has suggested such parodic intent on the part of the playwright in its composition.

Irony and parody have deep and virtually inextricable ties. They share vital structural features: both are double-voiced; the inversion common in much irony is a characteristic of parody; two levels of meaning coexist structurally in both. Hutcheon argues that because of this structural similarity, irony is the privileged rhetorical strategy of parody (*Theory* 25). While parody may often be more obvious than irony, its status as double allows for a kind of dialogue between the parody and the parodied (Schoentjes 236). Within that relationship, the original functions as an authority, whether it be a discourse or a specific text. A parody ridicules that authority, but at the same time it consecrates its status as authority, thereby simultaneously rendering homage to what it ridicules. Parody is thus both conservative and revolutionary, representing both the authority and its transgression.

The domain of what may be parodied is quite broad, extending from style and genre conventions to characters, specific situations, and ideas. Parody does not have a major presence in Corneille's theater, yet it has a recurring one. For example, on several occasions the playwright parodies the clichés of love, whether comic or tragic. Cliton and Lyse in *La Suite du Menteur* parody the budding relationship between Dorante and Mélisse, offering each other considerably less elevated sentiments than their masters. When Dorante addresses adoring stances to the portrait of Mélisse (ll. 917-33), Cliton's parodies his master by adding his own verse to the same portrait, focusing on her wealth instead of her beauty:

> Adorable et riche beauté,
> Qui joins les effets aux paroles;
> Merveille qui m'as enchanté
> Par tes douceurs et tes pistoles;
> Sache un peu mieux les partager
> . . . .
> Garde pour toi les confitures,
> Et nous accable de Louis.
>
> (ll. 939–48)[99]

More seriously, Corneille parodies the clichés of tragic love by having Arsinoé say to Prusias

Je n'aime point si mal que de ne vous pas suivre,
Sitôt qu'entre mes bras vous cesserez de vivre,
Et sur votre tombeau mes premières douleurs
Verseront tout ensemble, et mon sang, et mes pleurs.
(*Nicomède* ll. 1279–82)

In this case, Corneille uses parody to criticize Arsinoé, whose sincerity is very much open to question.

The ironic structure balancing homage and ridicule that is characteristic of parody is particularly noteworthy, because in Corneille's theater parody most often takes the form of self-parody. Corneille can be understood to imitate features of his own theater at times with a stance that both ridicules and pays homage to the themes and characters that made him famous. I don't want to underestimate how slippery this terrain is and how important the word *possible* is in this discussion of self-parody. Nonetheless, self-parody may be key to understanding the creative exuberance of Corneille. By parodying himself, Corneille sets himself up as an authority and at the same time calls attention to his ability to constantly evolve by ridiculing that very authority.[100] The intent implicit in self-ridicule and endemic to parody can only be intuited here, however, and thus the irony that attaches to parody is merely possible, not certain.

Generally, parody in Corneille's theater takes as its object his own plays. It may, for example, involve one character parodying another, as is typical of Cliton's treatment of Dorante in both *Menteur* plays. In *La Suite du Menteur*, Cliton parodies Dorante's attitudes concerning *être* and *paraître*. When Dorante explains to Cléandre why he automatically came to the latter's defense ("Chacun…sur son front porte écrit ce qu'il est," l. 809), Cliton immediately enjoins, "Par exemple, voyez, aux traits de ce visage [his own] / Mille Dames m'ont pris pour homme de courage" (ll. 811–12). In so doing, Cliton mocks Dorante's assumptions about how human worth and rank are manifested. At the other end of the spectrum an entire play may be seen to parody other plays. *Le Menteur* has long been considered in certain respects a parody of *Le Cid*.[101] Both involve young men who are eager to establish their reputation as men of valor and to lay claim to the woman they desire. The two heroes must contend with fathers who simultaneously abet and impede their success. Parody here is based on the move from Rodrigue's lofty sense of duty and obligation to Dorante's invented acts of bravery, from Rodrigue's true love to Dorante's flighty infatuation. The parodic features extend to the level of language. Dorante's description of his imaginary exploits ("Vaincre dans les combats, commander dans l'Armée / De mille exploits fameux enfler ma renommée," ll. 181–82) echoes Don Diègue's description of military leadership ("Attaquer une place, ordonner une armée / Et sur de grands exploits bâtir sa renommée," ll. 183–84), as Marie-Odile Sweetser notes ("Niveaux" 495–96). Corneille's parodic intent is ensured by the shift from tragedy (or tragicomedy, if one prefers) to comedy.

When the play in question is not a comedy, the issue of parody becomes more problematic and the question of possible parodic intent becomes harder to resolve. Corneille clearly worried about a possible parodic interpretation when he describes the danger of ending *Théodore* in the same fashion as *Polyeucte*: "[J]'eusse été ridicule, si j'eusse fait faire au sang de ces martyrs le même effet sur les cœurs de Marcelle et de Placide, que fait celui de Polyeucte sur ceux de Félix et de Pauline" (*Examen* 2:272). Note the playwright's choice of the term "ridicule." A fair number of examples of parody in Corneille's theater have been noted by critics, but only in a scatter-shot sort of way. In act 4, scene 5 of *Œdipe*, Jocaste sounds a great deal like Chimène when she tells Œdipe that she should hate him for having killed her husband, but that she loves him still and yet will follow her duty (Forestier, *Génétique* 339). The radical shift of context—from the frustrated hopes of sympathetic young lovers to the considerably less appealing married mother and son—suggests something beyond mere imitation of a successful scene. Similarly, it may be parody when Attila consults the two powerless kings, Ardaric and Valamir about his choice of bride (1.2), echoing the famous scene in *Cinna* where Auguste consults Cinna and Maxime about whether to abdicate the throne (2.1). Again, the difference between the two scenes, in the form of the contrast between both the motives of the rulers and the status of the men consulted, authorizes an interpretation of parody. Once embarked on this route, the possibilities are legion, but there is little grounding for such speculation. Is *Suréna* a parody of a Racinian play (La Charité and La Charité 103)? Is "Agésilas's reluctant gesture [accepting a union with Aglatide] . . . a parody of the sacrificial *générosité* of earlier heroes" (Carlin 126)? Is *Polyeucte*'s Sévère a parody of Christ (Lyons *Tragedy* 119)? While we may espy exaggeration and repetition, the terrain is unstable because Corneille's intent is so difficult to ascertain.

There is, however, a privileged domain for parody in Corneille's theater and that is the figure of the hero and the notion of heroism. Throughout much of Corneille's theater, he both glorifies heroism and at the same time treats it ironically. Heroism, by virtue of its inherent excessiveness, is ripe for parody: "La cuirasse de l'héroïsme a un défaut: elle sonne un peu fort. D'où le sentiment qu'elle pourrait à la limite sonner creux" (Serroy, "Préface *Menteur*" 11).[102] Thus the figure of the Cornelian hero, insofar as it is built upon exaggeration, lends itself to an ironic interpretation. What I have argued elsewhere concerning onstage tyrants holds for the hero as well: the acts that

[Marginal handwritten notes:]
- parodic intent clear in shift in genres.
- but harder to be certain for tragedies —
- unstable terrain for interp
- one domain clearer; glorifies heroism + treats it ironically
- fig of Cornelian hero built upon exagg ∴ lends self to ironic interp.
- ✱ recog limits of own approach

account for his heroic stature cannot be represented on stage because of the constraints, limitations, and *bienséances* of the seventeenth-century theater ("Staging" 116–17). Heroism, therefore, cannot be directly represented; it can only be conveyed on stage through language. The problem of the hero who speaks, rather than enacts, his heroism is that of such a speech's truth-value. Whatever the weight of historical reality that Corneille's heroic characters bring to his construction of their gravitas, the danger of exaggeration and ridicule remains. As Couton put it so well in reference to César in *Pompée*, "C'est une disgrâce qu'un conquérant soit toujours Picrochole par quelque côté et que leur langage ne permette pas de distinguer vrai et faux brave" (Corneille 1:1725). The possibility that the Cornelian hero may be perceived as a parodic figure is thus unavoidable and pervasive. Ironically, the strongest of heroes is perhaps the most vulnerable.[103] Corneille's heroes and their heroism have indeed occasioned numerous parodies on the part of other authors (Serroy, "Préface *Illusion*" 27), but the suggestion that Corneille himself intends parody interests us above all here. As we noted above, the Dorante of *Le Menteur* has long been considered a parody of the Cornelian hero of the tetralogy, especially of Rodrigue. The vehicles of the parody of heroism are not limited to comedy, however. Susan Read Baker believes that Othon, by his "failure to take action or even to speak wholeheartedly a discourse which provokes admiration" offers a "possibility...of parody which turns against an earlier form of Cornelian heroism" (*Harmonies* 137). *Pompée* offers a similar prospect by representing a series of historical characters, many of whom have been held up as heroes of one sort or another (Pompée, César, Cléopâtre), only to undermine all prospects for heroism in the play.[104] Clearly the ridicule is of a darker variety in these last two examples than in comedy.

The idea of Corneille parodying his own heroes is not a comfortable one for some, particularly for those who prize Cornelian heroism as the author's greatest legacy.[105] Indeed, the playwright's intent in this regard would remain completely impenetrable were it not for the character of Matamore, who provides a privileged vehicle for the parody of heroism in Corneille's theater.

Matamore, the very embodiment of exaggeration, appears fairly early in Corneille's *œuvre*; *L'Illusion comique* was first performed in late 1635 or early 1636. He offers a striking contrast to other characters in Corneille's early comedies: whereas the young playwright built his reputation on a new kind of comedy, Matamore is a stock character of a more traditional variety (Forestier, "Gageure" 817). Corneille's version of the *fanfaron* may be memorable, but Matamore was also certainly recognizable to the contemporary audience as an echo of a well-established theatrical tradition. The *Capitan* explicitly lays claim to the status of hero: his language is saturated with the fantastic feats he has performed,[106] but we do not see him do anything remotely heroic on stage. Matamore thus shares the verbal dimension of heroism with true heroes, a conjunction that allows for the possibility of parody. Of particular interest is that Matamore's style of verbal bravura reappears in a surprising number of Corneille's subsequent plays, contaminating ostensibly serious moments of heroism with the potential for ridicule because of such similarities. Thus, Corneille's concept of heroism does not merely run the danger of appearing at times excessive; his heroes also risk specific resemblance to Matamore. The subversive effect of this conjunction has long been noted and some have found it disturbing. Octave Nadal laments, "L'héroïsme serait-il ce gonfle-ment démeusuré, ou du moins commencerait-il par là? par cette exagération, par cette *ubris* verbale? Faudrait-il toujours supposer ce mensonge à soi dans les actes nobles, désintéressés?" (118).[107] The interpenetration of Matamore and the Cornelian hero is such that it has led to confusion between the two. Jean Serroy recounts that when Boileau sought to praise *le grand* Condé in *Épître* 4 he employed, no doubt inadvertently, Matamore's words: "Condé, dont le seul nom fait tomber les murailles, / Force les escadrons et gagne les batailles" ("Préface *Illusion*" 22).[108]

Before examining the specific resemblances between Matamore and a number of Corneille's heroes, I must mention that he is a highly unusual parodic character in that he precedes many of the heroes he parodies. While *L'Illusion comique* appeared on stage before *Le Cid*, the precise chronological relationship between the two is not entirely clear, particularly in terms of their conception.[109] The other heroic characters who bear a curious resemblance to Matamore all, however, appear after 1636. As Serroy puts it, "C'est comme si l'anti modèle précédait le modèle" ("Préface *Illusion*" 22). The effect of this reversal is that every Cornelian hero from the tetralogy onward labors under the onus of being a potential target for parody. The parodic potential of Matamore may also explain in part why *L'Illusion comique* was long rel-egated to obscurity.

The first and most famous object of parody is Corneille's classic hero, Rodrigue. The similarity of their bravura extends to their language. Matamore, devastated at the thought that his prospective father-in-law has become his enemy and fearful of the violence he might have to inflict on the man, sounds remarkably like Rodrigue: "Que n'ai-je eu cent rivaux à la place d'un père / Sur qui, sans t'offenser, laisser choir ma colère?" (ll. 737–38). Charles Mau-ron grasps the parodic mechanism at work here: "Matamore est un faux Cid auquel le vrai ressemble parfois un peu trop: en les juxtaposant, Corneille ne se moque-t-il pas de l'idéal qu'il nous propose?" (244). Not everyone agrees; there are those who reject the possibility of parody by focusing on the differ-ences between Matamore and Rodrigue rather than the similarities (Garapon

172–73; Doubrovsky 531). Resemblance to Matamore need not be limited to Rodrigue, however. Some, as far back as Georges de Scudéry, writing within the context of the *querelle du Cid*, find that Don Gomès, Chimène's father, has more than a little of the "Capitan ridicule" about him: "[T]out ce qu'il [Don Gomès] dit étant plus digne d'un fanfaron que d'une personne de valeur et de qualité" (Corneille 1:788). Don Gomès's language is indeed heroic, but his onstage acts do not conform to his pretentions ("Tout l'État périra plutôt que je périsse," l. 380). His actions in the play are limited to slapping an old man and being defeated by a novice swordsman.

César (*Pompée*) gives signs of a similar resemblance to Matamore. The emperor sounds like the *Capitan* when he describes himself as "N'ayant plus que les Dieux au-dessus de sa tête" (l. 1258). Rathé (*Reine* 88) and Couton (Corneille 1:1725) both point to César's offer to conquer for Cléopâtre any throne she might desire (ll. 1261–66), which seems to echo Matamore's offer to Isabelle: "Choisissez en quels lieux il vous plaît de régner: / Ce bras tout aussitôt vous conquête un Empire" (ll. 416–17). In the same vein, César describes the outcome of his imminent military forays as "[p]our faire dire encore aux Peuples pleins d'effroi / Que venir, voir, et vaincre, est même chose en moi" (ll. 1335–36).

Both Attila and Octar, his captain of the guards, use language strongly reminiscent of Matamore to characterize the Hunnish king. Attila describes himself to Ildione as "moi de qui l'âme altière / Cherche à voir sous mes pas trembler la Terre entière" (*Attila* ll. 817–18), and elsewhere as one of those "dont le nom fait trembler l'Univers" (l. 124). The word "trembler" is strongly associated with Matamore and serves the double function in *L'Illusion comique* of describing both the *fanfaron*'s fearsome force and his cowardice.[110] Describing Attila's philosophy of war, Octar uses language almost identical to that employed by Matamore: "Il [Attila] aime à conquérir, mais il hait les batailles, / Il veut que son nom seul renverse les murailles" (ll. 1109–10). Matamore brags, "Le seul bruit de mon nom renverse les murailles" (l. 233). More curious is the echo of Matamore heard in Octar's description of the Frankish king Méroüee. Octar says that the latter is capable of "[b]ouleverser les murs d'un seul de ses regards" (l. 572), which echoes not only Matamore's power over walls but also his threat to Clindor: "Je vais t'assassiner d'un seul de mes regards" (l. 244). That Méroüee was widely understood to be an allegorical representation of Louis XIV makes the echo of Matamore rather disquieting. Could Corneille possibly have been mocking the French king as well as his own heroes?

Aspar, the ambitious general in *Pulchérie*, also echoes Matamore when he boasts, "Moi, qu'on a vu forcer trois camps, et vingt murailles, / Moi, qui depuis dix ans ai gagné sept batailles" (ll. 317–18). The fondness for figures as well as the hint of enumeration are strongly reminiscent of Matamore who uses *mille* five times and favors extended enurmeration.[111] Enumeration is patently a manifestation of exaggeration, and, as such, "un signal privilégié et efficace de l'ironie" (Hamon 90). At the same time, it must be noted that Aspar's claims to heroism are certainly more dubious than those of Rodrigue, Don Gomès, César, or Attila. An echo of Matamore in the mouth of a character whose heroism is open to question is far less jarring than in that of a consecrated heroic figure. When Dorante, a thoroughly comic character, sounds like Matamore—"Je m'y suis fait quatre ans craindre comme un tonnerre" (*Le Menteur* l. 162)—the relation is no longer a question of parody, but becomes simple resemblance.

Alcandre, the wizard who controls the action in *L'Illusion comique*, anticipates Matamore, much as Matamore anticipates the Cornelian hero, appearing onstage before him and in a radically different context. Alcandre's attributes are indeed strikingly similar to Matamore's discourse about himself. Dorante describes Alcandre's cave as an invisible wall, a rampart "dont les funestes bords / Sur un peu de poussière étalent mille morts" (ll. 11–12). The same speaker employs hypocritical preterition to enumerate Alcandre's powers:

> Je ne vous dirai point qu'il [Alcandre] commande au
>   tonnerre,
> Qu'il fait enfler les mers, qu'il fait trembler la terre,
> Que de l'air qu'il mutine en mille tourbillons
> Contre ses ennemis il fait des bataillons,
> Que de ses mots savants les forces inconnues
> Transportent les rochers, font descendre les nues,
> Et briller dans la nuit l'éclat de deux Soleils.
> Vous n'avez pas besoin de miracles pareils.
>   (ll. 49–55)

The odd formulation "Je ne vous dirai point" may either suggest what Alcandre might be capable of in other circumstances or it may be read as a sign of unusually modest claims for a stage necromancer of the period, as Clifton Cherpack suggests (342). In any event, these disclaimed powers strikingly resemble the empty boasts made later in the play by Matamore. The passage is saturated with hyperbolic language, including figures ("mille" and the more modest "deux," rendered excessive by its union with "Soleils") and terms such as "trembler" and "tonnerre" associated with Matamore. The two men complement one another: Alcandre has the supernatural power without the bluster and Matamore the boastfulness without the power.

Matamore is thus not merely a figure of exaggeration, but his voice echoes through the mouths of a number of Corneille's ostensible heroes. The possibility of parody is thus placed front and center in a play that Serroy calls "le creuset matriciel" of Corneille's entire *œuvre* ("Préface *Illusion*" 27). The remarkable coupling of verbal similarity and substantive difference between Matamore and any of the characters we have compared him to works to support the likelihood of Corneille's parodic intent.

Parody is inherently tied to irony and specifically to exaggeration. The difficulty that one encounters with parody lies in establishing its status as such: that status is dependent both on the intent of the author and on the perception of the audience. "Cette *condition de lecture* [knowing the original model] fait partie de la définition du genre [parody], et—par conséquent, mais d'une conséquence plus contraignante que pour d'autres genres—de la perceptibilité, et donc de l'existence de l'œuvre" (Genette 26). Thus there exists the potential for considerable difference of opinion. Matamore, despite his chronologically inverted position in Corneille's theater, provides a solid example of the parody of Cornelian heroism, and thereby substantiates Corneille's affinity for parody and authorizes our suspicions of possible irony in other cases as well.

ALAZON

An *alazon* is an "imposter, someone who pretends or tries to be something more than he is" (Frye 39). The word "more" in Frye's description links the figure of the *alazon* to exaggeration. Matamore is an *alazon*, of course; to a certain extent, so is Corneille. The playwright, in his prefatory material, takes on a central characteristic of the *alazon*, that of making exaggerated claims. Furthermore, both Corneille in his prefatory material and Matamore in *L'Illusion comique* suggest the possibility of self-consciousness concerning their exaggeration. Thus the possibility of irony arises in both character and playwright both from the exaggeration inherent in the role of the *alazon* and from undercutting that role through self-awareness, evaluation, and critical judgment. Matamore claims to have lived on a diet of ambrosia and nectar in Isabelle's attic, but when pressed, admits "[c]ette Ambroisie est fade: / J'en eus au bout d'un jour l'estomac tout malade" (ll. 1189–90). By allowing nectar and ambrosia to leave their consecrated position of perfection as the food of the gods, Matamore indicates a consciousness of the absurdity of his own claims. The double voicing here—maintaining that he has access to ambrosia and criticizing its nutritional value—signals irony. In the case of Corneille's prefatory materials, exaggeration constitutes one of the primary signs that the playwright may have an ironic intent.

Corneille plays the *alazon* most obviously by his overuse of superlatives.

Superlatives are a stylistic feature of both Corneille's plays and his prefatory material. The possibility for irony increases through a combination of the exaggeration implied by superlatives with the playwright's evaluation of his own dramatic accomplishments, because both of these features are independent signals of possible irony. The prefatory material contains numerous examples of exaggeration combined with self-evaluation. I will only mention a few: Corneille says of *Le Menteur*, "Je me défierais peut-être de l'estime extraordinaire que j'ai pour ce poème, si je n'y étais confirmé par celle qu'en a faite un des premiers hommes de ce siècle" [Zuylichem] (*Au lecteur* 2:5). Of the fourth act of *Théodore*, he states, "[J]e ne crois pas en avoir fait aucun, où les diverses passions soient ménagées avec plus d'adresse" (*Examen* 2:271). On *Héraclius*: "Surtout, la manière dont Eudoxe fait connaître...le double échange que sa mère a fait des deux princes, est une des choses les plus spirituelles qui soient sorties de ma plume" (*Examen* 2:359). About *Œdipe*: "[J]'ai eu le bonheur de faire avouer à la plupart de mes auditeurs, que je n'ai fait aucune pièce de théâtre où il se trouve tant d'art qu'en celle-ci" (*Au lecteur* 3:19). Concerning *Othon*: "Si mes amis ne me trompent, cette pièce égale ou passe la meilleure des miennes" (*Préface* 3:461). There is no need to continue the litany; the point should be clear: Corneille engages in considerable, exaggerated self-praise. The question is how to interpret such statements. Is Corneille reveling in self-approbation, or is he perhaps playing an ironic game in which one voice speaks to a certain audience that takes his words at face value while another voice addresses an audience that perceives the note of irony in the exaggeration of his statements? The playwright does not simply speak highly of his own works with regularity, he also seemingly has more than one favorite play. Françoise Jaouën notes the problem of sincerity entailed in this multiplication:

> Faut-il par exemple croire Corneille quand il déclare dans ses discours de 1660 que *le Cid*, *Horace* et *Cinna* (ses plus grands succès) ne lui plaisent pas outre mesure, et qu'il préfère *Rodogune*, *Sophonisbe* ou même *Nicomède*? La question peut paraître naïve, elle l'est moins lorsqu'on comprend qu'elle met en cause le statut même de l'œuvre critique. (63)

How may we know whether Corneille is sincere in his prefatory texts or whether there is a gap between what he says and what he means?

Corneille's intent in using superlatives to praise his own work is certainly open to speculation. Georges May finds his boastfulness to be sincere: "La vantardise était une des faiblesses du poète, et il s['y] complaisait avec une certaine naïveté" (16). I believe rather that Corneille was not at all naive and thus am more ready to accept ironic intent on his part. There remains a third possibility: Corneille makes such statements as part of a public relations campaign to persuade his double audience—the public and the *doctes*—of the value of his plays. Such packaging and selling involve cynicism perhaps more than irony, but they are perfectly compatible with irony.

Eirôn

The opposite of exaggeration is litotes, or understatement, itself as much a signal of irony as exaggeration. Whereas the *alazon* is a figure of exaggeration and even hubris, the *eirôn*, associated with litotes, is a figure of dissimulation, modesty, and self-deprecation, a stance which may include deceit as well. Unlike the *alazon*, the figure of the *eirôn* is not at all characteristic of Corneille's theater. The playwright's characters do not often or long adopt stances of ignorance, naivete, or humility in order to ironically victimize their interlocutors. However, while his characters rarely play the *eirôn*, Corneille does so rather frequently in his prefatory material.

This type of irony, with its focus on dissimulation, is by its nature particularly diffuse and ambiguous. Given an instance of modesty, self-deprecation, self-criticsm, or naivete, the receiver must decide whether irony is present or not, as litotes typically trumpets neither its own presence nor its ironic intent. The classic representative of this form of irony is Socrates. As Muecke notes, the ironist "assumes his role of naïf and speaks, writes or behaves as if he really were the sort of person who might hold the views the irony is intent on destroying or subverting" (*Irony* 68). Thus, Knight wonders whether Corneille's "naïve surprise" at finding the Greek and Roman versions unhelpful to the adapter of the Œdipus myth in the *Au lecteur* and *Examen* is "genuine or over-played" (*Tragedies* 68). Corneille's intent cannot be ascertained here with certainty, but the possibility of irony most certainly exists.

The stance of the *eirôn* is self-reflexive: "The *eiron* is the man who deprecates himself" (Frye 40). One is struck by how often Corneille employs modesty and self-deprecation within the texts that accompany his published theater. He opens the *Préface* to *Sertorius* with a demurral: "Ne cherchez point dans cette tragédie les agréments qui sont en possession de faire réussir au théâtre les poèmes de cette nature" (3:309). After devoting over two pages of *Don Sanche d'Aragon*'s *Épître dédicatoire* to a discussion of his choice to call the play a *comédie héroïque*, the playwright defers humbly to his addressee: "Mais après tout, Monsieur, ce n'est qu'un *interim*, jusqu'à ce que vous m'ayez appris comme j'ai dû l'intituler" (2:553). Corneille's modesty concerning his own role in the success of *Andromède* has led to very different interpretations. He ends his *Argument* thus:

> Souffrez que la beauté de la représentation supplée au
> manque des beaux vers que vous n'y trouverez pas en si
> grande quantité que dans *Cinna*, ou dans *Rodogune*, parce
> que mon principal but ici a été de satisfaire la vue par
> l'éclat et la diversité du spectacle, et non pas de toucher
> l'esprit par la force du raisonnement, ou le cœur par la
> délicatesse des passions. Ce n'est pas que j'en aie fui ou
> négligé aucunes occasions, mais il s'en est rencontré si
> peu, que j'aime mieux avouer que cette pièce n'est que
> pour les yeux. (2:448)

Some, such as Marie-France Wagner, take Corneille's final statement that
the play "n'est que pour les yeux" at face value, saying that it confirms "la
primauté de l'image sur l'aspect verbal" ("Miroir" 164; see also Wood 685);
Christian Delmas, on the other hand, views Corneille's statement as false
modesty and perceives humor in Corneille's closing line (xiii–xiv). Corneille
exhibits the same questionable modesty in discussing his *Trois Discours sur le
poème dramatique* in a 1660 letter to l'Abbé de Pure: "[V]ous n'y trouverez pas
grande élocution ni grande doctrine" (3:7). Corneille criticizes *Horace*'s lack
of unity in the play's *Examen*, but David Maskell notes that while Voltaire
was satisfied by Corneille's self-denigration on this score, as well one might
expect, modern critics are reluctant to accept these comments at face value,
perhaps because one finds in other parts of the *Examen* the assumption that
the play does indeed have unity (269). Signs of contradiction in combination
with the modesty lead to a stronger possibility of irony. Corneille's odd logic
in humbly accepting the criticism that *Théodore* received from the public
makes one wonder whether he might be ironic here as well: he notes that
if he were to disagree with the public's low estimation of this play, then he
would be forced to reject their favorable judgment of his other plays (*Épître*
2:269). The fact that he makes this argument twice as long as it might have
been further arouses suspicion.

The stance of exaggerated self-denigration extends back to Corneille's
earliest plays, but it is more obviously playful in that context. The playwright
notes that in publishing *Mélite* he runs the risk that his readers may find his
simple and informal style to be base rather than naive, and he comments that
the play's publication is certain to give pleasure to his critics by providing
the opportunity to criticize and condemn him (*Au lecteur* 1:4). He humbles
himself in the *Épître dédicatoire*, saying that he is "un homme qui ne pouvait
sentir que la rudesse de son pays" (*Mélite*, 1:3). In the *Préface* to *Clitandre*,
Corneille observes that he has nothing but vanity in common with most
"Écrivains Modernes" (1:96). Are we then to read the opening of his first

tragedy's *Épître dédicatoire* in the same light: "Je vous donne *Médée* toute méchante qu'elle est, et ne vous dirai rien pour sa justification" (1:535)?

Some of the modesty and self-denigration we encounter in these texts may be explained in other ways. It seems clear that a tone of humility is the norm for the *épître dédicatoire* in general; asserting the unworthiness of one's play is part of the protocol of making a gift of it. Corneille opens his dedication of *Horace* to Richelieu with "[j]e n'aurais jamais eu la témérité de présenter à Votre Éminence ce mauvais portrait d'Horace, si..." (1:833). The entire letter is saturated with this tone of exaggerated humility. The stance of *eirôn* seems intrinsic to this highly conventional and almost ceremonial form of discourse in which the playwright marks gratitude and/or curries favor. The *épître* is a common feature of Corneille's theater, appearing in at least some editions of all of his first twenty plays. After *Don Sanche*, it disappears, with the sole exception of *Œdipe* (1659).[112] The *épître dédicatoire* lends itself particularly well to irony because, like theatrical discourse in general, it has a distinctly double addressee: the person named by the letter and the reading public. A gap in meaning can easily open up between the two, just as we have seen ironic gaps arise between the meaning of a character's words as they are addressed on stage and to the audience (see chapter 2). We note that Corneille chose in the later part of his career not to publish such letters with his plays. Having attained illustrious status as a playwright, he may have no longer felt the pressure to produce such self-abasing texts; indeed, beginning with the 1660 edition of his complete works, Corneille no longer included any of the *Épîtres dédicatoires* with his plays. One may even speculate that, given its general absence from the action of his plays, the *eirôn* stance was one with which Corneille was uncomfortable. Perhaps he found it difficult to control that voice and found himself confusing the sincere *eirôn* with an ironic *eirôn*.

Flattery is the complement to humility, and as such it is a frequent feature in the *épître dédicatoire*, used to elevate the addressee rather than humble the speaker. Flattery lends itself to the possibility of irony in two ways: first, because flattery almost inevitably entails exaggeration, and second, because of its inherently problematic relationship to truth; flattery and sincerity seem almost antonymous. Corneille combines humility and flattery in the *Épître* addressed to Montauron that precedes *Cinna*:

> Vous avez des richesses, mais vous savez en jouir, et vous en jouissez d'une façon si noble, si relevée, et tellement illustre, que vous forcez la voix publique d'avouer que la fortune a consulté la raison quand elle a répandu ses faveurs sur vous, et qu'on a plus de sujet de vous en souhaiter

le redoublement, que de vous en envier l'abondance. J'ai
vécu si éloigné de la flatterie que je pense être en possession de me faire croire quand je dis du bien de quelqu'un,
et lorsque je donne des louanges, ce qui m'arrive assez
rarement, c'est avec tant de retenue, que je supprime
toujours quantité de glorieuses vérités pour ne me rendre
pas suspect d'étaler de ces mensonges obligeants, que
beaucoup de nos modernes savent débiter de si bonne
grâce. (1:905–6)

The exaggeration here is obvious. Furthermore, the reversal between what he
is saying (that he is not a flatterer) and what he is in fact doing in this passage
(flattering) is structurally well suited to irony.[113] Hélène Merlin-Kajman has
brilliantly analyzed the ironic potential of the exaggerated flattery contained
in the *Épîtres dédicatoires* that accompany *Horace* and *Pompée*, dedicated to
Richelieu and Mazarin, respectively. In the first case, she interprets the gaps
between the Cardinal's status as minister of state, which is never mentioned,
and the abundant praise of his theatrical acumen as potentially highly ironic
(86–87). Indeed, these qualities, following Merlin-Kajman's argument, are
not only inappropriate to a man of state and of the church, but they right-
fully belong instead to Corneille (88). In the second case, Corneille uses
incongruity once again, implicitly assigning an inappropriate role to Mazarin
(ruler of the country) as well as the flattery of repeatedly equating Mazarin
and Pompée (78–79). In sum, the *épître dédicatoire* seems to be a privileged
site of possible irony for Corneille, albeit one he abandoned in the last part
of his career.

The stance of the *eirôn* may also spring from the gap between the
original publication date of the play and the 1660 *examens*, a gap that extends
up to a period of thirty-one years. The Corneille of 1660 is at times unable
to merge with the author of the earlier plays. Thus he dismisses Clitandre as
"un Héros bien ennuyeux" in the 1660 *Examen* (1:102), and describes his
goals in writing *Clitandre* thus: "[J]'entrepris d'en faire une [play] régulière
(c'est-à-dire dans ces vingt et quartre heures), pleine d'incidents, et d'un style
plus élevé, mais qui ne vaudrait rien du tout; en quoi je réussis parfaitement"
(1:101–2). We may legitimately wonder, however, whether Corneille is dis-
avowing his second play with this statement or mocking the rules governing
theater. The odd combination of self-denigration (*Clitandre* is a worthless
play) and bravado (I succeeded completely) makes it difficult to take the
playwright's statement at face value.

The role of *eirôn* is more complex than that of *alazon*: whereas the
alazon is faulted for self-delusion, the *eirôn* is viewed warily for his deceit

of others; the *alazon* is obvious while the *eirôn* wears a mask. Perhaps most
important, the *eirôn* attacks, unlike the *alazon*. While it would appear that the
alazon and *eirôn* are opposing and essentially incompatible stances, bringing
the two together adds the often ironic sign of reversal to the potential irony
inherent in the exaggeration of either taken separately. Thus when Corneille
oscillates between *alazon* and *eirôn* the irony is essentially inescapable. The
Préface to *Sophonsibe* provides an interesting example of the interaction of the
two. In it, Corneille engages in a long discussion of how Massinisse behaves
at the end of the play. The warrior's conduct is one of the crucial differences
between Corneille's version and Mairet's: while the latter had the despair-
ing Massinisse commit suicide on stage in the last scene, Corneille makes
Massinisse disappear from the stage before the final act begins. The little
that this later Massinisse does from afar—attempting to persuade Scipion
to accept his marriage and offering poison to Sophonisbe—is completely
ineffectual. Corneille responds in the *Préface* to criticism of his Massinisse
by adopting the stance of the *eirôn* with features of the *alazon*, creating a
highly aggressive irony directed at his critics. He opens with an exaggerated
enumeration of what Massinisse should have done: "J'accorde qu'au lieu
d'envoyer du poison à Sophonisbe, Massinisse devait soulever les troupes
qu'il commandait dans l'armée, s'attaquer à la personne de Scipion, se faire
blesser par ses gardes, et tout percé de leurs coups venir rendre les derniers
soupirs aux pieds de cette princesse" (3:384). Corneille then boasts of the
freedom he has left to the audience's imagination concerning Massinisse: "S'il
aime les héros fabuleux, il croira que Lélius et Éryxe entrant dans le camp y
trouveront celui-ci [Massinisse] mort de douleur, ou de sa main. Si les vérités
lui plaisent davantage, il ne fera aucun doute qu'il ne s'y soit consolé aussi
aisément, que l'histoire nous en assure" (3:384). The disparity between the
two options that Corneille allows the audience in this sentence signals the
likelihood of irony. Corneille moves again almost immediately to the role of
the *alazon*, bragging, "[J]e n'ai peut-être encore fait rien de plus adroit pour
le théâtre, que de tirer le rideau sur des déplaisirs [Massinisse's painful loss of
Sophonisbe], qui devaient être si grands, et eurent si peu de durée" (3:384).
The incongruity between the last two clauses undermines the possibility for
sincerity in his boast. Finally, Corneille moves to the position of the *eirôn*,
which he alternates with hostile jabs to conclude:

> Quoi qu'il en soit, comme je ne sais que les règles
> d'Aristote, et d'Horace, et ne les sais pas même trop bien,
> je ne hasarde pas volontiers en dépit d'elles ces agréments
> surnaturels et miraculeux, qui défigurent quelquefois nos
> personnages autant qu'ils les embellissent, et détruisent

> l'histoire au lieu de la corriger. Ces grands coups de maître
> passent ma portée; je les laisse à ceux qui en savent plus
> que moi, et j'aime mieux qu'on me reproche d'avoir fait
> mes femmes trop héroïnes, par une ignorante et basse
> affectation de les faire ressembler aux originaux qui en
> sont venus jusqu'à nous, que de m'entendre louer d'avoir
> efféminé mes héros. (3:384)

The stances of *alazon* and *eirôn* in Corneille's *Préface* to *Sophonisbe* combined despite their basic opposition, give a curious, shifting rhythm to the text and clearly signal irony.

*

I end this chapter on the varied possibilities for irony attached to ex-aggeration and its inverse, litotes, with a characteristic and playful example taken from the *Épître dédicatoire* to *Andromède*. In eight of Corneille's twenty *Épîtres*, the identity of the addressee is either completely absent or hidden behind initials, a choice that can comfortably be associated with the stance of the *eirôn*. In these cases, contemporaries and later editors have often tried to suggest a key to the addressee's identity. In the case of *Andromède*, the initials are M. M. M. M. Suggestions have been both fanciful and wide-rang-ing: Couton reports that Abel Lefranc suggested "À Mme de Motteville, mal mariée" and that, along the same lines, Delmas proposed "Madame de Mot-teville, mariée au monstre" (Corneille 2:1406); Maurice Rat follows Charles Marty-Laveaux in suggesting Madeleine Béjart (Rat 2:824; Marty-Leveaux 5:291); and Stegmann mentions the possibility of Mlle Mancini (*Héroïsme* 103–4). The initials, in fact, work against identification in this case, because of the improbably exaggerated, if not fantastic, repetition of the letter M. In what is no doubt a typographical error, and yet a telling one, Rat refers to this addressee as "M. M. M. M. M." (2:531). While the reader is never given any conclusive evidence that Corneille was not serious in his dedication, its combination of the modestly disguised dedication and the exaggerated repetition of letters may reasonably make us suspect that Corneille was ironi-cally mocking the conventions of the *épître dédicatoire*. Our interpretation is further supported by Corneille's paradoxical rhetorical stance within this *Épître*. While practically flirting with his unidentified addressee, he insists that he does not want her to be able to identify herself by reading the *Épître*: "Je…ne vous dis point en quoi les belles qualités d'Andromède approchent de vos perfections, ni quel rapport ses aventures ont avec les vôtres; ce serait vous faire un miroir, où vous vous verriez trop aisément, et vous ne pourriez plus rien ignorer de ce que j'ai à vous dire" (2:443). What then is to be the status of the the person to whom the play is dedicated? Neither the audience at large nor the individual concerned can make the identification while both are mocked for their desire to do so. How then can the dedication itself be anything but ironic?

it can only be ironic

*

Corneille frequently goes too far; exaggeration is a deeply embedded feature of his dramatic and rhetorical style. One has only to consider that the word "mille" appears 181 times in his theater, and in all but two of the plays, to recognize how far-reaching is Corneille's proclivity for exaggeration. It is also a critical portal to irony, often in its more playful forms. In gauging exaggeration, intent often remains clouded, as we have seen; because of such uncertainty, we may only entertain the possibility of irony through exaggeration.

exaggeration

"mille" – 181×!

Notes

[95]"Tout ce qui est démesuré, extraordinaire, appelle l'hyperbole. Le nez de Cyrano de Bergerac, par exemple…. [p]arce qu'il [the nose] est d'une dimension telle, que seule l'exagération peut nous le restituer dans toute son ampleur" (Perrin 84-85).

[96]Here is the example:

"Un conseil, évitez de mettre sur le tapis *la nouvelle affaire Dreyfus, le débat quasi théologique, que dis-je, métaphysique, qui coupe la France en deux, brise les ménages, brouille à jamais des amis de vingt ans*: la querelle de l'orthographe. Depuis ce funeste 6 décembre qui vit le gouvernement publier un rapport sur 'les rectifications de l'orthographe,' *le pays est au bord de la guerre civile* (*Le Nouveau Quotidien*)" (198, italics in original).

[97]Forestier discusses the role of the sublime at length in chapter 5 of his *Essai de génétique théâtrale* entitled "Une esthétique du sublime."

[98]While Hutcheon at times argues for a more neutral ethos for parody, she acknowledges that "'critical ridicule' remains the most commonly cited purpose of parody" (*Theory* 51). She notes that "Theodor Verweyen (1979) has separated theories of parody into two categories: those that define it in terms of its comic nature and those that prefer to stress its critical function. What is common to both views, however, is the concept of ridicule" (*Theory* 51).

[99]Marivaux will make much use of this structure wherein the servants echo the sentiments of their masters.

[100]Baker speaks of Corneille renewing his dramaturgy "by disrupting his own former practice" through parody and irony (*Harmonies* 148).

[101]Staves goes even further, calling *Le Menteur* a parody of *Le Cid, Horace,* and *Polyeucte* (520–21).

[102]Serroy traces the roots of Corneille's conception of heroism to the aristocratic code of the Castilian aristocracy, and goes on to say: "Le côté volontiers grandiloquent avec lequel celui-ci [honor] est affirmé et défendu et la façon chatouilleuse dont le moindre affront engendre aussitôt la volonté de vengeance lui sont apparus comme

empreints d'une outrance non exempte de ridicule" ("Préface *Menteur*" 11). Note that Serroy credits Corneille with recognizing the potential for ridicule.

[103]Lyons notes that "in negative evaluations of the hero of *Horace*—of which there have been a number in the twentieth century—Horace has been held up as almost a parody of Roman virtue" (*Tragedy* 120).

[104]See my "Pompée's Absence in Corneille's *La Mort de Pompée*" (270).

[105]Abraham does his best to foreclose any possible parodic reading: "En nous montrant le revers de cette médaille, Corneille n'en dément pas la face. Il ne se moque ni des héros, ni de l'idéal héroïque, mais de ceux qui, comme les Jourdain, veulent paraître généreux, ou glorieux, sans comprendre la signification soit de la générosité soit de la gloire, ceux, en somme, pour lesquels l'apparence fait office d'essence" ("Envers" 376). He inadvertently undermines is own position, however, by juxtaposing Corneille's heroes and Molière's M. Jourdain.

[106]For example, Matamore tells Clindor

> D'un seul commandement que je fais aux trois Parques,
> Je dépeuple l'État des plus heureux Monarques;
> Le foudre est mon canon, les destins mes soldats;
> Je couche d'un revers mille ennemis à bas.
> (*L'Illusion comique* ll. 237–40)

[107]Petit de Julleville takes the opposite perspective, voicing concern, not that Cornelian heroes sound like Matamore, but that Matmore sometimes speaks "le langage de la vraie bravoure," "quoique indigne" (iv).

[108]Matamore's precise words are "[l]e seul bruit de mon nom renverse les murailles, / Défait les escadrons et gaigne les batailles" (*L'Illusion comique* ll. 233–34).

[109]Abraham sums up the situation clearly:

> L'*Illusion* a été représentée avant *le Cid*, mais n'a été publiée qu'en 1639, deux ans après la publication du *Cid*. Puisqu'aucun texte antérieur à la publication ne subsiste, il est impossible de savoir à quel point la pièce telle que nous la connaissons correspond à celle de la représentation d'avant *le Cid*, ni si Corneille avait *le Cid* en tête lors de la facture de certain [sic] vers de *l'Illusion*. ("Envers" 365)

[110]There are five examples of *trembler* in *L'Illusion comique*: two fearsome (ll. 726, 766) and three cowardly (ll. 859, 1173, 1176). The most amusing occurs in Matamore's final appearance on stage when Lyse states baldly to his face that he ran to the attic out of fear: "Oui, vous tremblez, la vôtre [fear] est sans égale" (l. 1173). Matamore responds with his usual imaginative wit, providing a completely different explanation for his trembling: "Parce qu'elle [fear] a bon pas, j'en fais mon Bucéphale. / Lorsque je la domptai, je lui fis cette loi, / Et depuis, quand je marche, elle tremble sous moi" (ll. 1174–76).

[111]

> Oui, mais les feux qu'il jette en sortant de prison
> Auraient en un moment embrasé la maison,
> Dévoré tout à l'heure ardoises et gouttières,
> Faîtes, lattes, chevrons, montants, courbes, filières,
> Entretoises, sommiers, colonnes, soliveaux,
> Parnes, soles, appuis, jambages, traveteaux,
> Portes, grilles, verrous, serrures, tuiles, pierre,
> Plomb, fer, plâtre, ciment, peinture, marbre, verre,
> Caves, puits, cours, perrons, salles, chambres, greniers,
> Offices, cabinets, terrasses, escaliers.
> (*L'Illusion comique* ll. 747–56)

[112] *Œdipe* contains a variant of the *épître dédicatoire* in verse form, clearly addressed to Fouquet, but without the opening and closing formulae characteristic of a letter.

[113] Such a reversal is also suited to hypocrisy. Corneille aroused considerable criticism with this *Épître dédicatoire*. Couton notes that "[l]a dédicace de *Cinna* à Montauron...provoqua longtemps des commentaires sans indulgence," (Corneille 1:1598), and Stegmann calls it the source of "la légende d'un Corneille flatteur et avare" (*OC* 268).

gaps :
richest,
least mechanical
signs

irony:
I gap where
there should be
continuity

incongruity:

friction or
absence of logical
relation btwn
2 elts in proximity
↳ irony poss.

17th c. rules ⇒
harmony,
consistency

major ex
Rodelinde,
in Pertharite

(maternal
vs.
cruel —
which?

Chapter 7
Possible Irony III: Gaps

Gaps provide perhaps the richest and least mechanical signs of irony. Structurally, here as elsewhere, this form of irony involves two elements, but gaps require focus on the tension, or in more geometric terms, the space between two elements. Instead of more than one element where there ought to be only one (reduplication), there is a gap where there ought to be continuity. The signal of this type of possible irony is an unease with the juxtaposition of two elements. At one extreme, ironic gaps are delineated in terms of the geometric rigor of contradiction. In such cases, the irony is evident. In the domain of possible irony, however, the relationship between the two elements is rarely so clear cut. In this chapter, we will consider a variety of gaps or incongruities, ranging from the purely verbal (antithesis) to the logical (paradox) to the larger and more ill-defined, such as inconsistencies within characters or between registers within plays.

Incongruity

The *Oxford English Dictionary* defines *incongruity* as a "lack of harmony or consistency of parts or elements." These elements are considered in terms of difference rather than similarity, a difference that is not based primarily on a formal link such as repetition or reversal. Here, the friction or the absence of logical relation between two elements placed in close proximity signals the possibility of irony. What one perceives as harmonious or consistent is once again largely a matter of norms. Seventeenth-century dramaturgy, through rules concerning *vraisemblance* and the *bienséances*, codified the high value placed on harmony and consistency. It follows that incongruity was frowned upon and thus relatively uncommon in classical theater. Indeed, exaggeration is itself incongruous in the measured environment of seventeenth-century tragedy, and thus, as we considered in the last chapter, functions as a signal of possible irony. Given the focus on perception and norms, however, disagreement about what is and is not incongruous is inevitable, but that disagreement does not obviate the strong ties between incongruity and irony.

One of the more egregious examples of incongruity in Corneille's theater occurs in *Pertharite*. Grimoald pressures the unwilling Rodelinde to marry him by threatening to kill her son if she refuses. She responds by saying that she will marry him *only* on the condition that he kill her son first.

That a mother would make the murder of her son a condition for marriage is so aberrant and unexpected that we are confounded. Rodelinde increases our shock by saying that she will help him do it ("Fais, fais venir ce fils, qu'avec toi je l'immole," l. 907). One can only wonder, "Is she serious?" and on a broader scale, "Is Corneille serious?" That very question, regardless of whether it pertains to character or author, raises the possibility of irony. The excessive incongruity of this case has engendered varied critical responses as audiences have attempted to bridge the gap between what Rodelinde says and the norm of maternal protectiveness. That Rodelinde's motive is clearly to besmirch Grimoald and brand him as a cruel tyrant does little to diminish the incongruity. Furthermore, even with a "reasonable" motive in place, we have no assurance whether she intended to follow through on her demand or not. Knight insists Rodelinde is merely bluffing ("*Andromaque*" 21), while others have taken her offer at face value and either attacked or defended her for it.[114]

Pertharite was a resounding failure in 1651. When Corneille revised the play in 1660 and attempted to rectify the various shortcomings for which it had been attacked, he almost pointedly did not eliminate Rodelinde's criticized offer of infanticide. Not long before, in *Héraclius* (1646–47), Léontine's decision to sacrifice the life of her own son had been faulted as *invraisemblable* (Desfougères 503–4), as had Rodogune's demand that Antiochus or Séleucus kill Cléopâtre, which we will discuss shortly (*Rodogune*, 1644–45). Thus any suggestion that Corneille unknowingly had Rodelinde act in a manner that would be perceived as incongruous must be rejected. There is, however, one way to deal with the incongruity, to explain away the gap, and that is to frame her conduct in terms of Corneille's fondness for surprise. As we noted earlier, surprise is a recurring feature of Corneille's dramaturgy. Calling the incongruity a typically Cornelian surprise does not eliminate the possibility of irony, however, because of the close tie between surprise and exaggeration. Indeed, Rodelinde's offer is surprising and incongruous precisely because it is so excessive. Given the degree of criticism that the offer of infanticide has elicited, it seems fair to call it an infelicitous hyperbole, which, as we noted in chapter 6, is structurally identical to, and thus may be confused with, irony. Because critics communicated clearly to Corneille that this patricular element of surprise was problematic, his choice to retain it in later editions of *Pertharite* implies a decision to run the risk of an ironic reading. Rodelinde's provocation is dramatically superfluous: she could have simply refused to accede to Grimoald's pressure to marry him (Desfougères 503). More curious still, Corneille anticipated his critics by having Grimoald himself criticize Rodelinde's offer in terms that highlight its theatrical, ostentatious nature, and thus suggest that it is less than completely credible:

> Faire la furieuse, et la désespérée,
> Paraître avec éclat mère dénaturée,
> Sortir hors de vous-même, et montrer à grand bruit
> À quelle extrêmité mon amour vous réduit,
> C'est mettre avec trop d'art la douleur en parade,
> . . . .
> Les plus grands déplaisirs sont les moins éclatants,
> Et l'on sait qu'un grand cœur se possède en tout temps.
>   (ll. 943–50)

Within Corneille's desire to surprise his audience, there is a playful and *edged* urge to go too far, to deliberately challenge limits and court the possibility of irony. The predilection for surprise as well as an accompanying attitude of defiance can be dated back to the appearance of *Le Cid*. Chimène's behavior—that she received the man who killed her father in her own home, admitting that she still loved him, and may even marry him eventually—surprised everyone. It shocked and outraged the critics, and their reactions, voiced in *la querelle du Cid*, had a profound effect on Corneille, leaving him defensive and no doubt eager to have the last word. Perhaps more importantly, Chimène's behavior delighted audiences. From that moment of his career onward, Corneille sought to surprise and astonish his audience, and thereby to elicit admiration.[115] Corneille thus combines the desire to provoke with the aspiration to elicit admiration from his audience. Therein we may espy another potentially ironic incongruity deeply embedded in his dramaturgy, as surprise by no means necessarily elicits admiration.

We saw in chapter 5 that possible irony based on reduplication is widespread in *Rodogune*. Incongruity is a powerful signal in this play as well, although it is limited to one highly dramatic moment: Rodogune's demand that Antiochus or Séleucus kill their mother in order to win her hand. Rodogune's request of the brothers is perfectly symmetrical to that of Cléopâtre, who demands that one of her sons kill Rodogune in exchange for being named the elder of the two, except that matricide is a greater crime than simple murder. By demanding a crime in exchange for her hand in marriage, Rodogune moves from a position totally opposed to that of Cléopâtre (young versus old, desirable versus undesirable, good versus evil) to one where the similarities between the two women become more salient than the differences. Séleucus explicitly notes the resemblance between the two women when he says to his brother: "Que le Ciel est injuste! Une âme si cruelle [Rodogune] / Méritait notre mère, et devait naître d'elle" (ll. 1051–52). Furthermore, like Cléopâtre, Rodogune is incapable of envisioning a relationship other than that of enmity between Antiochus and Séleucus once she chooses one of the brothers and refuses the other: "Vous croyez que ce choix,.../ Pourra faire un heureux, sans faire un mécontent" (ll. 981–82). The gap between the two images of Rodogune is disturbing. The outrageousness of the act called for—matricide—resembles the incongruity of Rodelinde's demand for infanticide in *Pertharite* discussed above. In both cases, before making their ultimatum, the women are depicted as positive, desirable figures, victims of political forces beyond their control. Once the demand is made, it is difficult to see them again in the same rosy light. We may also note similarities with Sabine's reiterated requests to be put to death in *Horace*; in all three cases, supposedly virtuous women demand acts of terrible violence. Louis Herland discusses Rodogune's request as a kind of aporia in the play: "Le passage d'une phrase à l'autre [ll. 854–55] est parfaitement inintelligible, comme est saisissant le changement du ton: au langage de la pudeur, de la modestie, de la raison succède sans transition celui d'une furie vengeresse" ("Imprévisible" 241). Once this radical shift has occurred, the incongruity is compounded as Corneille seeks to maintain Rodogune as essentially virtuous: thus she is to be both similar to and the opposite of Cléopâtre.

Corneille was hardly unaware of these issues. In his *Examen* of the play, he goes on at considerable length discussing and justifying Rodogune's demand. He argues first that, unlike Cléopâtre, Rodogune did not really expect either of the men to carry out her wishes (2:202). Is Corneille suggesting that Rodogune was playfully ironic in demanding Cléopâtre's head? Rodogune, however, gives no indication in act 3, scene 4 that she means anything other than what she says. That she later tells Antiochus that she would have hated him had he obeyed her underlines the incongruity of her stance. In essence, Rodogune seeks to occupy two contradictory positions simultaneously:

> Votre refus est juste, autant que ma demande,
> . . . .
> Je voudrais vous haïr, s'il [your love] m'avait obéi,
> Et je n'estime pas l'honneur d'une vengeance
> Jusqu'à vouloir d'un crime être la récompense.
>   (ll. 1220–24)

Corneille maintains, although not very convincingly: "Il était de son [Rodogune's] devoir de venger cette mort [Nicanor's], mais il était de celui des princes de ne pas se charger de cette vengeance" (2:203). Corneille puts forth a second argument in defense of Rodogune's incongruous demand, claiming that it advances the play's action: "[E]lle conduit à l'action historique" (2:203). While it does lead to Séleucus's bowing out of the running for her hand and the throne, it does little else to move events forward. The third reason that

Corneille provides in the *Examen* is no doubt the most persuasive and the most revealing: "Quand cette proposition serait tout à fait condamnable en sa [Rodogune's] bouche, elle mériterait quelque grâce, et pour l'éclat que la nouveauté de l'invention a fait au théâtre, et pour l'embarras surprenant où elle jette les princes" (2:203). As in the case of Rodelinde in *Pertharite*, surprise appears to be of paramount value. Surprise, however, does not foreclose the possibility of irony. By its very nature, surprise throws the receiver off balance and we are left uncertain as to how to interpret it. The incongruity of Rodogune's demand makes the surprise all the more destabilizing.

While Corneille seems to revel in the incongruity he has created in Rodogune, others have been seemingly nonplused by it. Concerned about the instability occasioned by Rodogune's demand and perhaps mindful of the Roman Horace's prescription concerning consistency of character, a number of scholars have tried to minimize or deny the incongruity, essentially opting to explain away either the virtuous or the bloodthirsty aspect of Rodogune.[116] What is striking in the attempts to justify Rodogune is the laborious effort they require in order to recuperate the uncomfortable gap in her character. The awkwardness of these arguments and assertions reflects discomfort with the incongruity itself. Faced with both the virtuous Rodogune and the bloodthirsty Rodogune, one may deny or minimize one or the other, or one may accept the fundamental ambiguity of perceiving both concurrently. As we saw in chapter 1, the ambiguity stemming from the inclusion of two contradictory elements is characteristic of irony.

Incongruity, the result of a gap where there should be continuity or consistency, is a signal of possible irony. With its ties to surprise, exaggeration, and undecidability, it signals a moment that is ripe for ironic interpretation. Perhaps Corneille is commenting ironically, whether consciously or unconsciously, on the nature of the tragic heroine in these examples. Or he may be targeting the conventions of the tragic plot. Or the playwright may be merely seeking to dazzle and startle his audience with these awkwardly hyperbolic moments. All are possible interpretations.

Double Register

Ironic gaps are at times the result of a double register, two levels of discourse uncomfortably juxtaposed. In several plays, Corneille evokes two separate planes that both seem radically discrete and yet are placed in close proximity to one another. The juxtaposition of the two planes or discourses results in a kind of Flaubertian rubbing where each calls the other into question and each is a potentially ironic commentary on the other.[117] The most obvious examples of this situation are the two religious plays, *Polyeucte* and *Théodore*, which juxtapose the Christian and the pagan.

Marginal notes (handwritten):
- C. seems again to have wanted to surprise
- doesn't preclude irony —
- interp. uncertain
- critics have made great efforts to recuperate gap in Rodog's char. —
- don't like incong'y
- but can accept fundamental ambiguity as such —
- poss. irony.
- so: incongruity signals moment ripe for ironic interp.
- double register
- 2 levels of discourse uncomfortably juxtaposed
- eg Christian/ pagan

In *Polyeucte* the basic tension lies between the hero's earthly love for Pauline and his spiritual love for God, that is, between his affection and sexual desire for his wife and his aspiration to martyrdom and salvation. Polyeucte seems too entralled with his new wife to be an eager martyr and at the same time too committed to his divine calling to be so vulnerable to the physical attractions of Pauline.[118] The fundamental incompatibility of these two competing forces is at the heart of the tragedy. It is worth noting that the active zeal with which Polyeucte seeks death runs counter to Church doctrine in seventeenth-century France where martyrdom was taken to be a last resort in defense of the faith, not a goal in itself (Jaouën 64). Thus Corneille's choice to associate the religious plane in this play with martyrdom accentuates and even exaggerates the distance between the religious and the pagan.

Pauline provides Polyeucte with a most formidable obstacle to overcome in his chosen religious path, as both his "chère moitié" (l. 1166) and his "ennemie" (ll. 1091, 1166). In the earthly realm she is his beloved wife, but in the Christian sphere she is linked to the devil: Néarque tellingly refers to both the devil and Pauline as "ennemi" in the very first scene of the play (ll. 53, 104). The two planes are tied to gender as well. Pauline, the sole female protagonist, represents earthly pleasures while Christianity is associated with the male (see Greenberg, *Corneille* 122). Corneille makes an interesting move when he doubles the antithetical tension of Polyeucte's situation by giving Pauline two objects of affection—Polyeucte and Sévère—along with an attendant string of oppositions: present versus past, political marriage versus true love, sexual pleasure versus sexual attraction. Here, there is no double register, at least until the dénouement, in that Pauline's preconversion love for both men is strictly earthbound. While the double register of Polyeucte's situation and the discomfort it occasions are variants of the universally familiar conflict between the spiritual and the terrestrial, Pauline's conflict is highly unusual, particularly on the French stage, and has given rise to numerous readings that attempt to efface the scandal of her loving two men.[119]

Implicit in the tension between the Christian and the pagan registers are two very different conceptions of time. The Christian time of eternity cannot be reconciled with worldly time, yet Corneille calls attention to the double register. As Paul Scott notes, the play's action takes place only two weeks after Polyeucte's wedding rather than several years later, as in Corneille's sources ("Manipulating" 333). This displacement has consequences beyond simply rendering the force of sexual desire more powerful. In the fourth act, Polyeucte says to Pauline and Sévère, as he faces his own martyrdom, "Vivez heureux ensemble, et mourez comme moi" (l. 1310). How long should they live happily together? Would two weeks be enough? If Polyeucte is happy with Pauline, why the precipitation? Is the only way to be a Christian to die but critical of what, exactly?

immediately? How can Pauline and Sévère do what Polyeucte asks? How does one live happily and die a martyr simultaneously, and if it is not simultaneous, but consecutive, how does one begin to determine the juncture at which one moves from one to the other? The quandaries that follow from Polyeucte's directive lend support to the possibility of an ironic reading based on the gap between the two registers.

poss. ironic gap btwn 2

Corneille offers a synthesis at the end of *Polyeucte*, but it belongs to the realm of the *merveilleux* in its denial of the division between this world and the hereafter, and it does nothing to answer the questions posed above concerning the timing and necessity for martyrdom. Lemaître's reaction to the play reflects the unease occasioned by the double register: "Est-ce sublime? Est-ce révoltant? Est-ce simplement ridicule?" (289). His last question is not unrelated to the possibility of irony, and is made all the more disquieting when one considers that "the irreverent parodying of saints' lives was a feature of libertine writing of the 1630s and 1640s" (Paul Scott 332). Corneille's claim in *Polyeucte*'s *Examen* (1660) to have attained a fusion of registers in the play does not suffice to make it so.[120]

C's synthesis denies division btwn this world + hereafter —

problematic parodying of saints' lives in 17th c.

It seems altogether plausible that Corneille's attraction to the subject of the play reflects his own desire for fusion of what may have been the two most important domains of his life: theater and religion. Unfortunately for him, he lived in an era when the theater was not considered merely worldly, but base. While *Polyeucte* appears during a brief period in which plays with religious themes were in vogue, there was still resistance to, and debate surrounding, religious subject matter.[121] Thus the mere fact of a dramatic production of a religious subject reduplicates the double register of the pagan and the Christian and arouses considerable discomfort in the audience of the time.

tension: relig/theater => putting relig. story on stage => discomfort

> Ce public de croyants éprouvait un malaise à voir porter sur la scène un drame essentiellement religieux. Un miracle de la grâce transformé en divertissement profane, les vérités de la religion exposées sur les planches par la bouche d'excommuniés, l'Église au théâtre, un martyre de saint là où s'étaient poignardés tant d'amoureux, tout cela déconcertait, refroidissait les spectateurs. (Lemaître 287)

Indeed, the seventeenth-century audience was more taken with Pauline and Sévère than with Polyeucte (Cairncross 561). While the issue of intent poses certain problems here, clearly Corneille created the conditions that legitimize the possibility of an ironic interpretation. Whether Corneille intended irony or not, consciously or unconsciously, he left ample space for one to imagine that he might have.

can imagine that C may possibly have intended ironic interp

The same double register of the Christian and the pagan recurs in *Théodore*, although the issues raised are somewhat different. The first involves language, as religious terminology is applied to profane love. Baker finds that the commingling of the two discourses, as when Placide speaks of Théodore as "l'illustre objet des mes plus saints désirs" (l. 1005), constitutes irony ("*Théodore*" 7). The conflation of the two registers is even more problematic when it cannot be ascribed to the hyperbolic expression of true love, as when Marcelle is said to "idolâtre" Placide (l. 32), her stepson. Furthermore, *Théodore* is notable not only for incorporating a religious vocabulary, but for being probably the most sexually explicit of Corneille's plays. The subject of prostitution caused considerable consternation among his contemporaries.[122] We find three occurrences of the word *lit*, twice with sexual overtones.[123] Thus the juxtaposition of incompatible languages carries the potential for an ironic reading by virtue of its incongruity. A second site for possible irony involves antiphrasis through equivocation. Attempting to convince Marcelle that she has no designs on Placide, Théodore swears, "J'atteste ici le Dieu qui lance le tonnerre" (l. 539). Her words have two referents: Théodore ostensibly refers to Jupiter, who is associated with lightening and thunder, but in fact she is speaking of the Christian God. Unlike the normal situation of verbal irony, Théodore does not want the victim (Marcelle) to doubt or question the sincerity of her words. She fails, however, as Marcelle is quick to suspect Théodore's dodge. The audience for her irony can only be the spectator.

Finally, the double register in *Théodore* raises the possibility of parody. Baker notes:

> The radical failure of the plot to join its human and transcendental planes is not just unsatisfactory, however. It also threatens parody of the higher plane by the lower. Until the death of the martyrs, Corneille artfully juxtaposes his double register. Forced thereafter to witness their violent divorce in Act V, the spectator/reader is confined to the disobliging thought that sainthood has small effect on the world here below. ("*Théodore*" 12)

The same knife that is used to kill Théodore and Didyme subsequently serves as Marcelle's instrument of suicide and finally of Placide's attempted suicide. The instrument of sacred martyrdom is in no way differentiated from that of profane self-slaughter. Why would Corneille choose such a parallel? Why would the martyrdom of Théodore and Didyme have no effect on stage beyond a lover's despair? The gap between the two registers remains unresolved, in part because of the lack of differentiation in the dénouement. In its resistance to satisfactory synthesis, the gap invites an ironic reading.

The issue of double register is not limited to Corneille's religious drama. In *Œdipe* the Greek myth mixes uncomfortably with a love plot typical of both the novel and the theater of mid-seventeenth-century France. Thésée and Dircé seem to belong to an entirely different play than the other characters do.[124] Louvat and Escola refer to the situation as "deux pièces" and stress the lack of harmony between them, particularly in the dénouement ("Statut" 466). They read Corneille's *Œdipe* as a conflation of two different plays, one a tragedy and the other a *comédie héroïque* ("Statut" 470); the rivalry between Dircé and Œdipe reflects the competition between the two dramatic genres within the play itself (466). The possibility of irony arises when we note that the plot of the *comédie héroïque* occupies a far greater portion of the play than the original material of the tragedy, so that Œdipe seems diminished in his new environment. The two registers remain separate and the young lovers are never integrated into the myth, revealing an ungainly gap.

We find a similar conflict between freedom and fate in *La Toison d'or* where Jason mocks Aète's credulity for believing the gods' edict that, without the Toison, Aète is destined to lose his throne:

> Vous présumer perdu sur la foi d'un scrupule
> Qu'embrasse aveuglément votre âme trop crédule,
> Comme si sur la peau d'un chétif animal
> Le Ciel avait écrit tout votre sort fatal?
> (ll. 1040–43)

The environment in which this play takes place, however, where Médée's supernatural powers are manifest and gods come on stage, is an incongruous one in which to argue the individual's freedom from divine control.

While Corneille typically integrates the public universe of the political with the private love story in his theater, nowhere does he do it so awkwardly as in *Agésilas*. With the exception of the relatively elderly Lysander, all of the characters, from the trivial Aglatide (who is captivated not by a man, but by a throne) to the king Agésilas, are torn between private desires and politically motivated unions. More surprising is the fact that everyone, until the final moment, gives preference to the personal as they attempt to alter the political situation in order to make the love matches possible. Even the older Lysander, who should logically represent the pragmatic politics of carefully arranged marriages, is incongruously susceptible to the arguments of true love. Discussing the situation with his two prospective sons-in-law, Lysander waxes poetic over the power of love:

Je sais trop que l'Amour de ses droits est jaloux,
    Qu'il dispose de nous sans nous,
Que les plus beaux objets ne sont pas sûrs de plaire.
L'aveugle sympathie est ce qui fait agir
    La plupart des feux qu'il excite.
              (ll. 541–45)

The political and the personal registers remain uncomfortably separate throughout, as the political seems undermined by its ungainly juxtaposition with the dominant personal register.

Are these gaps between registers signs of clumsiness on Corneille's part, failed attempts at fusion and synthesis? Or are they possibly ironic commentaries on myth, love, politics, or the theater itself? The incongruous gaps between registers in these plays rarely permit completely satisfying explanations; they do set out the conditions that would allow for the possibility of an ironic reading.

Allegory is a particular variant of double register featuring tension between two discrete realms. The similarity between irony and allegory has long been noted. Allegory, however, lacks the evaluative or critical edge of irony (Hutcheon, *Edge* 2); furthermore, it is based on resemblance while irony is structured on a relation of difference (*Edge* 65). Still, the double dramatic channels at play as well as the gap between them are reminiscent of the examples of possible irony that we have been considering. Corneille presents allegorical portraits of Louis XIV in both *Attila* and *Tite et Bérénice*. In the former, the Frankish king Méroüée is twice compared to Louis at considerable length (ll. 221–30 and 557–89), in terms that Couton indicates are crystal-clear to the audience and that include abundant and specific historical references (Corneille 3:1544, 1547–48). In *Tite et Bérénice*, in a much shorter passage, Tite describes himself in a fashion that similarly brings to mind Louis.

Mon nom par la victoire est si bien affermi,
Qu'on me croit dans la paix un Lion endormi:
Mon réveil incertain du monde fait l'étude,
Mon repos en tous lieux jette l'inquiétude,
Et tandis qu'en ma Cour les aimables loisirs
Ménagent l'heureux choix des jeux, et des plaisirs,
Pour envoyer l'effroi sous l'un et l'autre pôle,
Je n'ai qu'à faire un pas, et hausser la parole.
              (ll. 397–404)

Again, Couton argues convincingly that seventeenth-century spectators would recognize the allegory immediately (Corneille 3:1621–22). The choice of Louis XIV as the figure allegorized makes it unlikely that irony was intended. The fact remains, however, that the double encomium in *Attila* is so heavy-handed and disruptive of the flow of the play's action that we are caught short and may legitimately wonder whether Corneille's motives were limited to flattery.

Another variant of double register involves the obverse of the possibly ironic gap: a situation where the gap is concealed, so that what appears seamless in fact conceals a significant and problematic breach. The primary example comes from *L'Illusion comique*, in which the gap between acts 4 and 5—the fact that they are not situated on the same diegetic level—is carefully camouflaged so that a first-time spectator would not know that Clindor has, in the space between the two acts, passed from his life to a role on the stage. The disparity between Clindor's life as an actor and as a courtier to a prince is enormous, but Alcandre (or rather, Corneille) makes that break invisible. The gap between the two is possibly ironic—an acid social commentary on the relationship between *être* and *paraître* perhaps—but the concealment of the gap itself is not. The camouflage does allow for a highly dramatic surprise when it is revealed, which, of course, is an effect that Corneille favors.

Character Contradictions

Similar to the tension between registers in certain of Corneille's plays are the contradictions to be found within various characters. Incompatible character traits or actions give rise to gaps that may be perceived as ironic. It has often been noted that several of the names the playwright chooses for his characters seem to contradict their personalities—Angélique in *La Place Royale*, Sévère in *Polyeucte* (Félix, equally ironic, comes from Corneille's avowed source), Valens and Placide in *Théodore*, and Honorie in *Attila*—thereby granting ironic shading to these characters. It is worth noting that Corneille makes such a choice of names in both of his religious tragedies.

Faced with double registers, we find the possibility for irony in the disjunction; the gap may lead us to wonder whether one register might be an ironic commentary on the other. Contradiction within a character may provide an even stronger marker of possible irony because it counters Corneille's own statements on the importance of consistency of character. In the *Discours du poème dramatique*, he extols "l'égalité, qui nous oblige à conserver jusqu'à la fin à nos personnages les mœurs que nous leur avons données au commencement" (3:132). He then quotes the Roman Horace: "Qu'il soit jusqu'au bout ce qu'il était au commencement, semblable à lui-même" (Couton's translation, Corneille 3:1401).[125] Despite such statements,

Corneille shows a marked predilection for contradictory characters.[126] We
have already considered such contradictions in Rodogune and Rodelinde
under the heading of incongruity. Similarly Polyeucte, as the embodiment of
the double register we found above, does not cohere as a character. Corneille
never explains the leap from enraptured newlywed to determined martyr.[127]
In *Le Cid*, Don Diègue vaults from despair to hope without explanation in
his monologue after Don Gomès's insult (Margitic 39). Much ink, including Corneille's, has been spilt over whether Horace's attack on his sister
follows from or contradicts his earlier and equally violent victory over the
three Curiace brothers. Bérénice's reversal, from her secret arrival in order
to win back Tite to her renunciation of any claim on him and her willing
departure, may reasonably strike one as contradictory. Auguste's sudden
about-face in the fifth act of *Cinna* has also been viewed as problematic, as
Napoleon's reaction attests.[128] In general, the contradictions in these cases are
tied to chronology: the character changes in a fashion that could not have
been forseen, whence the traditional criticism of psychological implausibility
leveled against Corneille.

Ptolomée in *Pompée* provides a clear example of the problems raised by
such chronologically grounded contradictions in character. Until the moment
when his death is announced (5.3), Ptolomée demonstrates poor judgment,
ruthlessness, cowardice, and resentment of his sister. Achorée's *récit* of the
king's final battle and his demise contains a radical shift:

> Mais il est mort, Madame, avec toutes les marques
> Que puissent laisser d'eux les plus dignes Monarques;
> Sa vertu rappelée a soutenu son rang
> Et sa perte aux Romains a coûté bien du sang.
> Il combattait Antoine avec tant de courage,
> Qu'il emportait déjà sur lui quelque avantage,
> Mais l'abord de César a changé le Destin!
> Aussitôt Achillas suit le sort de Photin,
> Il meurt, mais d'une mort trop belle pour un traître,
> Les armes à la main en défendant son maître.
> Le vainqueur crie en vain qu'on épargne le Roi,
> Ces mots au lieu d'espoir lui donnent de l'effroi;
> Son esprit alarmé les croit un artifice
> Pour réserver sa tête à l'affront d'un supplice.
> Il pousse dans nos rangs, il les perce, et fait voir
> Ce que peut la vertu qu'arme le désespoir,
> Et son cœur emporté par l'erreur qui l'abuse
> Cherche partout la mort que chacun lui refuse.

Enfin perdant haleine après ces grands efforts,
Près d'être environné, ses meilleurs soldats morts,
Il voit quelques fuyards sauter dans une barque;
Il s'y jette, et les siens qui suivent leur Monarque
D'un si grand nombre en foule accablent ce vaisseau,
Que la mer l'engloutit avec tout son fardeau.
C'est ainsi que sa mort lui rend toute sa gloire.

(ll. 1633–57)

Here, Ptolomée is presented as courageous and worthy of the throne he occupies. However, despite the abundant praise, especially in the opening and
closing lines, Ptolomée's redemption is undermined. If we consider what
the king actually does in this *récit*, we find that he fights bravely, he flees
when surrounded, and he dies because the boat he boards is then swamped
by his own soldiers. The first action is normally classified as heroic, the second as cowardly, and the third as an unfortunate (or even ironic) accident.
The narrator, Achorée, listed as "écuyer de Cléopâtre," has little reason to
be anything but objective when he speaks to his mistress and Cornélie, as
it is very rare for Cornelian confidants to have a persuasive agenda when
recounting events for the benefit of characters on stage and the audience.
Yet Achorée frames the disparate events as purely heroic (ll. 1633–34, 1657).
Is Achorée being ironic? Is Corneille being ironic through Achorée? There
have been radically different interpretations of this passage. Both Couton
(Corneille 1:1722) and Louis Marin (148) find redemption for Ptolomée
in the fact that he dies nobly. Goodkin reads Achorée's comment about
Ptolomée's death being worthy of a king as "scathingly ironic" and is distressed
that anyone could read it as "straight" (253), while Doubrovsky notes the
unheroic nature of a death by drowning (277). Neither side of this debate
ventures any explanation for the character inconsistencies within the *récit*
itself. Does it matter that Corneille takes Ptolomée's flight and death from
historical sources (Corneille 1:1752)? It might indeed, as those are the two
parts of the *récit* that are most difficult to reconcile with the narrator's praise
of the Egyptian king. The situation is further complicated by what Achorée
says in the same passage about Achillas's death. The qualification "traître"
can be read to distinguish Achillas from Ptolomée *or* to provide a reductive
double for the king who authorized Achillas's murder of Pompée. Achillas,
unlike Ptolomée, actually does die a heroic death in battle, but Achorée
declares him unworthy of his death (ll. 1641-42). As framed by Achorée, it
seems clear that Achillas's death is ironic. But how does Achillas's experience
relate to Ptolomée's? Does it signal that we are to read the latter's death as
ironic as well? In the final analysis, we have more questions than answers.

To credit such complexity to the relatively unengaged Achorée would seem to be unwise; the responsibility for the contradictions and the possible irony belongs rather to Corneille.

Contradictions of character in *Pompée* are not limited to Ptolomée. César's inconsistencies extend across the play. Here, however, the element of chronology is absent: César does not undergo a shift, but manifests distinctly incompatible traits throughout. I would suggest that simultaneous character inconsistency may be more likely to invite an ironic reading than a chronological, albeit radical, shift because the latter may often find an explanation (divine grace in Polyeucte's case, force of will in Auguste's, etc.). The essential disjunction in César's character involves whether he is truly magnanimous or whether his *générosité* is motivated by self-interest. Hero or hypocrite?[129] César speaks at length of virtue and is impressively aggrieved at Pompée's assassination, but he has other, baser interests clearly in view, interests that suggest that this death is very convenient for him. Achorée explicitly calls César's sincerity into question: "Je ne sais si César prendrait plaisir à feindre" (l. 737). Indeed a significant gap lies between César's language and his achievements. César describes for Cornélie the glorious scene of reconciliation he *would have* organized for Pompée had he not been killed (ll. 1039–56); the conditional mode conveys the strong potential for irony (Hubert, "Function" 125–26). He promises revenge but avoids condemning Ptolomée. Throughout the play, as Corneille himself notes in the *Examen*, the style of expression is elevated and grandiloquent (1:1077); however, it lacks a concrete referent. In César's hands even Pompée's funeral moves off to the unreal domain of "demain" (l. 1808).

We find a similar gap in Cléopâtre, albeit attenuated. When she lectures Ptolomée about the need for royal *vertu*, he deflatingly suggests an alternate interpretation for her noble stance: "[D]'un faux zèle ainsi votre orgueil revêtu / Fait agir l'intérêt sous le nom de vertu!" (ll. 279–80). As her rival for the throne, Ptolomée is hardly objective, however. Her response, "la seule vertu me fait parler ainsi" (l. 284) is equally suspect, insofar as Pompée, whom she defends, is carrying her father's will naming her to share the throne with her brother.

There are several plausible explanations for the multiple contradictions of character in *Pompée*. Chronologically based contradiction (as in the case of Ptolomée) provokes surprise that, as we have seen, Corneille desired. The non-chronologically based contradictions (César and Cléopâtre), in contrast, create uncertainty, one might even say suspense, as we await a resolution that some would say never comes. Milorad R. Margitic's suggestion of the "esthétique baroque du discontinu" (39) provides a useful framework, describing the contradictions but not orienting them with any specificity. Finally,

the possibility of irony in the depiction of characters here has implications
for interpretation: we may speculate that Corneille, by parading before his
audience the famous characters of *Pompée*, all of whom are unable to live
up to their supposed grandeur, is making a wry commentary on the heroic
status of any historical figure.[130]

The same argument concerning heroism, contradictory character, and
irony can be made in the case of Othon. An incongruity clearly underlies the
gap from the opening lines of the play, when Albin describes him antitheti-
cally: "Othon, dont les hauts faits soutiennent le grand nom, / Daigne d'un
Vinius se réduire à la fille" (ll. 8–9). The contradiction involves more than
social class. On the one hand, Othon is the virtuous hero, worthy of the
emperor's throne and of the love that Plautine and Camille pledge to him.
On the other hand, he is fundamentally passive: when Vinius urges him to go
to the army and attempt a coup, he does nothing (4.2). "In the ironic world
of *Othon*…the hero defines himself by his refusal to act" (McDermott 651);
Knight sums up the situation: "there is a gap where one expected to find the
hero" ("Othon" 593). The contradictions in Othon's character are pervasive,
both contemporaneous and based on chronology. He was once one of Néron's
courtiers and companions, accompanying his emperor in debauchery and
willing to cede his own wife to him. Corneille makes a number of references
to his unsavory past and underlines the contrast with his worthy present.
The multiplication of contradictions in the character of Othon makes the
possibility for irony greater. Curiously, while literary critics have tended to
resolve the contradictions in César by choosing one option or the other, in
the case of Othon there is a far greater acceptance of the fact of contradiction, and thus of irony, in the play as a whole. This difference in reception
may be related to César's greater and enduring fame. There is far less doubt
that the target of the irony in Othon's case is the concept of the hero, but
perhaps because it is attached to an emperor not normally associated with
heroism, the possible irony is less unsettling for the receiver.

Contradictions in character not grounded in chronology exist in
other plays as well. Dorante in *Le Menteur* is constructed as a contradictory
character, juxtaposing morally dubious mendacity and noble courage. In the
context of a comedy such inconsistencies pass far more comfortably than in
tragedy; indeed they contribute to the comic in *Le Menteur*. The resulting
incongruity is itself a source of humor. This fact does not preclude irony,
however; a reading of *Le Menteur* as an ironic commentary on social class
and the mores imposed on youth is entirely possible. Dorante's lack of coherence as a character may be viewed as a critical reflection of the contradictory
expectations placed on him as a young man.

The language of a character may provide a source of contradiction.

Lovers' discourse has led to the perception of contradictions in the characters of both César (*Pompée*) and Attila. Such larger-than-life historical figures of enormous power and political acumen speaking the language of the humble and tender lover—to Cléopâtre and Ildione, respectively—allow ample space for an ironic reading. Attila tells Ildione:

> Quels climats voulez-vous sous votre obéissance?
> Si la Gaule vous plaît, vous la partagerez,
> J'en offre la conquête à vos yeux adorés,
> Et mon amour…
>
> (ll. 874–77)

Attila

while César regales Cléopâtre with flowery words:

> C'est l'effet des ardeurs qu'ils ["vos divins appas"] daignent
>   m'inspirer;
> Et vos beaux yeux enfin m'ayant fait soupirer,
> Pour faire que votre âme avec gloire y réponde,
> M'ont rendu le premier, et de Rome, et du Monde.
>
> (ll. 1275–78)

César

Their lovers' discourse is radically dissimilar from their language in other contexts in the two plays, leaving a gap which lends itself well to irony.[131] The audience is left wondering whether Corneille is mocking the legendarily powerful leaders he has put on stage.

ANTITHESIS AND PARADOX

Antithesis and paradox both involve the double required by all irony as well as the opposition, contradiction, or tension between the two elements that results in a gap, a conceptual space where there should be seamless continuity. Antithesis, the foundation upon which paradox is built, is defined by the *Oxford English Dictionary* as "an opposition or contrast of ideas, expressed by using as the corresponding members of two contiguous sentences or clauses, words which are the opposites of, or strongly contrasted with, each other." Schoentjes calls antithesis "une des figures de prédilection de l'ironie" (176). Antithesis is primarily a verbal manifestation of possible irony, with ties to the most basic form of verbal irony, antiphrasis. While antithesis and antiphrasis share a "rapport de connivence" (Hamon 11), their operation differs significantly: antithesis involves inclusion (what is posited *and* its opposite are present) while antiphrasis uses substitution (what is said is the opposite of what is meant). Because irony is so often reduced to

antithesis =>
- double
- oppositional tension/ contradiction

primarily verbal

unlike antiphrasis both X and its opposite = present

antiphrasis in the public imagination and deeply linked to all forms of opposition and inversion, the force of opposition which typically attaches itself
to antiphrasis may lend a note of irony to all antithesis because the latter is by
definition a figure of opposition. The opposition characteristic of antithesis
is also reminiscent of other formal signals of possible irony such as repetition and symmetry (see chapter 5); furthermore, it endows the gap with an
elegant and clearly defined outline. The other possibly ironic gaps that we
have discussed in this chapter are not as highly structured; incongruity in
particular rarely has much structural support. Despite its balanced structure,
however, antithesis is rather thin as an ironic vehicle. In terms of Corneille's
plays, the simplest tie of antithesis to irony can be found in the vast number
of oppositions constructed at the ends of successive lines. The playwright's
affinity for antithesis has of course been frequently noted; Boorsch says that
it is "si chère à son esprit qu'elle est vraiment une des formes essentielles
de sa pensée" (116). We saw in chapter 5 how Sabine (or Corneille) uses
the antithetical tension between the last words of successive lines to signal
ironic intent according to Newmark (*Horace*, ll. 621–22 and 623–24).[132]
Such examples are legion (e.g. *Le Cid*: vengeance / allégeance, ll. 699–700;
Héraclius: magnanime / crime, ll. 205–6; *Pertharite*: obstacle / miracle, ll.
979–80; *Attila*: hâter / arrêter, ll. 155–56), but do not of themselves provide
much foundation for interpetation. By clearly leaving an unbridgeable gap,
they may be suggestive of ironic intent, but are inadequately substantial to
signal more than possible irony.

   Antithesis does not need to be limited to words. The story of Œdipus
is based on the antithetical notions of free will and fate. The tension between
the two is at the heart of Sophocles' play: it is the mistaken confidence shared
by Œdipus, Laïus, and Jocasta that they are free to avoid what an oracle
foretold that leads to the tragedy, and it is Œdipus's free choice to take full
responsibility for his acts at the dénouement that marks his tragic grandeur.
While working with the same basic antithesis, Corneille changes the balance
in *Œdipe*, reducing the role of fate and multiplying assertions of free will.
We made reference briefly to the issue of free will as it pertains to the irony
of fate in chapter 4; here I would like to consider in more detail how Corneille alters the balanced configuration of fate and free will he inherits from
earlier versions. In Sophocles' play, free will is situated at the margins of the
play, stationed both at the extradramatic origin of the tragedy—the three
characters decide to attempt to circumvent their fate long before the play
opens—and at the dénouement with Œdipus's acceptance of his fate and thus
his responsibility, coupled with his freely made choices to blind himself and
demand exile. Corneille makes significant changes at these liminal moments
as well as other alterations between them. First, Œdipe makes no free choice

to avoid his fate, as he is completely unaware of it in Corneille's version. At the dénouement his free will is not rooted in a paradoxical acceptance of his fate, but is rather a simple act of defiance against the gods. Instead of choosing to no longer cast eyes on his own crime, Corneille's Œdipe portrays his act of self-blinding thus:

> Ne voyons plus le Ciel après sa cruauté,
> Pour nous venger de lui, dédaignons sa clarté,
> Refusons-lui nos yeux, et gardons quelque vie
> Qui montre encore à tous quelle est sa tyrannie.
>   (ll. 1991–94)

Dircé asserts Œdipe's triumph over fate when she says, "Il s'est rendu par là maître de tout son sort" (l. 1975). Corneille multiplies assertions of free will within the body of the play as well. Thésée explicitly attacks fate and champions volition:

> L'âme est donc toute esclave, une loi souveraine
> Vers le bien, ou le mal incessamment l'entraîne,
> Et nous ne recevons, ni crainte, ni désir
> De cette liberté qui n'a rien à choisir,
> Attachés sans relâche à cet ordre sublime,
> Vertueux sans mérite, et vicieux sans crime:
> . . . .
> Le Ciel juste à punir, juste à récompenser,
> Pour rendre aux actions leur peine ou leur salaire,
> Doit nous offrir son aide, et puis nous laisser faire.
>   (ll. 1153–70)

He then proceeds to enact his theory by freely assuming the role of Jocaste's supposedly dead son. He thereby champions free will through a kind of theatricality (see Hubert, *Metaphors* 168), as he invents a role for himself: Dircé's long-lost brother. Œdipe, upon discovering that he is not the son of Polybe as he had believed himself to be, trumpets the freedom of the self-made man, ironically of course, because he is anything but self-made.[133] Jocaste offers Dircé the freedom to escape being sacrificed to the oracle that has called for Laïus's blood: "Et le Roi même.../ Vous offre sur ce point liberté toute entière" (ll. 836–38), seemingly suggesting that she run off with Thésée ("Agissez en Amante aussi bien qu'en Princesse" l. 866). Dircé refuses this freedom. Indeed, it is ironic on another level entirely to have Dircé, the freest character in the play—free because she is Corneille's fictional creation—serve as the mouthpiece for fate: she responds to her mother's suggestion that she escape the fate awaiting her by saying

> C'est assez vainement qu'il [Œdipe] m'offre un si grand
>   bien [freedom],
> Quand le Ciel ne veut pas que je lui doive rien,
> Et ce n'est pas à lui de mettre des obstacles,
> Aux ordres souverains que donnent ses Oracles.
>   (ll. 839–42)

Her response clearly indicates that Corneille was fully aware of the traditional role of fate in the subject of Œdipus. Thus in the place of the powerfully antithetical balance of fate and free will Corneille places a larger, more ungainly gap, favoring free will and yet clearly acknowledging the crucial role of fate, as is evident from Dircé's comment to her mother. In so doing, Corneille creates a second potentially ironic gap between his version and Sophocles', a gap whose incongruity has both baffled critics and also led to rich interpretations of Corneille's version (see, for example, Louvat and Escola, Dalla Valle, Biet, Matzat, and Theile).

Paradox is built on antithesis, but its ties to irony go beyond apparent contradiction to undecidability and doubt. Thus, as Perrin notes, "Le propre de l'ironie ne tient pas au fait de mentionner un point de vue que le locuteur cherche à disqualifier mais au paradoxe qui en découle" (125). Paradox is related to the undecidability at the heart of irony, which entails the inclusiveness of two seemingly incompatible elements (see chapter 1). Corneille demonstrates a decided proclivity for paradox. In several of his prefatory texts, he aggressively asserts a paradoxical stance; the aggressivity heightens the possibility for irony. In the *Au lecteur* to *Héraclius* he is explicit: "J'irai plus outre, et quoique peut-être on voudra prendre cette proposition pour un paradoxe, je ne craindrai point d'avancer que le sujet d'une belle tragédie doit n'être pas vraisemblable" (2:357), and he brags in the *Épître dédicatoire* to *Pompée*, "À bien considérer cette Pièce, je ne crois pas qu'il y en ait sur notre Théâtre, où l'Histoire soit plus conservée, et plus falsifiée tout ensemble" (1:1074). In this last example he marries exaggeration to paradox. Forestier points to a paradox in the *Préface* to *Othon* that he believes could serve as an epigraph for all of Corneille's serious theater: "Je n'…ai encore mis aucune [historical episode] sur le théâtre à qui j'aie gardé plus de fidélité, et prêté plus d'invention" (3:461) ("Poète" 37). The delight with which the playwright wields paradox in these prefatory texts strongly suggests the possibility of a mockingly ironic intent on his part. The plays themselves provide abundant examples, ranging from purely verbal formulations such as Honorine's "Je

[marginal notes:]
C. aware of traditional role of fate in Oedipus—

but wilfully increases gap

↓

+ gap btwn self + Sophocles.

paradox

related to undecidability—

inclusiveness of 2 seemingly incompatible elements

plenty of paradoxes in C's own prefaces

↓

in plays
(eg. Chimène)

meurs s'il [Attila] me choisit, ou ne me choisit pas" (*Attila* l. 444) or Dymas's description of Œdipe at the end of the play: "Qu'il vit, et ne vit plus, qu'il est mort, et respire" (*Œdipe* l. 1982), to paradoxical situations like Orode's mistrust of Suréna in *Suréna*, Chimène's position in *Le Cid* (Don Diègue: "Chimène le poursuit, et voudrait le sauver," l. 1345), or Eduïge's vis-à-vis Grimoald in *Pertharite* ("Et la Princesse alors par un bizarre effet, / Pour l'avoir voulu Roi, le perdit tout à fait," ll. 109–10). Neither paradox nor antithesis, however, is of itself necessarily ironic, but both, through their structural ties to irony, may often function as signals of possible irony.

CINNA

To conclude this chapter I propose to examine in some detail the possible irony engendered by Corneille's handling of Livie's advice to Auguste in *Cinna*. In this play, the playwright takes a series of three causally connected events from his source material, explicity and ostentatiously disrupts the causality by reversing the second event, and then seemingly denies the existence of the gap engendered by that reversal. The basic source material is Seneca's *De Clementia* as well as Montaigne's translation of the passage from Seneca, both of which Corneille cites in the play's prefatory material. In both, as well as in Cassius's version of the same events,[134] 1) Livy counsels her husband to exercise clemency towards Cinna, 2) Augustus accepts her advice gratefully, and 3) acts upon it, which leads to a positive outcome. Corneille's version opens in a fashion identical to that of his sources: in act 4, scene 3, Livie approaches her husband, who is distraught at having learned that his trusted advisor and protégé is leading an assassination plot against him. She begins by asking, as is the case in the sources, "Mais écouteriez-vous les conseils d'une femme?" (l. 1197), and goes on to to argue that because harsh retaliation has not been effective, serving only to encourage other would-be assassins, Auguste should try a different tactic, specifically clemency: "Après avoir en vain puni leur insolence, / Essayez sur Cinna ce que peut la clémence" (ll. 1209–10). Here, in stark opposition to what is found in the sources, Corneille's Auguste immediately rejects her advice and dismisses her ("Ne m'en parlez jamais, je ne consulte plus," l. 1220). Livie persists nonetheless and presents a second argument for clemency that is unique to Corneille. Whereas the emperor perceives clemency as weakness ("Régner, et caresser une main si traîtresse / Au lieu de sa vertu, c'est montrer sa foiblesse" l. 1241–42), Livie sees it as a gesture of strength and self-mastery ("C'est régner sur vous-même, et par un noble choix / Pratiquer la vertu la plus digne des Rois" ll. 1243–44). Once again, Auguste rebuffs her crudely ("Vous m'aviez bien promis des conseils d'une femme; / Vous me tenez parole, et c'en sont là, Madame" ll. 1245–46) and accuses her of personal ambition. Finally, in the last scene of the tragedy, Corneille rejoins the source material: Auguste pardons Cinna, along with Émilie and Maxime, and we learn of the success of this strategy through Livie's prophecy: there will be no further conspiracies against Auguste for the duration of his reign. The causality governing this favorable outcome is underlined by both Montaigne (125) and Corneille ("Après cette action, vous n'avez rien à craindre" l. 1757).

In Seneca's version as well as in the other sources, it is clear that Augustus accepts Livy's advice. In Corneille's *Cinna*, Auguste rejects that same advice and yet seems to do exactly what she suggested. It is precisely this reversal—from acceptance to rejection—that gives rise to the possibility of irony by creating a gap between the first and third moments. The structure of reversal and the seeming contradiction of both rejecting and accepting Livie's advice are classic signs of irony. Corneille's choices thereby set up the possibility for an ironic reading.

Logically, Auguste cannot both reject and accept Livie's advice, as many have noted. Voltaire is blunt about the consequences: "Auguste répond à Livie: *Vous m'aviez bien promis des conseils d'une femme, vous me tenez parole*; et après ces vers comiques, il suit ces mêmes conseils. Cette conduite l'avilit" (54:155–56). Before considering the range of solutions this logical paradox has engendered, it is important to acknowledge the complicating role that gender plays here. The female source of the counsel is hardly a neutral factor, as Voltaire's comment makes clear. F. E. Sutcliffe states the issue plainly: "Bref, pour qu'elle acquière ses titres de noblesse, la clémence doit se présenter comme une vertu mâle" (247). As an explanation of Corneille's choice, his potential discomfort with female wisdom or influence seems inadequate here, however, and all the more so when we consider the prophetic power that the playwright accords Livie.

Throughout much of the eighteenth century and at least half of the nineteenth, Livie was simply eliminated from performances of the play (Georges 269). This solution to the problem she poses is the most brutal, although it has the advantage of dealing with both the question of logic and that of male superiority. The radical nature of such a move points to the threat that Corneille's Livie poses. Explaining away the logical inconsistency has been a more common and less drastic solution. The possibility of imperial marital strife has been used to motivate Auguste's uncivil response to Livie's advice (Baker, "Strategies" 78; Tiefenbrun, *Signs* 200). P. J. Yarrow has attempted to fill in the gap between Auguste's rejection of Livie's suggestion and his enactment of it by positing an offstage meeting between the two during which Livie is able to sway her husband.[135] The most common defense against the logical inconsistency, however, has been to deny the identity between Livie's suggestion and what Auguste finally decides to do. If Auguste's gesture of clemency in act 5, scene 3 can be understood to differ significantly from Livie's suggestion in act 4, scene 3, then the gap disappears. The line of argument is as follows: the clemency that Livie proposes is based on pragmatism, Machiavellian precepts, self-interest, political ruse, or calculation and is therefore not a virtuous recommendation (see, for example Georges 273). In all cases, her motives are inferior to those of Auguste. Alternatively, some choose to extol Auguste rather than denigrate Livie. For Sutcliffe, "Le geste d'Auguste est plus large: il pardonne, mais il fait aussi don de sa personne" (250). Forestier argues the sublimity of Auguste's act, while explaining away the latter's reaction to Livie:

> Tout le texte est construit de telle sorte que, de degré en degré Auguste soit acculé à punir—et c'est pourquoi on le voit récuser à l'acte IV le conseil de Livie l'invitant à la clémence—, d'où sort, *in extremis*, son geste proprement royal, mais extraordinaire aux yeux des hommes et proprement invraisemblable. (*Génétique* 213)

Elevating Auguste provides the double advantage of accentuating his heroism and masking the discomfort caused by the logical inconsistency. Whether denigrating Livie or elevating Auguste, readers have clearly devoted considerable energy to denying the kinship between Livie's suggestion and Auguste's act of clemency.

A final alternative is to grant Livie the inspirational role that Auguste would seemingly deny her. Timothy Reiss states clearly that "cette clémence, nous l'avons vu, vient…de l'intervention de Livie" (52).[136] We noted in our description of the events in Corneille's version that the playwright added Livie's insistence on the notion of self-possession ("C'est régner sur vous-même" l. 1243). A clear echo of her statement is to be found in Auguste's famous line "Je suis maître de moi comme de l'Univers" (l. 1696), spoken at the moment he grants clemency. The striking similarity between Auguste's formulation and Livie's second reason for suggesting clemency supports the idea that she has indeed influenced the emperor (Yarrow, "Réflexions" 550). While arguing the centrality of Livie's role acknowledges the apparent identity of her suggestion of clemency and Auguste's granting of same, it has the logical disadvantage of disregarding Auguste's almost brutal rejection in act 4, scene 3.

A further complication comes from the role of the divine. Livie explicitly becomes a prophet in the final lines of the play ("une céleste flamme / D'un rayon Prophétique illumine mon âme; / Oyez ce que les Dieux vous font savoir par moi" ll. 1753–55). While her final speech seems to entail a

— open-ended reading — ∅ solid —
lots of possible endings

she becomes
prophet in
end —
mouthpiece
of gods —

supernatural transformation of some sort, it can hardly be viewed as a co-incidence that the favored mouthpiece of the gods is the same person who earlier advises Auguste to grant clemency. In act 4, scene 3 Corneille explicitly points to the role the divine will play in Auguste's decision when he has the emperor dismiss his wife with "Le Ciel m'inspirera ce qu'ici je dois faire" (l. 1258).[137] Given that he decides to do precisely what she suggested and that she

what to
make of this?

is later the voice of the gods, is it not reasonable to tie the divine inspiration of which Auguste speaks to Livie? Indeed, if one denigrates Livie's suggestion in act 4, scene 3, calling it Machiavellian, for example, does one not run the risk of implicitly disparaging her prophetic speech? One of my students read the dénouement of the play in a distinctly unprophetic fashion: she believed that Livie makes up the words she claims are divinely inspired in order to impose her own version of Auguste's legitimacy. André Georges is careful not to go that far in dismissing Livie: he interprets Auguste's decision as divinely inspired, but accords Livie a marginal role nonetheless.[138]

La Harpe
(contemporary)
criticized C
for staying too
faithful to
sources —

Jean-François de La Harpe chastises Corneille for misjudging the need for historical fidelity: "Ici l'exactitude historique trompe l'auteur, qui ne s'aperçut pas que ce conseil de Livie était du nombre des faits que le poète dramatique est le maître de supprimer" (81). This admonition is itself ironi-cally incongruous, because Corneille was hardly one to enslave himself to history, even this early in his career. It seems unlikely that Corneille would have blindly followed what the sources said about Livie's advice while utterly reversing Auguste's reaction in those same sources. The mixture of fidelity and departure admits of no simple solution, although it does recall Corneille's paradoxical description of *Othon* quoted earlier ("Je n'…ai encore mis aucune

no simple
solution

[historical episode] sur le théâtre à qui j'aie gardé plus de fidélité et prêté plus d'invention").

In the final analysis, we still have to ask why Corneille created the logical inconsistency of rejecting and then seemingly following Livie's advice. The similarity between what she suggests and what he finally does is patent. Corneille could easily have made some distinction had he wanted one. From

too many poss.
explanations!

our discussion of this situation, it is clear that there are too many possible explanations, none of which is satisfying. Is the playwright ironically mocking the authority of his sources? Looking at the specific reversal, it seems reason-

is C mocking A?

able to suppose that Corneille is making some pejorative commentary on Livie, but because of the logical gap, it is ultimately just as legitimate to posit

is he eliciting
the sublime?

the opposite: that he is denigrating Auguste. Or is the illogical gap a means of eliciting the sublime? The gap opened up by Auguste's reversal, through its stubborn incongruity, carries the possibility of an ironic interpretation, but does not provide assurance that it is the correct one.

what would ironic reading be?
does she say?

*

Ironic gaps are particularly undecidable and notably difficult to see as anything more than possible, because they involve an absence and rely far less than other forms of irony, as a rule, on structural signals. Gaps are more often a matter of logical incompatibility than of opposition or reversal. Thus, the level of doubt and the potential for disagreement are high. In the next chapter, the gaps will be on a larger scale, involving the margins between one play and another, between prologue and play, or between Corneille and his sources or the authorities he invokes. A gap at a margin is far more visible, and thus the level of uncertainty will not not be as high as in this chapter.

Notes

[114]Voltaire calls her offer an "atrocité absurde" (55:794); Desfougères talks about "les fureurs de cette mégère inapprivoisable" (503); Stegmann finds Rodelinde to be "un masque figé, inhumain, ostentatoire" (*Héroïsme* 2:431), calling her provocation "un défi incroyable de la plus haute invraisemblance et de la plus grande immoralité" ("L'Humour" 327). In her defense of Rodelinde, Baker does not see her as overacting, nor as preposterously histrionic; rather, Rodelinde is adopting the language of male power and insensibility (*Harmonies* 86). Doubrovsky defends her as well, saying: "Rodelinde va lui [Grimoald] donner l'exemple de la Maîtrise, en sacrifiant sa maternité à sa vengeance" (331).

[115]Baker says that "the constant thrust of Corneille's dramaturgy was to seek out the extraordinary subject" ("*Théodore*" 2), and Forestier describes at length Corneille's preference for *le sujet extraordinaire* (*Génétique* 112).

[116]According to Couton, the famous eighteenth-century actress Mlle Clairon played Rodogune as a fury, Voltaire found the princess to be odious, and Faguet thought her to be "du côté des coquins" (Corneille 2:1288). Couton himself, however, rationalizes and excuses Rodogune's demand of matricide and joins Corneille in calling her 'vertueuse' (2:1288–89). Couton also cites Saint-Évremond's assertion that Machiavelli would have found her demand to be a political virtue, not a crime, and that Cléopâtre is so cruel that her murder would be just (Corneille 2:1288–89). Herland excuses Rodogune by asserting that she is possessed by Nicanor: "[C]e n'est plus elle qui parle, elle obéit aux mânes de Nicanor dont la volonté s'est substituée à la sienne propre" ("Imprévisible" 243). Forestier uses the concept of the sublime as a means of justifying Rodogune's demand:

> S'il invente ensuite de toutes pièces la manière dont Rodogune se défend en demandant aux princes qu'ils vengent sur leur mère l'assassinat de leur père, il ne se livre donc qu'à un travail d'extrapolation du vrai—permettant l'accroissement de la *grandeur* des émotions tragiques; permettant d'atteindre au sublime—, qui demeure par là dans l'espace du croyable.
> (*Génétique* 291)

[117]"Just as there is a certain dialectic inherent in irony, so, too, there is a certain irony inherent in dialectic, as each statement tends to undercut the opposite view to which it is juxtaposed, and vice versa" (Monson 570).

[118]"Corneille's martyr creation is radical in its presentation of a sexualized saintly hero" (Paul Scott 328).

[119]Fumaroli provides an interesting reading, one that is exceptional in not seeking to dismiss the claims of the couple Pauline-Sévère. It also offers the distinct advantage of linking the problem to the tension between the earthly and the divine:

> Alors que, dans les pièces précédentes, l'amour naturel et le lien sacramentel découlaient pour ainsi dire l'un de l'autre, pour des couples à proprement parler insécables, ici, Pauline et Polyeucte, mariés par Félix sous la loi païenne, sont la proie d'un malaise: leur mariage est fondé sur la rupture d'un couple antérieur, uni spontanément par une « vraye amité », celui de Sévère et de Pauline. Le souvenir de cette union naturelle, rompue par la loi injuste imposée par Félix, est une fêlure dans l'union légale et au demeurant heureuse, de Polyeucte et de Pauline. Pour que cette fêlure disparaisse, pour que le couple soit totalement soudé, il faut que Polyeucte quitte Pauline, se donne au Dieu chrétien, subisse le martyre, et que Pauline le rejoigne en Dieu. Ce que le mariage païen n'avait pas réussi, les noces de sang du martyre chrétien vont l'accomplir. (*"Cid"* 411)

Even Fumaroli is forced to admit, however, that "cette fusion de l'amour pastoral et de l'amour chrétien était trop audacieuse pour les puritains doctrinaires" ("Fils" 54). It is worth noting that his explanation is based upon the construction of another double register—*l'union naturelle* and *l'union légale*—that may potentially itself be subject to an ironic interpretation.

[120]"Les tendresses de l'amour humain y font un si agréable mélange avec la fermeté du divin, que sa représentation satisfait tout ensemble les Dévots et les gens du Monde" (Corneille 1:980).

[121]Couton notes that, "Les problèmes techniques particuliers posés par la 'comédie de dévotion' interfèrent pendant ces années (1638–1644) avec un débat plus vaste qu'on appelle ordinairement la querelle de la moralité du théâtre et qui en fait met en question la licéité et l'existence même du théâtre dans une société chrétienne" (Corneille 1:1630).

[122]Corneille refers to the issue of prostitution in the *Épître dédicatoire* as "la prostitution que l'on n'a pu souffrir" (2:269), a general reaction echoed by d'Aubignac: "[T]out le Théâtre tourne sur la prostitution de Théodore, [et] le Sujet n'en a pu plaire" (57).

[123]The first example refers to Flavie's sickbed ("Flavie au lit malade" l. 63), not a sexually charged site, although she is dying of unrequited love and, presumably, desire for Placide. The last two examples, referring first to Marcelle's bed (Placide: "Je vous irais chercher jusqu'au lit de mon père" l. 232) and then Placide's (Théodore: "Plutôt que dans son lit, j'entrerais au tombeau" l. 518), do carry a sexual charge.

[124]Hubert points out that "[b]y observing the strict but obviously ludic rules of *amour-estime*, rules that can only apply to seventeenth-century French literature, Dircé and Thésée erect a cultural barrier between themselves and the myth" (*Metaphors* 165).

[125]Corneille, quite typically, goes on to qualify Horace's dictate, but in a fashion that sanctions only surface inconsistency: "L'inégalité y peut toutefois entrer sans défaut, non seulement quand nous introduisons des personnes d'un esprit léger et inégal, mais encore lorsqu'en conservant l'égalité au-dedans, nous donnons l'inégalité au-dehors selon l'occasion" (3:133).

[126]Herland is particularly struck by this tendency in Corneille's theater:

> Nous nous trouvons à certains moments, dans ces pièces, en présence de sentiments, de paroles, de décisions, non seulement soudaines, non seulement imprévues et peu conformes à ce qu'on devait attendre du personnage, mais absolument contraires aux paroles mêmes qu'il vient de prononcer et

au sentiment dont il est plein à ce moment même. ("Imprévisible" 239)

[127] Devant nous, dans le déroulement de la pièce, il y a deux Polyeuctes [sic]: celui d'avant le baptême, tout possédé de sa femme, celui d'après, tout possédé de Dieu, très éloigné de l'autre, autant dire contraire; à quel moment l'autre est devenu l'un, par quels secrets cheminements, quelles altérations insensibles, quels muets passages, nous ne le savons pas, nous n'en saurons rien: ils s'affrontent sans se rejoindre. (Chauviré 6)

[128]See chapter 1. Apparently, Napoleon was not the only one to prefer character consistency to nobility of character in their interpretation of the emperor. According to Clarke, "Auguste's pardon of Cinna, as told by Seneca, was retold and interpreted in the 17th century with almost total unanimity as a political manœuvre. The pardon was admired as a subtle change of tactics intended to consolidate Auguste's position as Emperor" ("Prudence" 328).

[129]Critical evaluation of César has ranged from one extreme to the other. On the one hand, Lemaître (296), Sweetser (*Dramaturgie* 129–31), and Forestier (*Génétique* 250–52) accord him heroic status; Sellstrom chooses to believe in his nobility of character while admitting that there are signs of possible hypocrisy (836). On the other hand, Gérard makes the case that César is motivated by nothing more lofty than ambition (345), Hubert presents him as an actor ("Function" 122), and Soare constructs a devastating assault on César's virtue that invokes Matamore and Tartuffe (195, 197).

[130]This includes Pompée who is presumed to be heroic, but never credited with specific acts that would support that assumption (see Ekstein, "Pompée's Absence").

[131]Doubrovsky makes the point clearly in his discussion of César: "L'exagération du langage précieux ne doit pas dissimuler la contamination réelle du dessein héroïque par le propos amoureux" (280). Of Attila, Gossip says, "Critics have had a field-day deriding 'les scènes sentimentales, avec leur jargon de ruelles' [Descotes, p. 91], suggesting that 'Attila est autant Céladon que fléau de Dieu;…son tonnerre devient constamment chanson de rossignol et murmures de brise langoureuse' [Mornet, p. 100]" ("*Attila*" 159).

[132]"The emphasis on the last words in the lines, the first contradicting the second, is…characteristic of Corneille's irony" (Newmark 6).

[133] Ce revers serait dur pour quelque âme commune,
Mais je me fis toujours maître de ma fortune,
Et puisqu'elle a repris l'avantage du sang,
Je ne dois plus qu'à moi tout ce que j'eus de rang.
(ll. 1717–20)

[134]*Histoire romaine*, as described by Georges (270).

[135]He bases his argument on Livie's final lines in 4.3: "Il m'échappe, suivons, et forçons-le de voir / Qu'il peut en faisant grâce affermir son pouvoir" (ll. 1263–64) ("Réflexions" 549-50). Gossip disagrees, arguing that we find clear mention of Livie's offstage meetings with Euphorbe and Émilie, but no reference whatsoever to such a meeting with Auguste (*Cinna* 66).

[136]Sutcliffe concurs that Auguste bases his decision on Livie's advice (249), as do Reed (219) and Yarrow ("Réflexions" 550).

[137]Indeed, Defaux asserts that Auguste rejects Livie's suggestion in order that he may say "Le Ciel m'inspirera" (744).

[138]Reed suggests a distinctly Christian reading of the situation, saying that "more might be made of the irony that in Corneille's world as in the Christian world the last come first and that the solution to Auguste's dilemma is suggested by a woman" (221).

CHAPTER 8
POSSIBLE IRONY IV: MARGINS

Irony is always about a relationship between two elements. As in the preceding chapter, our focus will be on the gap between the two, but here the gap will be located at a plainly discernable margin between the two elements in question. The signal of possible irony is not the margin itself but, as discussed in chapter 7, incongruity or a surprising degree of difference where one might reasonably expect resemblance and continuity. Corneille's work as a playwright may be associated with a great variety of margins: moving from the inside to the outside, we will examine specific examples of several different sorts. First, we will consider the margin between plays based on the order in which they were composed, focusing at length on the margin between *Le Menteur* and its sequel, *La Suite du Menteur*. Second, we will examine the margin between prologue and play, where the prologue makes clear reference to the political context in which Corneille wrote. The extradramatic world is thus juxtaposed with the dramatic. Third, we will consider the relationship of certain of Corneille's plays to their literary or historical sources. Finally, we will turn to the margin between Corneille's writings on dramatic theory and the various authorities who preside over the norms of seventeenth-century theater. As we move from inside to outside, we will note a wide range in the degree to which irony is plausibly present, from the questionable to the almost certain. In the last section particularly, the observation of irony is abetted by the added note of aggression and the frequent tone of *raillerie*.

MARGINS BETWEEN PLAYS

Corneille wrote his plays in a certain order, but we have little information concerning the extent to which he might have seen each play in relation to the preceding one. In chapter 4, we noted the ironic juxtaposition of *Le Menteur* and *Pompée*. In that particular case, Corneille took pains to call the reader's attention to the discordance between the two works (*Épître*, 2:3). In those comments, the playwright describes a radical opposition between the two in terms of seriousness and level of language.[139] In chapter 6, we commented both on the similarity between *Le Cid's* Rodrigue and the figure of Matamore and on the problematic margin between the plays themselves: it is unclear whether *L'Illusion comique* chronologically preceded *Le Cid* or vice-versa. The similarities between Rodogune and Matamore—specifically their verbal claims of heroic valor—raise the possibility of irony, a possibility made more likely by the existence of that proximal margin between the two plays. The issues raised by *L'Illusion comique* and *Le Cid* may be extended to the entire tetralogy. Critics have long noted that the sequence of Corneille's most famous tragedies is framed by two comedies, *L'Illusion comique* and *Le Menteur*, plays that call into question the very notion of Cornelian heroism championed by the tetralogy.[140] Was Corneille ironically mocking his own heroes? The potential for speculation concerning the margin between the tetralogy and these two comedies is both considerable and yet problematic in that it is based solely on a limited, albeit elegant, structure.

There is one example, however, where the margin between two plays explicitly calls for attention and interpretation: the one that we find between *Le Menteur* and *La Suite du Menteur*. I would like to examine this case in detail because it illustrates how Corneille plays with the margin between the two comedies, both spurring and discouraging efforts to link the two across the gap separating them. *Le Menteur* and *La Suite du Menteur*, performed only a year apart (1643–44 and 1644–45), were Corneille's final comedies. The latter is often dismissed or neglected in discussions of Corneille's theater. I would suggest that its reception in large measure results from the problematic nature of the ties between the two plays. *La Suite du Menteur*, while presenting a number of the same characters as *Le Menteur* and making frequent reference to events and characters of the first play, is nonetheless jarringly different in numerous ways. It is the combination, itself incongruous, of strong similarities and glaring differences between the two that gives rise to a strong likelihood of irony.

Corneille aggressively advertises the continuity from one play to the next in several fashions. The most immediately obvious is the use of the word *suite* in the title. While *suites* were not uncommon in seventeenth-century France, Corneille was apparently the first to write a sequel to a comedy and the first to compose a sequel to one of his own works (Lancaster 2, 2:447). Sequels are invariably motivated by the desire to capitalize on the success of the original, a success which in this case was considerable.[141] At the same time, the very nature of the sequel seems to invite the possibility of irony. According to Thomas Carmichael,

> The sequel is a narrative production whose claim to authority ironically rests upon its intertextual traces. Every image and figure in the sequel stands in differential relation to an earlier representation, with which it is affiliated and from which its authority derives, and to the extent that

a narrative is recognized or recognizes itself as a sequel,
it inevitably also calls attention to the conventions that
govern its own narrative logic. (175)

As we shall see, the notions of authority, intertextuality, and self-referentiality
all enhance the likelihood of irony. While the sequel indeed involves "repetition with a difference" (Carmichael 175), it does not, in contrast to parody,
imply any mocking of the original. The irony is of an entirely different sort,
focused not on ridiculing the original, but on broader notions of literary
conventions and literary authority.

The similarities and continuities between *Le Menteur* and *La Suite
du Menteur* take multiple forms. Most obviously, Dorante appears in both
plays and tells frequent lies in each. The crucial site of linkage between the
two plays is the exposition of *La Suite du Menteur*, which serves to explain
how the about-to-be-married Dorante in Paris at the end of *Le Menteur*
finds himself unattached and in a Lyon jail. Two other characters—Cliton,
Dorante's valet, and Philiste, Dorante's friend—also appear in both plays. The
two men make frequent references in *La Suite* to the characters and events of
the first play, references which ensure that the ties between the two cannot
be overlooked. These include the *festin sur l'eau*, Dorante's supposed duel
with Alcippe, and the protagonist's invented marriage. Cliton calls particular
attention in the second play to Dorante's lies in *Le Menteur*: "N'aurons-nous
point ici de guerres d'Allemagne?" (l. 104), he inquires pointedly.[142] One of
the primary functions of the eight scenes in which Cliton and Dorante are
alone together on stage in *La Suite du Menteur* is precisely to remind us of
these links between the two plays. Philiste plays a role similar to that of Cliton
in this regard: like the valet, he makes frequent reference to specific events
in *Le Menteur*, and both men register surprise at the changes in Dorante's
actions and attitudes. While Cliton's judgments of Dorante are often comical,
Philiste's social standing makes his judgments and his doubts about Dorante's
veracity far more serious. At the same time, Philiste has an additional role as
storyteller: he has converted Dorante's earlier adventures into comic narratives
told for his pleasure and that of his audience.[143] Thus from the two ends of
the social spectrum, Cliton and Philiste actively underline the similarities
linking the two plays.

While both men have considerably larger roles in *La Suite* than in *Le
Menteur*, the spectators are perfectly comfortable assuming that these are the
same Cliton and Philiste as in the earlier play, in part because of the references they make and in part because neither is a very complex or developed
character. The same is not true in the case of Dorante. The inconsistencies of
character between the two Dorantes are so glaring that one is indeed forced

Margin handwritten notes:
- eop. as concerns: authority, intertextuality, self-referent'ty
- nb doesn't mock original — bigger ? of literary convention + lit authority
- similarities / continuities
  - Dorante — his lies
  - Cliton + Philiste
  - ref to 1st play (esp Cl/D)
- both Ph + Cl note changes in D from one to other.
- Ph retells stories from first.
- easy to recog Ph + Cl as same chars as in 1st play —
- but D= radically diff

to wonder if it is the same individual (see Adam 2:394–95 and Mallinson 216). The site of Dorante's similarity to his former self *and* of his radical difference is his defining characteristic, the lie. "Menteur vous voulez vivre, et menteur vous mourrez" (*La Suite* l. 374), Cliton says to him. Dorante tells five lies in *Le Menteur* and another four in *La Suite du Menteur*. The lies in the second play are themselves ironic reflections of the lies in the first, because they are contrary in intent. Whereas the first incarnation of Dorante uses lies to impress others and avoid unpleasant situations, the Dorante of *La Suite* tells lies only for selfless, noble reasons. The gap between the two kinds of lies is the main source of comedy in the sequel. In his strong sense of honor, in his *générosité*, in his humility even, the Dorante of *La Suite* bears almost no relation to the character of the same name in *Le Menteur*. And yet, of course, the two are continually presented as one and the same. Cliton, himself a major source of continuity between the two plays, repeatedly calls attention through both his skepticism and his astonishment to the ungainly combination of gaps and similarities at work between the two Dorantes. For example, in *La Suite* Dorante denies to the Prévôt that Cléandre is the man who was involved in the fatal duel and who then stole his horse; subsequently he reveals to Cliton that Cléandre is indeed the man in question. Dumbfounded, Cliton says, "Je ne sais où j'en suis, et deviens tout confus. / Ne m'aviez-vous pas dit que vous ne mentiez plus?" (ll. 357–58). Here, as elsewhere, Cliton serves to cue the audience that *La Suite du Menteur* is an ill-fitting sequel.

The tonality of the two plays is radically different. Whereas *Le Menteur* is a light comedy in which violence is merely fictional and the "dead" miraculously resuscitate after a duel, *La Suite* opens upon a duel that is fatal to one of the combatants and lands Dorante in jail. Unlike its predecessor, *La Suite* belongs to the Spanish *comedia* tradition of novelesque tragicomedy (Serroy, "Préface *Menteur*" 21). Given two plays dealing with the same characters and the same central theme, this shift from comedy to tragicomedy is unsettling.

The ungainly gaps between *Le Menteur* and *La Suite du Menteur* are to some extent an inevitable function of the relationship of sequel to original. The dependence of the sequel on the original creates a significant imbalance between the two plays, as even Corneille noted.[144] The extent of that dependence on the first play can be gauged by the fact that the first sentences of both Corneille's *Épître* and the *Examen* of *La Suite du Menteur* contain references to *Le Menteur*. The prison, in which much of the action of *La Suite* transpires, functions well metaphorically in this regard: the author is imprisoned by the first play when he writes a sequel. We might go even further and suggest that just as Dorante's cell is not what one normally expects of a prison, resembling rather a comfortable inn in which the protagonist is able to receive his guests, so too this sequel deviates from the norm.

The gaps between the two plays have given rise to many explanations. Their very variety makes the possibility of irony all the more plausible. Some simply accuse Corneille of dramatic clumsiness (for example Mallinson 213–14; Petit de Julleville ix); any gaps are therefore unintentional, and thus not ironic. The problem with such an interpretation is that it calls into question Corneille's skill as a playwright, a prospect that is even more awkward for most than the gaps themselves. A second means of recuperating the gaps is to attribute them to a problem with the plays' sources. Amusingly enough, Corneille himself was apparently a victim of the irony of fate: he thought that the Spanish originals upon which he based *Le Menteur* and *La Suite du Menteur* were both written by Lope de Vega (*Au Lecteur* to *Le Menteur* 2:4). The source of Corneille's error, as Serroy explains, is that Alarcón's *La Verdad sospechosa* (which became *Le Menteur*) erroneously appeared in volume 22 of an edition of Lope de Vega's *Comedias*, published in Saragossa in 1630 ("Notice *Menteur*" 298). Furthermore, Lope's *Amar sin saber a quién* followed *La Verdad sospechosa* almost directly in this edition (Serroy, "Notice *Menteur*" 305). The proximity between the two, both physically in the same volume and figuratively, in that Corneille thought they were both written by the same author, might explain why the playwright decided to make one the *suite* of the other. Beyond this misunderstanding, however, it is clear that the two Spanish plays have very little in common: "Il fallait toute l'ingéniosité de Corneille pour percevoir entre *Amar sin saber a quién* et *La Verdad sospechosa* un rapport de sens qui permît à leurs adaptions respectives de se présenter comme un diptyque" (Picciola 2:292).[145]

A third option for dealing with the gaps between the two plays is to paper them over, not explaining the differences, but rather reconciling them on some other plane. Serroy makes two such attempts, both focused on the site of greatest disjunction: Dorante. He says: "[D]ans les deux cas, Dorante est fidèle à lui-même: simplement, dans *Le Menteur*, il est fidèle au personnage qu'il se compose, alors que dans *La Suite* il laisse parler sa nature profonde" ("Sincérité" 134). Elsewhere, he explicitly unifies the two through Dorante's heroism, as embodied by his sword ("Préface *Menteur*" 12). Indeed, Dorante carries a sword in both; in the first play he wears it throughout and once is about to use it in a duel, and in the second play he pulls out a sword to prevent two other men from dueling, but too late. To associate the sword with heroism is something of a leap, however, and to paint the first Dorante as heroic because he was eager to duel without even knowing Alcippe's grievance against him is hardly convincing.

A fourth and more common way of dealing with the gaps between the two plays is to acknowledge intent and suggest a motivation for the disjunction. One explanation is that Corneille wrote *La Suite* in order to rehabilitate Dorante whose exuberant pleasure in lying in the first play was found in some quarters to be immoral and offensive.[146] Emmanuel Minel motivates the gaps by reading the two plays as a series of oppositions.[147] Serroy as well relies on an opposition to justify the gap between the two Dorantes: the protagonist of *Le Menteur* suits the "cadre artificiel du Paris mondain" while the second Dorante's "honnêteté" fits provincial Lyon ("Sincérité" 132).[148] None of these explanations is very convincing. Interestingly, Cliton engages in precisely the same interpretive activity within *La Suite* itself, as he struggles to reconcile the Dorante of two years earlier to the man he has found in jail. His particular explanation is conversion: "Il s'est bien converti…/ C'est tout un autre esprit sous le même visage" (ll. 599–600). This is not merely a casual comment; Cliton returns to the subject in the following scene: "Tout de bon à ce coup vous êtes converti" (l. 673). Given that Cliton is a comic character and that the play is in no way religious, the incongruity of the valet's suggestion itself raises the possibility of irony, which in turn colors our reading of other explanations for the apparent differences between the two Dorantes.

Crucial to an argument for intentional irony here is the exposition of the *Suite*. The plot of *La Suite du Menteur* requires that Dorante be free of all romantic entanglements and filial obligations as the play begins. Where Corneille might have chosen to dispatch Lucrèce by means of an untimely death, he instead covers Dorante in disgrace by having him desert his bride the night before the wedding and steal her dowry. He goes further still by implying strongly that Dorante is responsible for his father's death. The latter, Géronte, married Lucrèce himself in order to save her from humiliation and ruin, but then died two months later. It is not clear whether the father dies from despair, shame, or sexual exertion; but Corneille takes pains to link Géronte's death to Dorante's flight with the word "poste." Dorante describes his flight by saying: "Je pars de nuit en poste" (l. 49), while Cliton, fewer than twenty lines later, presents Géronte's death with the expression "il prend la poste à l'autre Monde" (l. 68). The exposition of *La Suite*, while it painstakingly links the action of the two plays, simultaneously subverts linkage. First, the rapid succession of surprising events—Dorante flees, Géronte marries Lucrèce in his place, Géronte dies—undermines verisimilitude. Second, Dorante's role in these events makes him appear to be a more pernicious character than either of the plays themselves would suggest. Corneille thus takes his own site of continuity—the exposition of the second play—and creates dissonance. The author seems to be using Dorante's gratuitously despicable behavior in order to poke fun at the idea of a sequel, the idea of seamless continuity. Some literary scholars take the exposition at face value,

[Margin notes:]
(✓)
acknowledge gap + suggest motive—

ex: rehabilitate Dorante?

ex: plays = opposites

ex: city vs province

Cliton does same exercise of trying to reconcile…

↓
poss. irony

'exposition = crucial

links action of two plays (gets rid of fiancée, etc)

yet subverts linkage—

so: w/c site of continuity (exposition), C creates dissonance

∴ pokes fun at sequel

Some say authorial incompetence; Ekstein says no, Irony

another alt: both end happily (impending marriage) but expo of Suite ⇒ M. ended badly, so Suite will, too.

also, sequel → another sequel: no closure

+, D's fear of marriage

+use of conditional @ dénouement

ref. In Examen makes irony of "happy ending" obvious

and reproach Corneille for it. Henry Carrington Lancaster finds that "it was a strange blunder [on Corneille's part] to prepare us for a reformed liar by making him guilty of theft and of conduct that was dishonorable to his fiancée and caused his father's death" (2, 2:449). Unless we accept the explanation of authorial incompetence, irony provides perhaps the only coherent means of accounting for the radical differences between the Dorantes of *Le Menteur*, of the exposition of *La Suite*, and of the action of *La Suite*.

The exposition of *La Suite du Menteur* raises a second and independent possibility of irony, this time in relation to the earlier play's dénouement. Both *Le Menteur* and its *Suite* end on the same happy note of traditional comedy: an impending marriage. Their very resemblance works to suggest that the outcome of *La Suite* will be no more happy in the long run than was that of *Le Menteur*. The complete reversal of the ending of *Le Menteur* articulated in the exposition of *La Suite* invites the expectation of a second reversal after the the lights dim on the happy scene of Mélisse and Dorante's projected union. Such a reversal, by its very nature ironic, is buttressed by two other considerations. First, it is in the nature of the sequel to generate yet another episode, another sequel. If the original text can be opened to continuation, then the sequel is all the more susceptible. It is thus difficult to ascribe complete closure to *La Suite*. Second, Verhœff notes a constant trait in Dorante's character across both plays that, while more subtle than his heroism, is far more convincing: his fear of marriage (*Comédies* 129). Other similarities between the two dénouements may also suggest the possibility of reversal: at the beginning of the fifth act of *La Suite*, when all obstacles have seemingly been eliminated, Lyse says to Cliton, "Et s'il [Dorante] l'aime [Mélisse] en effet, je tiens la chose [marriage] faite" (l. 1642). Note the conditional *si*. We find a similar *si* at the very end of *Le Menteur* in the mouth of Lyse's parallel character, Sabine: "Si vous [Dorante and Lucrèce] vous mariez, il ne pleuvra plus guère" (l. 1798). The proposed unions are equally uncertain, equally conditional. That Corneille deliberately played with the ironic potential of the parallel endings may be inferred from a comment he made in the *Examen* to *Le Menteur*: he explains that he altered the rather harsh dénouement of *La Verdad sospechosa* "afin…que la comédie se termine avec pleine tranquillité de tous côtés" (2:8). Given that the *Examen* was written in 1660, that is, fifteen years after the publication of *La Suite du Menteur*, the words "pleine tranquillité" are perfectly ironic; Corneille both means what he says and means the exact opposite as well.

While the exposition of *La Suite* is the central focus of irony, there are other features that suggest irony as well, a number of which are rarely found in Corneille's other plays. We discussed in the first chapter the fact that theatrical speech involves two discrete channels of communication: from character to character and from playwright to audience. The character-to-character channel operates in the realm of fiction, while the one connecting playwright and audience involves a nonfictional, albeit virtual, realm. Irony may arise if the separation between the two channels breaks down, both because of the change of register and because of the incongruities to which such a breakdown gives rise. There are several varieties of this breakdown between channels in the course of the two *Menteur* plays. References to another play are frequent and function to remind the audience that what they are witnessing is equally fictional. The simplest is the reference in *Le Menteur* to *Le Cid* (l. 62).[149] Far more elaborate and frequent are the references to *Le Menteur* as a play within *La Suite*. As Alexander Leggatt notes, theatrical sequels tend to be metatheatrical (62). Cliton reveals to Dorante that a play entitled *Le Menteur* and portraying his escapades has been written and produced in Paris. This is not a mere allusion, but rather a discussion of the play that extends for thirty-six lines (ll. 271–306). At the end of *La Suite*, the subject returns. In another lengthy passage (sixty-one lines), one which Corneille chose to eliminate in the 1660 edition of his complete works, Philiste presents Dorante with a printed copy of *Le Menteur*, and the full cast of the play goes on to discuss the possibility of the author's writing a sequel. Dorante finds this to be an excellent idea and proposes that they stage it themselves once it is written. Near the end of this section, Dorante refers to himself as character and spectator/reader simultaneously when he says, "Allons voir comme *ici* [in the copy of *Le Menteur*] l'Auteur m'a figuré" (2:1263, italics mine). By explicitly presenting himself as real and fictional at the same time, the onstage Dorante reminds us that he is not real at all, but rather an actor depicting a fictional construct. The playfulness of such metatheatrical references is obvious.[150] Similarly, the lines between actor and character are blurred when Cliton says that his role in *Le Menteur* is being played by "le Héros de la Farce, un certain Jodelet" (l. 281); he insists particularly on the close resemblance between Jodelet and himself: "C'est l'original même, il vaut ce que je vaux" (l. 285; see also l. 826). The audience, of course, was perfectly aware that they were watching Jodelet play the role of Cliton in the *Suite* as well as in *Le Menteur*. He was a famous actor at the time, endowed with a distinctive nose and voice (Couton, Corneille 2:1248). Thus every reference Cliton makes to Jodelet unambiguously reminds the audience that what they are watching is not reality. The interference between channels may explain Antoine Adam's uneasiness about these references, made clear when he says, "On a l'impression que Corneille a poussé trop loin la complaisance pour l'acteur Jodelet qui s'était chargé de ce rôle" (2:395). Even in the final lines that Corneille retained in the 1660 edition of *La Suite*, we find a breakdown between channels as Cliton addresses the audience directly:

"Ceux qui sont las debout se peuvent aller seoir, / Je vous donne en passant cet avis, et bonsoir" (ll. 1903–4). This ending parallels what we find in the final line of *Le Menteur*, where Cliton enjoins the audience, "Par un si rare exemple apprenez à mentir" (l. 1804). Elsewhere, the playwright duplicates in *La Suite* the collision between two discrete channels when he treats the famous *Astrée* as both fact and fiction. Referring explicitly to the novel as a "Roman" (l. 1238), Lyse nonetheless claims to be from the same village as the heroine and in fact to be related to her (ll. 1239–40). Furthermore, she goes on to specify that the old willow tree that Céladon and Astrée used to hide their correspondence is on the corner of her grandfather's property; "Et l'on m'a dit que c'est un infaillible signe / Que d'un si rare Hymen je viens en droite ligne" (ll. 1245–6). The logical leaps are breathtaking and the breakdown between diegetic levels is total. The irony here is of a particularly playful sort, taking aim at the referentiality of theatrical discourse.

Another form of playful irony that we find in these plays involves self-deprecation. The *raillerie* typically associated with French irony is particularly in evidence as Corneille playfully turns it on himself. We find two such examples here, one in each of the *Menteur* plays. The reference to *Le Cid* in the early editions of *Le Menteur* is accompanied by the implication that esteem for Corneille's play is a sign of an out-of-touch provincial: "J'en voyais là [in Poitiers] beaucoup passer pour gens d'esprit, / Et faire encore état de Chimène et du Cid" (2:1225). In *La Suite*, Cliton passes judgment on Corneille's *Le Menteur*: "La pièce a réussi, quoique faible de style" (l. 295). The metatheatrical self-disparagement is both playful and unquestionably ironic.

Were *La Suite du Menteur* endowed with a different title and the allusions to *Le Menteur* eliminated, it would stand alone as a play without difficulty. The repeated allusions and strategies linking it to *Le Menteur* all open the door to irony through the subversion of the second play's autonomy (see Rosenmeyer 33). The result goes well beyond the possibility of irony to virtual certainty.

PROLOGUE AND PLAY

The margin between a play and its prologue offers similarities with that between a play and its *suite*. In both cases, the search for meaning at the margin is authorized by more than mere juxtaposition. The margin between two plays, for example *Horace* and *Cinna*, may indeed be open to an ironic reading; but such a reading is not explicitly authorized. Calling a play a *suite* or attaching a prologue to a play solidifies the ties between them to a degree that any gap can reasonably be presumed to be intended and thus significant. A major difference between the two in the case of Corneille is that the

[margin notes:]
direct address to audience at the end

reg to L'Astrée as both fiction + fact

self-deprecation (C mocks self)

irony < subversion of Suite's autonomy

⌐ margin between prologue + play

(margin = play + sequel = non-threatening)

most successful are extended application of ideas to particular plays, esp Suite margin separating prologue and play has political implications, while the one separating a play and its *suite* does not. Claiming to find playful irony in the conjunction of the two *Menteur* comedies is relatively unthreatening. After all, who is the victim of this irony? Corneille may be gently poking fun at the spectator who is easily led by his generic expectations; he may be commenting ironically on theatrical conventions; perhaps he is mocking himself as well. Prologues present a decidedly dissimilar situation, because in seventeenth-century France they customarily incorporate direct praise of the king. The presence of the king in the prologue makes any suggestion of ironic intent potentially dangerous politically.

Prologues appear attached to only two of Corneille's plays, and it is no accident that they are his two machine plays, *Andromède* and *La Conquête de la Toison d'or*. Whereas prologues were common in plays of antiquity, in seventeenth-century France, they are associated above all with opera, a genre to which the machine play has often been linked (Hémon 380). Indeed, Voltaire credits Corneille with furnishing the model for the prologue—including praise of the king—for the later operas of Quinault and Lully (55:825).[151] In antiquity, prologues were solidly tied to the action of the play. As they gradually disappeared, so did the sense of natural linkage between prologue and play. When we consider Corneille's machine plays or the operas of Lully and Quinault we find considerable ambiguity. Prologue and play/opera seem completely independent and at the same time profoundly linked, as Buford Norman observes (45). He considers the ties between prologue and opera in the eleven libretti that Quinault wrote for Lully and concludes that "all but three…contain explicit links between prologue and tragedy" (65). Because of the close ties between Corneille's prologues and Quinault's, as well as the classical doctrine emphasizing harmony, which Sylvain Cornic extends to prologue and work (49), it seems reasonable to assume that such linkage is the norm in Corneille's machine plays as well.

The situation in the prologue to Corneille's first machine play, *Andromède*, is perfectly straightforward. Melpomène, the muse of tragedy, explicitly offers examples for the young King Louis (he was twelve years old at the time) to follow: "Je lui montre Pompée, Alexandre, César, / Mais comme des Héros attachés à son char" (ll. 53–54). Persée, the hero of the play proper, can be assumed to be another of these exemplary heroes that Louis is destined to emulate. Wagner sees the link between prologue and play as strong: "[L]'image royale du prologue déborde dans la fable et va contaminer les figures mythologiques qui, ainsi, perdent leur dimension référentielle presque infinie, au profit d'un seul personnage, le roi moderne" ("Miroir" 170). The gaps between the king and Persée are rationalized within the prologue itself: Louis's extreme youth is explained away by repeated reference to his destiny ("je lis chaque jour son destin dans les cieux" [l. 68], says Melpomène) and Persée's divine status is understood conventionally to represent the superiority of the king to his subjects. There is thus little room for the possibility of irony.

The same is not the case in *La Toison d'or*. The second and last of Corneille's machine plays is preceded by an allegorical prologue which does not simply praise the king, but considers actual events. Through figures such as La Victoire, La France, Mars, and La Paix, the prologue enacts France's suffering in war and its joy at attaining peace with Spain through Louis's marriage with the Spanish Infanta, Marie-Thérèse. The king, while not on stage, is the major focus of the prologue, along with his queen, who appears in the form of a portrait on the shield of the figure L'Hyménée. The play itself tells the story of how Jason procures the Golden Fleece in Colchos with Médée's aid in order to return home and claim the throne of Thessalie from his uncle, Pelias.

The prologue to *La Toison d'or* is more than twice as long as the one preceding *Andromède*. What is immediately striking in this second case is that it is not merely a site of flattery: the prologue opens with a long complaint, voiced by La France, about war, victory, and its consequences for Louis's subjects. Corneille is not timid:

> Et la gloire du Trône accable les sujets.
> . . . .
> Je me lasse de voir mes villes désolées,
> Mes habitants pillés, mes campagnes brûlées.
> (ll. 32–38)[152]

The potential affront to the king may be excused: the peace treaty and royal marriage mark the end of such suffering by removing the need for war (Lancaster 3, 2:505).[153] Despite such reasoned explanations of Corneille's choice of subject matter, the description of misery is unsettling in itself.

Of central concern here is the margin between the prologue and the play. We find both substantial similarity and jarring incongruity between Corneille's second machine play and its prologue. The thematics are comparable: both involve kings, queens, war and peace, marriage, and ascent to the throne. Indeed, a number of these elements are doubled within the play itself, which both intensifies the links to the prologue and simultaneously complicates them. There are two kings: Aète, king of Colchos; and Jason, about to become the king of Thessalie. Similarly, we find two queens: Hypsipyle, queen of Lemnos, and Médée, who is about to become Jason's queen. The play ends with the promise of two marriages: between Jason and Médée;

and between Hypsipyle and Médée's brother, Absyrte. Abby E. Zanger, in an
excellent and far-reaching examination of the prologue and play, notes that
both involve male heroics, cross-cultural love, empire building, and stolen
riches (111). For some, the analogies between the two are straightforward: the
play parallels the prologue (Wagner, "Évocation" 214; Lancaster 3, 2:503–4).
The power of Marie-Thérèse's image on the shield, which causes Discorde and
Envie to disappear and the chains imprisoning La Paix to break and fall away,
parallels Médée's power; the misery of the people caused by constant war is
echoed in the wars endured by desolate Colchos and even in Aète's sorrow
at losing his throne. The links between the two extend to the extratheatrical:
the King of Spain was the Grand Master of the Order of the Golden Fleece
and the myth of the Golden Fleece was the theme of the fireworks set off in
Lyon in December 1658 to celebrate the initial agreement to the marriage
(Zanger 99).[154] For a play that has received relatively little critical attention,
a remarkable amount of effort has been expended on finding links between
prologue and play.

Despite all of these ties, unsettling disjunctions between the two are
difficult to avoid. It is in the disjunction that the possibility for irony arises
and with that irony, attendant political danger. As mentioned above, the
marriage of Louis and Marie-Thérèse represents the attainment of peace
for France and Spain. Jason brings peace to Colchos as the play opens, but
through arms, not marriage. And by making off with the Golden Fleece,
Jason assures the downfall of a legitimate king in order to secure a place on
the throne of his own land. Furthermore, whereas the prologue ends in joy-
ous celebration, La Toison d'or concludes with flight, betrayal, and loss, and
only the distant promise of dynastic redemption. A particularly disquieting
incongruity involves the issue of procreation. In the play's final scene, Jupiter announces that Aète will regain his kingdom and his line will carry on,
not through any issue of his son and Hypsipyle, but through a child named
Médus who will be born to Médée. Médée is a problematic maternal figure,
as everyone knows that she will kill the children she has by Jason. This is
not the picture of dynastic succession that a newlywed Louis XIV would be
pleased to take as a model.

The crux of the matter, the primary site of both resemblance and
difference in the margin between prologue and play, is identity, specifically
between the couple glorified in the prologue, Louis XIV and Marie-Thérèse,
and the central couple of the play, Jason and Médée. Is Louis to see himself
in Jason, the man who tricks Aète, who callously abandoned Hypsipyle and
who, as the audience knows, will do the same to Médée? Despite the links
between Louis and Jason outlined above, which boil down to heroism, as-
cension to the throne, and a new bride, equating the two is extremely risky.

Indeed, few seriously suggest a simple identification of the two men.[155] An identification between Louis and Aète is even more problematic, as the latter is an old king who is tricked out of the fleece and thereby loses his kingdom. Amy Wygant offers a provocative alternative: "[I]n becoming himself, Louis XIV will become not Corneille's Jason, but rather his Medea" (540). While Wygant thereby provides Louis with a powerful double, one has only to consider that Médée betrays her father and uses sorcery to further her love interests to conclude that Médée is at least as problematic a stand-in for the young French king as Jason. The same problem arises when we turn to Marie-Thérèse. Is she to be identified with Médée? Leaving aside the thorny issue of sorcery, Médée is disloyal to her father in order to marry the man of whom she has become enamored. Marie-Thérèse, in contrast, is marrying Louis on behalf and for the benefit of her father, the King of Spain. Is an identification to be made with Hypsipyle, the abandoned and betrayed queen? Wygant argues this position, linking the two women through their role as political brides (540). Hypsipyle, however, is far more focused on the man rejecting her than on the role of bride that she accepts at the dénouement. Other associations with Marie-Thérèse involve Medusa's head and the Golden Fleece (Zanger 116, 122–23). In essence, there are no comfortable identifications to be made, only partial possibilities and disturbing incongruities. Thus any identification runs the risk of being perceived as ironic. The critical stance of irony, its "edge," is provided by the political context explicitly referenced by the prologue.

Faced with these difficulties in harmonizing prologue and play and the need to do so because of their proximity, critics have made numerous efforts to reconcile the two, to bridge, erase, or explain away the gaps. Wagner and Couton have no difficulty reconciling prologue and play, as they simply deny the existence of any incongruity, equating Jason with Louis XIV, as we noted above.[156] Another critical move has been to deny the contiguity between prologue and play: Niderst argues that Corneille began his play as early as 1656, long before either the peace treaty or the marriage (93). Such a position concedes that Jason and Médée are problematic stand-ins for Louis and Marie-Thérèse but refuses to assign any meaning to that incongruity. Lancaster tries to finesse the issue by refusing a global identification between individuals in favor of the equating of specific events.[157] The most creative ways of dealing with the relationship between prologue and play come from Zanger. Indeed, she offers several. She suggests that the indeterminacy of the relationship between prologue and play may be intentional, figuring the enigma, a salon game that was very much in vogue at this time and that involved interpreting mythic and emblematic images (121). Zanger notes that the visual depiction in an enigma often represents an object or idea seemingly unlike the apparent subject (121). Implicit in this solution is the existence of a final, correct identification of the characters in the prologue with those of the play, albeit one that is difficult to arrive at. As we just saw, however, any such identification opens the door to irony. In a second effort to bridge the gap, Zanger focuses on a pairing of Marie-Thérèse and Médée, and argues that "in brandishing the figure of Medea, such spectacles rehearsed the symbolic activities of kinship exchange by explicitly staging danger and its containment" (99). She does not retreat from the dangers posed by Médée as a stand-in for Marie-Thérèse, calling her an "explosive symbol" (112), but rather ascribes those very dangers, in symbolic form, to the new queen. Marie-Thérèse's power—her ties to her father's throne—is contained and employed for the benefit of France, just as Médée's powers are contained by Jason and used to advance his own political ambitions. There is another side to the dangers posed by both Marie-Thérèse and Médée, that of their power to bear children, that is much more difficult to accommodate. The bride has the central role in the generation of the state (Zanger 127). The example of Médée is a disquieting illustration of that truth: not only will she kill her children, but the son she will bear who is destined to reinstate Aète on the throne—Médus—will be the son of a foreign king (Égée). Legitimacy passes through the woman, whether foreign princess or sorceress. Even Zanger finds Corneille's depiction of the power of female generativity to be politically dangerous, and so she proposes soothing attenuations. She argues that the wealth of the Norman Sourdéac, for whom Corneille originally wrote *La Toison d'or*, allowed Corneille to make a more "explosive parallel" between the royal and the mythological couples than had the play been part of the civic celebrations of the marriage in Lyon or Paris (128). Zanger also contends that Corneille moderates the dangerous possibilities for analogy by removing Médée and Jason from stage at the end of the play (128). Finally, in a cascade of deflections, she uses the play's production history to show how the danger might have been attenuated:

> Corneille's spectacle, the most detailed (and therefore most unsettling) version of the Golden Fleece myth, was not staged during the marriage celebration. It was staged in its aftermath, in November 1660, after "the Golden Fleece" had been "stolen" and taken to Paris…And the play did not premier in Paris, but in the provinces, in Normandy. It was not staged in Paris until January 1661. Due to the death of Mazarin, furthermore, it was not seen by the court until 1662. By this time, Louis XIV was firmly in control. He no longer needed Médée's agency to enrich

his state. Indeed, the birth of a dauphin in late 1661, like the Médus of Corneille's play, displaced the queen in importance, shifting the story away from potential loss and putting mastery and gain in sight. (129)

I have described at length Zanger's eclectic strategies for reducing the danger of the analogy between Médée and Marie-Thérèse in order to demonstrate how much energy is required in order to reduce that danger. The fact that the avenues she employs do not seem to coalesce into a unified design that might be attributed to Corneille serves to suggest that despite such heroic efforts on her part, the danger cannot be fully contained.

The fact remains, however, that Louis did not, by all accounts, interpret the juxtaposition of the laudatory prologue and the considerably darker play as irony at his own expense. Corneille was not arrested or exiled. As Hutcheon has argued very cogently, "[I]rony isn't irony until it is interpreted as such…Someone attributes irony; someone makes irony happen" (6). The interpreter of irony has considerable power over the situation: Corneille may or may not have had an ironic intent in setting up the incongruous juxtaposition of prologue and play, but his intent is not sufficient either to make those situations ironic or unironic. Even if he had no such intent, had Louis XIV found irony in this particular juxtaposition, then that irony would exist. The interpretation of irony lies squarely with the audience. The potential political dangers of the situation for Corneille make it likely that the signs of irony in the margin, of which we have noted several, will be as inconclusive as possible, offering the indeterminacy of possible irony and nothing more.

The case of *La Toison d'or* suggests the possibility of irony through analogy between the onstage universe and actual events of Corneille's time. *La Toison d'or* clearly plays with the margin between the two discrete referential domains, current events in the prologue and myth in the play. Discordant analogies between events in other plays by Corneille and the historicopolitical context in which they were composed contain limitless potential for the discovery of possible ironies. For example, Marine Corlouer suggests that *Don Sanche* is perhaps an ironic reflection on the questionable paternity of Louis XIV (64). While I by no means want to denigrate such an avenue of ironic interpretation, I have chosen not to pursue such possibilities because they require, in my opinion, too high a degree of conjecture concerning authorial intent. While it is common practice to posit specific analogies between current events and Corneille's plays, to suggest that Corneille is making some ironic comment thereby on the actual events is to go considerably further down the path of conjecture. The gaps I have considered as possibly or probably ironic all involve the margin between two events or statements entirely under Corneille's control. If we discuss Louis XIV in this chapter, it is because the playwright makes unambiguous reference to him and the celebration of his marriage in *La Toison d'or*'s prologue. While the margin between dramatic fiction and political affairs inevitably contains the potential for ironic interpretation, it is an avenue that I will leave to others.

*

The margin between *Le Menteur* and *La Suite du Menteur* is itself both different from and similar to that between *La Toison d'or* and its prologue. *La Suite du Menteur* and *La Toison d'or* share the position of coming second, existing under the shadow of the margin separating them from what precedes. It is thus not an accident that both of these plays are among the most neglected in Corneille's *œuvre*. To what extent this neglect is a function of the ironic potential of the margins we have examined in these two cases is impossible to ascertain, but it certainly seems plausible. Coincidentally, *La Toison d'or*, like *La Suite du Menteur*, shares characters with an earlier play: Corneille presented another facet of the myth of Medea in his *Médée* twenty-five years earlier. No two other plays in the playwright's *œuvre* share onstage characters.[158] There is no margin to speak of, however, between *Médée* and *La Toison d'or*, first because of the time elapsed between the appearance of the two, and second because the later play is a prequel, not a sequel, to the earlier play. Furthermore, Corneille makes no allusion in *La Toison d'or* to his earlier play. Thus the margin between *Médée* and *La Toison d'or* in no way suggests the possibility of irony. The margins between *Le Menteur* and *La Suite du Menteur* and between *La Toison d'or* and its prologue are proximal sites of considerable incongruity. Margins exist further afield as well, separating Corneille's dramatic universe from the past as well as from the context in which the works are written.

SOURCES

It was traditional practice in seventeenth-century theater, and especially in tragedy, that the basic plot outline of a play be taken from history or mythology. Sources, whether obscure or well known, were typically mentioned in a published play's prefatory material. At the same time, playwrights, Corneille perhaps more than most, made significant changes to the received plots. Indeed, Forestier's far-reaching work on the playwright focuses on making sense of how Corneille combines repetition of his source (the characters, the situation, and especially the dénouement) and difference (many features of the plot leading up to the dénouement). In and of itself, the combination of resemblance and difference does not suffice to suggest the possibility of irony.

An additional sign of irony is needed, such as, for example, incongruity or reversal. Given that the source material is, generally speaking, substantially distant in time and space from Corneille's interpretation of it, it is difficult to presume that the audience would have perceived such signals of irony in Corneille's version. But to the extent that there is such awareness and perception on the part of the audience, an ironic reading is entirely possible.

Thus, we may assume that in order for the possibility of irony to arise, there has to be knowledge of the historical episode or mythological plot on which the play is based. Corneille frequently chose rather obscure sources for his plays, so the potential for espying significant departures from the source would be restricted in most cases to a very limited portion of the play's audience.[159] Given the foregrounding of sources in Corneille's prefatory material, it is clear that such an audience did exist, although it may have been limited largely to the *doctes*. Examination of the sources reveals several patent reversals on Corneille's part. A particularly unambiguous example can be found in *Nicomède*. Whereas the source material (primarily the historian Justin) presents a king who seeks to kill one of his sons in order to favor another, and a son who has his father killed in retaliation, Corneille relieves Prusias of infanticidal intentions and has Nicomède forgive his father and restore him safely to the throne. Forestier underscores this reversal in his discussion of the play's hero: "Corneille s'est ici astreint…à transformer profondément une histoire qui présentait une violente situation tragique" (*Génétique* 79). In the case of Othon, the shift concerns character more than action: the man whom the historian Tacitus depicted as ruthlessly ambitious is, in Corneille's play, considerably more devoted to his betrothed than to his own political interests. Elsewhere Corneille reverses the tone of the dénouement. In Alarcón's *La verdad sospechosa*, Don Garcia is forced by his father to marry the young woman he mistakenly identified as his chosen as a form of punishment for his lies. "Perdí mi glorias" (I have lost my glory), he laments. In Corneille's version, *Le Menteur*, Dorante happily makes the switch from one woman to the other, and the play ends lightly with Cliton's advice: "Par un si rare exemple apprenez à mentir" (l. 1804).[160] Just as it is more common in the case of verbal irony for praise to signal blame rather than vice-versa, the possibility for irony is attenuated, but not entirely eliminated, by the ameliorative nature of these three reversals. No critical or evaluative edge is present when Corneille makes the outcomes and situations more palatable to the audience. Such is not always the case, however. Attila's preoccupation with choosing between Ildione and Honorie for his wife seems incongruous in the context of the historical source that indicates that Attila had numerous wives.[161] Of course, seventeenth-century mores did not allow for polygamy, but it is nonetheless curious that Corneille would have chosen to center his plot on an issue that was completely alien to the source material.

Few of Corneille's plays are based on material that was well known to his audience, but in that handful of cases, any significant deviation from the source is glaringly obvious. The resulting discordance may well allow for multiple explanations, but an ironic stance vis-à-vis the source must legitimately be one of them. In *Médée*, Corneille has Jason think of killing his children before Médée does. Like Médée, he is motivated by the desire to make his spouse suffer:

> C'est vous, petits ingrats, que malgré la nature
> Il me faut immoler dessus leur [Créuse and Créon's]
>   sépulture,
> Que la sorcière [Médée] en vous commence de souffrir,
> Que son premier tourment soit de vous voir mourir.
>   (ll. 1565–68)

Corneille's desire to eclipse his predecessors, Euripedes and especially Seneca, may provide an unironic explanation (Couton, Corneille 1:1405), as might clumsiness or inexperience on the young playwright's part. Nonetheless, Corneille's move to suggest that Jason first thought of the defining act of Médée, an act that simultaneously conveys both the horror that the character inspires and the depth of her anguish, is a radical one. The very thought of infanticide marks a significant and disturbing gap between the legendary Jason and the Cornelian Jason, a gap that William O. Goode does not hesitate to call the "supreme irony" of this play (812).

In chapter 7 we discussed the double register in *Œdipe*. Here we may understand that double register as a function of the gap between Corneille's version and those of his sources, Sophocles and Seneca. Corneille invents the character Dircé who almost engulfs the traditional plot with her political ambitions and her love for Thésée. The latter's presence in the play is equally surprising, but at least the character is not invented out of whole cloth by the playwright. For all their individual attempts to involve themselves in the plot, Thésée and Dircé remain completely exterior to it, revealing an ungainly gap. We discussed earlier the changes Corneille made to the number and kinds of oracles upon which Sophocles built his play. The notion of the tragic is thereby seriously compromised in Corneille's version (see chapter 4), and Œdipe's consequent diminishment as a tragic hero allows for the possibility of an ironic interpretation as well. The changes made by Corneille to the source material are such that Louvat and Escola conclude, "Si *Œdipe* a été aussi souvent mal jugé, c'est que cette concurrence est perçue par les critiques, pour qui le texte de Sophocle chronologiquement antérieur fait logiquement autorité, comme proprement scandaleuse" ("Statut" 463). The question of ironic intent is a thorny one in this context. As we noted earlier, *Œdipe* is not a parody of Sophocles' or Seneca's tragedy: there is no indication of an intent to ridicule the source(s). There is, however, the same kind of Flaubertian rubbing that I noted in the context of the double register, only here it occurs at a greater distance, between the play and its source. Each version calls into question the other.

In the case of *Œdipe*, we also find a type of intertextual competition that keeps the source constantly in view, a competition that Corneille clearly relished. Forestier calls it a "gageure folle" to rewrite the tragedy that served as Aristotle's touchstone in his *Poetics*: "[O]n n'adapte pas un chef-d'œuvre absolu, même lorsqu'on s'appelle Corneille" (*Génétique* 332). However, that challenge may indeed have been what made the subject an attractive one for Corneille. We find the same impulse at work when he writes a *Sophonisbe* that competes with Jean Mairet's masterful *La Sophonisbe*. The latter, although written twenty-nine years earlier, was still being staged in 1663 when Corneille produced his version.[162] In both cases, however, Corneille went to considerable lengths to underscore his distance from his sources. He claims that one cannot compare his *Œdipe* to the versions of Sophocles or Seneca, or his *Sophonisbe* to Mairet's chef-d'œuvre of 1634, because his plays are radically different from theirs. "Comme j'ai pris une autre route que la leur [Sophocles and Seneca], il m'a été impossible de me rencontrer avec eux," he asserts in the *Au lecteur* of *Œdipe* (3:19); in the case of *Sophonisbe* he claims "une scrupuleuse exactitude à m'écarter de sa [Mairet's] route," so that "on ne peut faire aucune comparaison entre les choses, où l'on ne voit aucune concurrence" (*Préface* 3:381). Yet the debts to his sources that Corneille denies so emphatically are enormous. Is Corneille winking ironically at his audience, or a portion of his audience, or does he believe his own claims? Even more subject to an ironic reading is his contention that he is not trying to best his forerunners. He explains the changes he made in *Sophonisbe* in relation to Mairet's version by saying, "[Ç]'a été par le seul dessein de faire autrement, sans ambition de faire mieux" (3:382). Are we really to believe that Corneille did not seek to outdo his rivals? Structurally, a desire on Corneille's part to best his rivals, whether near (Mairet) or distant (Sophocles or Seneca), is by no means incompatible with an ironic intent, as irony is an effective tool for undermining a rival. The margins between certain of Corneille's plays and their sources contain such unwieldy gaps that the conditions for irony are present and the possibility of irony may legitimately be entertained.

AUTHORITY

In *L'Ironie littéraire*, Hamon reserves a privileged place for the voice of authority, which he terms *le gardien de la loi*. Both because of its rigidity—which provides a clear margin—and its consecrated position, it may easily become a target for irony:

> Le matériau de prédilection de l'énoncé ironique ne serait-il pas constitué plutôt, et plus généralement et plus 'abstraitement,' de l'ensemble des systèmes de valeurs (normes, hiérarchies, orthodoxies, axiologies) qui régissent une société: systèmes moraux, esthétiques, idéologiques, technologiques, etc.? (Hamon 9)

The system of values in this context is the French neoclassical theater and its body of rules. Hamon notes how Sperber and Wilson's theory of ironic echoic mention (see chapter 5) works well here because the voice of authority, being relatively stable, provides the ideal "contexte de substitution" against which irony can be grasped (152).

As we have seen, sources are one form of authority against which Corneille measures himself; in his prefatory material he regularly signals similarities and differences, camouflaging and/or underlining the gaps between his play and those of his predecessors. Another incarnation of authority involves the various writings and pronouncements on dramatic theory of the period. One must look no farther than the opening sentences of the first of Corneille's *Trois Discours sur le poème dramatique* to find the playwright simultaneously bowing in the direction of authority and challenging it: "[I]l faut suivre les préceptes de l'art, et leur [the audience] plaire selon les règles. Il est constant qu'il y a des préceptes, puisqu'il y a un art, mais il n'est pas constant quels ils sont" (3:117). Lyons notes that to begin his major work of poetics in this fashion "reveals an attitude toward regularity that is at the least ambivalent and probably ironic" (*Kingdom* 15).

In seventeenth-century France, it was a standard rhetorical move within the prefatory texts accompanying a play for a playwright not simply to cite his sources, but also to make reference to respected authorities in the area of dramatic theory in order to justify decisions made in writing the play in question. The same acknowledgement of authorities is normal practice in any writings on dramatic theory as well. Corneille's manipulation of the margins between himself and various authorities allows him to ally himself with certain ones and distance himself from others. The potential for irony is considerable and often becomes evident irony in those cases where the playwright patently constructs margins as a form of attack on an authority.

The authorities most frequently cited by Corneille are the ancients, chief among them Aristotle, whose *Poetics* is the theoretical touchstone for the dramatic principles of seventeenth-century France. Aristotle's name is ubiquitous in Corneille's *Trois Discours sur le poème dramatique*. Appearing first as the fourth word of the first *Discours*, Aristotle is invoked a total of seventy-four times. The repetition of the name is sufficiently excessive so as to itself suggest a possible signal of irony. Corneille's main goal in citing Aristotle is not to mock the ancients, however, but to buttress his arguments through alliance with an unassailable authority. Instead of calling attention to a gap between himself and Aristotle, a gap which exists and that the playwright only rarely acknowledges,[163] Corneille camouflages the margin, suggesting almost seamless continuity. Ever an admirer of the Romans, Corneille also makes repeated references to Horace and the authority of his *Ars Poetica*; he cites Tacitus, Juvenal, and St. Ambroise as well. In a similar vein, the only prefatory material Corneille provides to accompany *Tite et Bérénice* are two brief passages translated from Greek to Latin, relating to the action depicted in the play.[164] That they are not translated into French highlights the fact that they are ancient and therefore, by implication, authoritative. The absence of the French might be seen to contain an element of ironic playfulness in that the passages require a certain level of erudition, gratuitous in this context, in order to read them. Another curious example is the playwright's use of sources in the prefatory material accompanying *Rodogune*. He points to three historians as his sources, the first two from from the first or second century AD and the third somewhat more recent, thus bowing in three directions of the ancient horizon: the Greek Appian of Alexandria, the Roman Justinian, and the Jewish historian Josephus. Couton notes tellingly that Corneille in fact drew little from any of these sources in creating *Rodogune*. The play is largely Corneille's invention. Examining the playwright's motives, Couton is forced to admit the possibility of irony: "Toute révérence gardée, il faut avouer qu'il jetait à l'occasion de la poudre aux yeux de lecteurs ou de critiques disposés à une sévérité historique qu'il estimait déplacée" (Corneille 2:1274).

By and large, however, Corneille does not cite the ancient sources ironically. Rather, using such sources for legitimation, he manipulates the respect that their authority elicits and, much as he hid the gap between acts 4 and 5 of *L'Illusion comique*, Corneille actively camouflages the gaps between his dramatic practice and the pronouncements and practice of the ancients.[165] Thus, while he does not criticize or mock the ancients, his advertised adherence is nonetheless ironic in the sense that he manifestly does not conform to his stated reverence of their precepts. Very early in his career, in the *Préface* to *Clitandre* (1632), Corneille makes a telling statement: "Je me donne ici quelque sorte de liberté de choquer les Anciens, d'autant qu'ils ne sont plus

en état de me répondre" (1:95). He will shortly change tactics and choose
to hide his intentions, instead claiming the ancients as the guarantors of his
own authority in matters of dramatic theory.

The second nexus of authority cited by Corneille is modern rather
than ancient and involves the rules governing seventeenth-century theater
as well as the *doctes* who formulate them. Here Corneille's attitude is considerably less deferential, even on a superficial level. We may venture that
the playwright describes his own attitude towards the *doctes* as well as his
motivation for writing the *Trois Discours sur le poème dramatique* when he
says that Aristotle "écrivait pour le [Platon] contredire" (3:146). Corneille's
prefatory and theoretical texts often entail dialogue with his contemporaries, but these are dialogues in which he manipulates and mutes the voice
of the other. By and large, although the playwright responds frequently in
the prefatory material to specific issues his contemporaries have raised, he
refrains from naming those contemporaries.[166] Corneille acknowledges his
tactic in a letter to l'Abbé de Pure concerning the *Discours*: "[B]ien que je
contredise quelquefois M. d'Aubignac et M[essieu]rs de l'Académie, je ne les
nomme jamais, et ne parle non plus d'eux que s'ils n'avaient point parlé de
moi" (3:7). D'Aubignac stands out among the *doctes*, particularly in 1660
when Corneille's *Discours* and *Examens* were published, because his highly
influential *Pratique du théâtre* had just appeared in 1657. Furthermore, it
is likely that d'Aubignac irked Corneille by claiming a role of authority in
matters of dramaturgy despite being quite unsuccessful as a playwright.[167] On
one occasion, in the *Préface* to *Sophonisbe*, Corneille does choose to identify
his contemporaries, but irony is evident in the excessive profusion of names:
along with d'Aubignac, we find Tristan l'Hermite, Hardy, M. de Scudéry,
Boisrobert, Benserade, and Mairet.[168]

The rules themselves do not fare better than their formulators and
defenders. Indeed, Corneille's resistance to conforming to the rules is universally recognized. His experience with the *querelle du Cid* certainly worked
to harden his stance of basic enmity towards the authority of both rules and
the rule givers. As we saw in the opening of the first *Discours*, Corneille
acknowledges the authority of the rules and yet is eager to question their
soundness. He discusses rules a great deal, as though to colonize and thus
dominate the problematic terrain, "occupying it ironically" in Lyons's words
(*Kingdom* 16).[169] Discussion of the rules is by no means limited to the *Discours*, but is a regular feature of the prefatory texts throughout Corneille's
career. Irony is a weapon in his engagement with the rules and his opposition
to their authority.

Corneille's preferred strategy vis-à-vis authority, and one that inevitably
entails irony, is to pit one authority against another, creating margins between

them. It is well known that playwrights of the period, particularly successful ones, were regularly subjected to virulent criticism for any infringement of the rules in the eyes of the dramatic theorists and scholars (see Barnwell, "Introduction" 56). Thus Corneille's attacks stem first from the need to defend himself. Constructing conflicts between various authorities was an excellent means of disarming his adversaries. This device is ironic because it opens up gaps where none should exist. The most common variety involves pitting Aristotle against the *doctes*, an ironic atttack on the latter who claim to be Aristotelians (see Forestier, *Génétique* 70).[170] In the *Épître dédicatoire* to *La Suite du Menteur*, Corneille defends his controversial position that a play has no obligation to be *utile*, but only to give pleasure: "Quant à Aristote, je ne crois pas que ceux du parti contraire aient d'assez bons yeux pour trouver le mot d'utilité dans tout son *Art poétique*" (2:96). It is obvious that Corneille enjoys mocking his critics as he makes reference to not only Aristotle, but Horace as well, the very Horace who famously spoke of art as both pleasing and useful:[171] "[M]ais pour moi qui tiens avec Aristote et Horace que notre art n'a pour but que le divertissement" (2:95). Furthermore, he explicitly calls the reader's attention to his own tactics: "[J]e suis bien hardi tout ensemble de prendre pour garant de mon opinion les deux maîtres dont ceux du parti contraire se fortifient" (2:95–96).

Similarly, Corneille pits the public against the rule-makers, establishing another margin and casting the *doctes* as the "other." In the *Épître dédicatoire* to *La Suivante*, the playwright divides his audience into two groups, the public and the *Savants*, and then offers a solid reason to concern oneself with satisfying the former rather than the latter: if one does not please the public, the *Savants* "n'oseront se déclarer en notre faveur, et aimeront mieux dire que nous aurons mal entendu les règles, que de nous donner des louanges quand nous serons décriés" (1:387–88). The authority of the public is thus shown to be superior to that of the troublesome *doctes*. The success of a play, something that can come only from the public and not the *doctes*, is indeed the primary authority for Corneille. In his discussion of *Horace*'s lack of unity in the play's *Examen*, Corneille admits that his work is defective according to the rules (1:840), but "if the rules condemn the play, then its success condemns the rules" (Maskell 270; see also Lyons, *Kingdom* 18). Corneille uses the same strategy in the *Examen* to *L'Illusion comique*, criticizing the play's irregularity while noting its success with the public.[172] Furthermore, by criticizing his own plays, Corneille lays claim to the position of *docte* for himself, thereby manipulating the *doctes*' voice of authority and pretending that no margin exists between him and them. At the same time, he undermines their lofty position of consecrated critical judgment by presenting the competing authority of the public, which he acknowledges to be superior to that of the *doctes*.

On one occasion, Corneille pits the authority of the Church against that of the *doctes*. Corneille was criticized by the latter for the licentiousness of the subject matter of *Théodore*, specifically that the eponymous character is condemned to be a prostitute. The gap between what the playwright says in the following passage and what he means, itself ironic, is a reflection of the hypocrisy of his critics:

> Ce n'est pas toutefois sans quelque sorte de satisfaction
> que je vois que la meilleure partie de mes juges impute ce
> mauvais succès [of *Théodore*] à l'idée de la prostitution que
> l'on n'a pu souffrir…Et certes il y a de quoi congratuler à
> la pureté de notre théâtre, de voir qu'une histoire qui fait
> le plus bel ornement du second livre des Vierges de saint
> Ambroise, se trouve trop licencieuse pour y être supportée.
> (*Épître dédicatoire* 2:269)[173]

Corneille continues to mock his critics by conjuring up the lascivious scenes he deliberately chose not to include. He conveys a possibly ironic intent by exaggeration: going on too long, saying considerably more than necessary to get his point across ("Qu'eût-on dit si comme ce grand docteur de l'Église j'eusse fait voir Théodore dans le lieu infâme, si j'eusse décrit les diverses agitations de son âme durant qu'elle y fut, si j'eusse figuré les troubles qu'elle y ressentit au premier moment qu'elle y vit entrer Didyme?" 2:269), all the while buttressing himself with St. Ambroise ("et c'est pour ce spectacle qu'il [Ambroise] invite particulièrement les vierges à ouvrir les yeux" 2:270).

Another authority that Corneille advances in opposition to the rules of the *doctes* is that of pragmatic necessity. Corneille points out in the *Examen* to *Le Cid* that people often walk and talk at the same time; however, such verisimilitude must be sacrificed on the stage because "ils échapperaient [while walking] aux yeux avant que d'avoir pu dire ce qu'il est nécessaire qu'ils fassent savoir à l'Auditeur" (1:705). Similarly, Corneille does not bring any of Don Diègue's five hundred friends on stage because such silent bit players "ont toujours mauvaise grâce au Théâtre, et d'autant plus que les Comédiens n'emploient à ces Personnages muets que leurs moucheurs de chandelles et leurs valets, qui ne savent quelle posture tenir" (1:706). The mocking humor and the abrupt shift in context from character to actor in this last sentence also work to signal the possibility of irony. In the *Examen* to *Don Sanche*, Corneille discusses his infringement of the rule forbidding the introduction of new characters late in the play. Speaking of the fisherman who materializes in act 5 (albeit off stage), the playwright says that the latter was en route to Castille "de son seul mouvement" (2:557), thus once again denying the

174 *Corneille's Irony*

distinction between the dramatic universe and reality; "et il n'a point de
raison d'arriver ce jour-là plutôt qu'un autre, sinon que la pièce n'aurait pu
finir s'il ne fût arrivé" (2:557). Against the authority of the rule concerning
new characters Corneille thus contrasts the pragmatic necessity of bringing
the play to a close. In this last example, the victim of the irony, as is evident
from the light tone of the sentence, is at least as much the playwright himself
as it is the authority of the rules of dramaturgy.

In the *Épître dédicatoire* to *Don Sanche d'Aragon*, Corneille calls into
question the appropriate stance to take vis-à-vis consecrated authorities by
treating two such authorities in an opposite fashion in rapid succession. After
bowing in the direction of Aristotle, Horace, and even Plautus, Corneille takes
up the subject of whether his play might be called a tragedy. The playwright
thinks not, but does cite Averroès, the Arab philosopher who translated and
wrote a commentary on Aristotle. Averroès offers a very broad definition of
tragedy ("*un art de louer*" 2:552), which may be considered to include *Don
Sanche*. Corneille does not accept that accommodation and essentially refuses
the authority of Averroès:

> Mais j'aurais mauvaise grâce de me prévaloir d'un auteur
> arabe, que je ne connais que sur la foi d'une traduction
> latine, et puisque sa paraphrase abrège le texte d'Arsitote
> en cet article, au lieu de l'étendre, je ferai mieux d'en croire
> ce dernier, qui ne permet point à cet ouvrage de prendre
> un nom plus relevé, que celui de comédie. (2:552–53)

Just a few lines later he defends the absence of risibility in what he is calling a
comédie by citing Heinsius, who says that laughter does not make a comedy.
In this case, Corneille welcomes the wisdom of authority, and for no other
reason than that Heinsius is an authority: "Après l'autorité d'un si grand
homme je serais coupable de chercher d'autres raisons" (2:553). In essence,
Corneille suggests that he will use authority when it suits him and refuse it
when it does not. The obvious opposition between the treatment Corneille
accords Averroès and Heinsius works to signal irony.

Corneille even pits a consecrated authority against that self-same
authority, creating a gap where one would hardly expect to find one. In the
extremely brief *Au lecteur* preceding *Agésilas*, the playwright foregrounds two
quotes by Horace that express positions that are at least in part contradictory: 1) one ought to consult Greek models day and night, 2) Roman writ-
ers deserve praise for having "osé abandonner les traces des Grecs" (3:563,
Couton's translation). It seems to me that Corneille is saying several things
with this paradoxical pairing of quotes, some of which are ironic. He is seri-

ously using the authority of Horace to argue the importance of invention as well as historical example, and to set out a nuanced relationship between the two. He acknowledges the authority of the ancients and their rules, but shows that the margin between ancients and moderns is both relative and universal. The irony comes from the gap between Horace's two statements and the ironic edge from the context in which these statements appear: Corneille's *Au lecteur* to *Agésilas* in which he implicitly and forcefully defends himself against the rival authority of the *doctes* and their prescriptions. That the playwright does so by citing the authority of Horace, an authority that he renders problematic through partial contradiction, suggests the likelihood of ironic intent on Corneille's part.

Occasionally in these texts Corneille deals with the notion of authority by ironically mocking it. Such *raillerie* is at times subtle and at others obvious, and is often directed at the rules against which he chafes. When the playwright claims that *Cinna* has met with universal approval strictly because the play conforms so well to the rules of *vraisemblance*, even as it strays from the truth (*Examen* 1:910), are we not justified in seeing, along with Forestier (*Génétique* 304–5), a measure of irony? Corneille mocks the issue of *vraisemblance* as it pertains to place in both *Clitandre* and *Andromède*, abandoning authorial control of where the action occurs: "[J]e laisse le lieu de ma Scène au choix du Lecteur" (*Préface* to *Clitandre* 1:96); "[V]ous le [the name of the city] lui donnerez tel qu'il vous plaira" (*Argument* to *Andromède* 2:447), and assures the reader, "[O]ù vous l'aurez une fois placée, elle s'y tiendra" (1:96). He uses the authority of religion ironically by conflating it with the authority of the *doctes*, calling the latter "les grands Réguliers" (*Examen* to *La Galerie du palais* 1:303) and mockingly suggesting that they bring a religious orthodoxy to the issue of dramatic theory. A few lines from the end of the last of the three *Discours*, Corneille concludes, "[V]oilà mes opinions, ou si vous voulez, mes hérésies, touchant les principaux points de l'Art" (3:190). The playwright thereby sets up an opposition between his opinions (which, as we have read throughout the *Discours*, are eminently well reasoned and sound) and the term "hérésies" (with its slight note of hysteria and its complete inappropriateness to the context). The incongruous juxtaposition of the two registers—dramatic theory and religion—provides the irony.

The margins between Corneille and the varied authorities with which he had to contend provide a fruitful site for irony because these margins are vigorously contested and thus regularly subject to evaluation and judgment. In his prefatory texts and writings on dramatic theory we hear Corneille's voice directly, not channeled through the voice of a character, and it is a voice that has repeated recourse to irony throughout his career. In his long struggle with regularity, rules, and the figures of authority standing behind them, both ancient and contemporary, Corneille employs irony in the service of the articulation of his own dramaturgical space. Irony allows Corneille to take a stand against the powerful authorities with which he had to contend, and it provides a potent weapon against those who would constrain him.

*

Margins over which Corneille exerts significant control exist on many scales: between scenes, between acts, between plays, between plays and their sources, between the individual work and the authorities Corneille invokes or with which he must contend. In this chapter we have examined the presence of irony at some of the larger margins. When such margins take on surprising characteristics—difference in place of resemblance, resemblance in place of difference, discontinuity or gaps in place of continuity, *raillerie* in place of respect—we find the possibility of irony. The prospect for irony here is anchored by Corneille's control and even manipulation of the margins in question.

NOTES

[139]It may be worth considering, given that Corneille himself suggests juxtaposing the two plays, that César's possible hypocrisy (discussed in chapter 7) is not without relation to Dorante's mendacity.

[140]"Ainsi les serments liant à jamais le Cid à Chimène et Pauline à Polyeucte apparaissent, dans les œuvres complètes, ironiquement encadrés de désaveux badins" (Mauron 244). See also Serroy ("Préface *Illusion*" 26).

[141]"Common-sense generalizations about the sequel...explicitly place the phenomenon in the marketplace" (Budra and Schellenberg 4). It is thus perhaps not an accident that the topos of money has such a strong presence in *La Suite*.

[142]Cliton recalls Dorante's explanation of his hasty nuptials: "Et le cheval surtout vaut en cette rencontre / Le pistolet ensemble, et l'épée, et la Montre" (ll. 135–6). He even calls attention to structural similarities, as when he notes the recurrence in *La Suite* of the window scene in which Dorante speaks to his beloved in the dark and there is a misidentification: "Ces fenêtres toujours vous ont porté malheur. / Vous y prîtes jadis Clarice pour Lucrèce" (ll. 1552–3). The window scene in *La Suite* involves a misidentification on Mélisse's part: she believes she is talking to Dorante when in fact it is Philiste.

[143]"Cent fois en cette ville aux meilleures maisons / J'en ai fait un bon conte en déguisant les noms, / J'en ai ri de bon cœur, et j'en ai bien fait rire" (*La Suite* ll. 613–15).

[144]"L'obscurité que fait en celle-ci [*La Suite*] le rapport à l'autre a pu contribuer quelque chose à sa disgrâce, y ayant beaucoup de choses qu'on ne peut entendre, si l'on n'a l'idée présente du *Menteur*" (*Examen* to *La Suite* 2:99).

[145]It would appear that it was only shortly before writing the *Examen* to *Le Menteur* in 1660 that Corneille discovered that *La Verdad sospechosa* was in fact written by Alarcón. In this *Examen*, Corneille says of *La Verdad*: "On l'a attribué au fameux Lope de Vègue, mais il m'est tombé depuis peu entre les mains un volume de don

Juan d'Alarcon, où il prétend que cette comédie est à lui, et se plaint des imprimeurs qui l'ont fait courir sous le nom d'un autre" (2:7).

[146]Nadal intuits such a motivation from Corneille's words in the *Suite's Epître*:

> Si j'étais de ceux qui tiennent que la poésie a pour but de profiter aussi bien que de plaire, je tâcherais de vous persuader que celle-ci [*La Suite*] est beaucoup meilleure que l'autre [*Le Menteur*], à cause que Dorante y paraît beaucoup plus honnête homme, et donne des exemples de vertu à suivre, au lieu qu'en l'autre il ne donne que des imperfections à éviter. (2:95) (Nadal 221–22)

Corneille hardly seems to take such charges, if they even existed, seriously, for he goes on to say, "[M]ais pour moi qui tiens avec Aristote et Horace que notre art n'a pour but que le divertissement, j'avoue qu'il [Dorante] est ici bien moins à estimer qu'en la première comédie, puisque avec ses mauvaises habitudes il a perdu presque toutes ses grâces" (2:95).

[147]The confusion and interchangeability of feminine identity in *Le Menteur* contrasts strongly with the idealized unique object in *La Suite du Menteur*; there are similar contrasts in the role of money and the strength of authority in the two plays. However, the ungainly nature of the gaps between the two often resists such simple opposition. For example, Minel opposes the weak authority of the father in the first play with the strong authority of "la justice carcérale, puissante, rigoureuse" in the second (221). It is difficult, though, to reconcile the prison in *La Suite* with Minel's description; Dorante has a steady stream of visitors of both sexes and has no problem obtaining permission to leave for an evening rendezvous. In fact there is no jailor; only a *prévôt* who appears in a single scene. The father's authority in *Le Menteur* may indeed be weak, but the prison in *La Suite* is hardly rigorous or strong.

[148]Out of frustration, perhaps, Serroy moves beyond the play to explain the differences in terms of Corneille's career: "*Le Menteur* et *La Suite du Menteur* représentent précisément ce moment où la tonalité bascule, et où le théâtre de Corneille choisit définitivement sa voie. C'est l'univers tragique qui va l'emporter" ("Préface *Menteur*" 33). It does seem odd, however, to argue for a major turning point in the playwright's œuvre being a play entitled *Suite*.

[149]In 1643–44, *Le Cid* was virtually synonymous with the name Corneille. Staves discusses how this reference, which Corneille removed after the 1656 edition, operates in the play: "Corneille was extremely aware of the artificiality of his own work and seems to have felt compelled to draw attention to it. In lines he gives Dorante about Poitiers he laughs at himself and at the controversy over the *Cid*—thereby also calling attention to the 'playness' of the play in which the lines are spoken (ll. 60–62)" (520).

[150]While Corneille moved to reduce such references in his 1660 edition, he nonetheless retained the majority of them. One explanation for the elimination of the original dénouement may be that the discussion of theatrical matters came at the expense of the plot. Specifically, Dorante's concerns with secrecy regarding Cléandre's murder of his rival in a duel as well as with the details of the courtship of Dorante and Mélisse seem to evaporate amid talk of a sequel.

[151]As the century progressed, almost all dramatic works that made use of music were accompanied by encomiastic prologues (Canova-Green 143).

[152]Stegmann says of this portion of the prologue: "Ce texte courageux ne déplut pas en 1660" (*OC* 593). He notes that later in Louis's reign such criticism would not be tolerated: "En 1690, Campistron rétablit ces vers dans son *Tridate* et ils furent censurés

par la police: la situation était plus sévère et le mécontentement grondait" (593).

[153]Zanger goes even further and calls the image of the country ravaged by war a *topos* of treaty literature (197), while Niderst suggests that Corneille may have sought in this prologue to defend a peace treaty that had been much criticized (3, 1:94).

[154]Zanger notes that the Golden Fleece was also the centerpiece of the fireworks set off for the king and queen's entry into Paris in August 1660. On the other hand, she points out that "Medea and Jason are, however, not found in the allegorical arsenal used by the poets who wrote sonnets for the marriage. Nor are they found in Colletet's early allegorical reports on the treaty negotiation" (99).

[155]Wagner does identify Jason and Louis XIV: "Sous le masque dramatique de Jason se dissimule une présence historique, le grand roi Louis XIV à l'aube de son règne en 1660" ("Évocation" 214). Less directly, Couton suggests, "Le personnage de Jason convenait à un roi jeune et conquérant," and he equates Jason with Apollo, Hercules, and Alexander, other fictional reincarnations of Louis XIV (Corneille 3:1417–18).

[156]Later, in her introduction to an edition of *La Toison d'or*, Wagner takes the opposite position, asserting that there is no tie whatsoever between prologue and play. "La pièce de circonstance qu'est le prologue est ajoutée à la fable et indépendante de celle-ci. C'est une pièce en raccourci…dont l'argument est sans aucun rapport avec l'intrigue de la tragédie et dont les personnages disparaissent à la dernière scène" ("Introduction" 57).

[157]"He [Corneille] would hardly have dared represent Louis XIV by Jason or his Spanish bride by Medea, but he evidently meant to indicate the parallel between Jason's quest and Louis's war, between amorous Medea securing the Fleece for her lover and Marie-Thérèse's bringing peace and territorial gains to her royal mate" (Lancaster 3, 2:503–4). Wygant points out the weakness in Lancaster's argument: "In short, then, the King must be Jason, but the King cannot be Jason" (540).

[158]*Pompée* and *Sertorius* come closest, but Pompée never appears on stage in the former and does not have the lead role in the latter.

[159]In the *Notice* to *Attila*, Couton says: "Corneille aimait que son public eût déjà quelque connaissance du sujet, mais point trop précise, cars alors il serait devenu exigeant" (Corneille 3:1536).

[160]Smith notes that "making a comedy, 'quelque chose d'…enjoué qui ne servît qu'à…divertir', out of *La verdad sospechosa* involved…profound change. Alarcón is rated the sternest moralist among the Spanish dramatists of his generation. An embittered man, he used his plays to present a moral lesson to his contemporaries, especially the degenerate members of the nobility. In *La verdad sospechosa*, lying is shown to be a vice especially dishonorable to a nobleman" (67).

[161]Couton quotes Jornandès, one of Corneille's primary sources, as saying that Attila had "d'innombrables femmes comme c'est l'usage de cette nation" (Corneille 3:1540).

[162]The subject of Sophonisbe was thus well known to seventeenth-century audiences. I discuss Corneille's efforts to rival Mairet in my "Sophonisbe's Seduction: Corneille Writing Against Mairet."

[163]Corneille takes issue with Aristotle's notion of catharsis (3:145–46), suggests that pity precedes terror (3:142–43), and reverses the hierarchy of plot types (3:153).

[164]Couton explains that these excerpts come from a Latin translation by Guillaume Blanc d'Alby of a Greek text written by a monk in Constantinople, itself an abridged version of a history of Rome written by Dion Cassius in the third century AD (Corneille 3:1616).

[165]Lanson says of Corneille, "Il a su trouver dans la *Poétique* d'Aristote et dans les règles tout ce qu'il lui importait d'y trouver, et il a peut-être inventé plus de règles qu'il n'en a subies" (61).

[166]For example, d'Aubignac suggested that Corneille should have had Camille run into Horace's sword rather than allowing a brother to slay his sister. Corneille points out the problem in d'Aubignac's reasoning—Horace should not even have drawn the sword—in the *Examen* to *Horace*, but does not utter d'Aubignac's name (1:839). Stegmann calls Corneille's silence in this instance "une discrète ironie" (*OC* 248). Similarly, in the same *Examen*, the well-informed reader would know that when Corneille argues that he is making Valère act as a Roman, not a Frenchman, would (1:843), he is attacking d'Aubignac who sought to reconcile ancient and modern mores.

[167]Discussing the use of *stances* in the *Examen* to *Andromède*, Corneille attacks d'Aubignac without mentioning his name: "[J]e ne puis m'empêcher de demander qui sont les maîtres de cet usage [of *stances*], et qui peut l'établir sur le théâtre, que ceux qui l'ont occupé avec gloire depuis trente ans [Corneille and his cohort, but not d'Aubignac], dont pas un ne s'est défendu de mêler des stances dans quelques-uns des poèmes qu'ils y ont donnés" (2:455–56).

[168]Corneille's decision to acknowledge his contemporaries in this particular context is motivated, in my opinion, by a desire to drown out the importance of Mairet as a source for *Sophonisbe*.

[169]Lyons makes the point that "the term *règle* often appears in Corneille's writing with a curiously indefinite ontological status, as if marked by quotation marks and suspended for examination as a hypothesis" (*Kingdom* 16).

[170]Interestingly, Corneille accused Scudéry of using the same tactic in the "Lettre apologétique du Sieur Corneille" in the context of the *querelle du Cid*: "[V]ous vous êtes fait tout blanc d'Aristote" (1:801).

[171]"Omne tulit punctum qui miscuit utile dulci, / lectorem delectando pariterque monendo" [That which mixes the useful and the agreeable satisfies everyone at the same time by simultaneously giving pleasure to and advising the reader] (*Ars Poeticas* ll. 343–44).

[172]"Je dirai peu de choses de cette Pièce: c'est une galanterie extravagante qui a tant d'irrégularités qu'elle ne vaut pas la peine de la considérer, bien que la nouveauté de ce caprice en ait rendu le succès assez favorable pour ne me repentir pas d'y avoir perdu quelque temps" (1:614).

[173]Concerned, perhaps, that he was not signaling the irony clearly enough, Corneille changed "la meilleure partie de mes juges" to "la meilleure et la plus saine partie de mes juges" when he incorporated the *Épître dédicatoire* into the play's *Examen* in 1660 (2:271).

CHAPTER 9
CONCLUSION

has covered
wide range
of topics

As we look back upon the previous eight chapters, it is difficult not to be struck by the breadth of terrain covered. In terms of irony's sources, while the focus has been decidedly on Corneille's intent, I have examined a range of gradations, from the dramatist's ascertainable intent to be ironic, to possible intent, to a more or less directed choice of ironic reception on the part of the audience. In order to better evaluate the breadth of the irony we have encountered, let us focus on a single play, *Attila*, as emblematic of Corneille's entire dramatic *œuvre*. Revisiting and reuniting the different aspects of irony found in this single play will enable us to see how diverse kinds of irony may be threaded together within a work to create meaning.

close look,
finally at
Attila,
to sum it
up

bring all
categories of verbal
together – very

esp Attila himself
as source of irony
– exaggerates
– uses sarcasm
– uses raillerie
– verbal echo
of less
powerful
chars

Attila brings together almost all of the various categories of irony we have examined. In reviewing them, I would like to take special note of the large role that the eponymous hero takes as a source of irony. Attila dominates the different types of verbal irony in the play. It is because of the exaggeration in his opening words to Ardaric and Valamir that we first suspect irony on his part ("Rois amis d'Attila, soutiens de ma puissance, /…" ll. 73–76). Later Attila verges on sarcasm when he calls the two men "nobles gladiateurs" (l. 1545) and "mes illustres amis" (l. 1515), and he is frankly sarcastic when he tells Honorie "Et remerciez-moi de suivre ainsi vos lois" (l. 1240) concerning a "suitable" marriage partner for whoever refuses to wed the king. Attila uses *raillerie* with the two dispossessed kings, mocking them for not being sufficiently devoted to him to kill his rival (ll. 1519–22). Valamir and Ardaric explicitly place Attila's comments in that ironic framework when the first says to the second as soon as the tyrant leaves the stage, "À l'inhumanité joindre la raillerie, / C'est à son dernier point porter la barbarie" (ll. 1529–30). Attila assails Honorie with the verbal echo of her words (ll. 1237 and 1069) as well as reversing her cruel proposal to marry Ildione to his captain of the guards and applying it to her ("Songez donc sans murmure à cet illustre choix [marrying Attila or Octar]" l. 1239). He suggests a similar reversal as he warns Ildione, "Si vos tyrans d'appas retiennent ma franchise, / Je puis l'être [tyrannical] comme eux de qui me tyrannise" (ll. 889–90). Attila's last word in the scene where he tells Ardaric to kill Valamir or be killed is the highly incongruous "ma tendresse" (l. 1362). Irony is thus clearly a weapon of choice for the tyrant. While the two captive kings do not employ verbal

weapon of
choice for
tyrant

irony, Honorie and Ildione make minor forays into this domain of a fashion in keeping with their respective personalities. Ildione's irony is gentle: she teases Attila for his explanation of his choice to marry Honorie: "Ses honneurs [Honorie's projected marriage to Attila] près des miens [Attila's affection for Ildione] ne sont qu'honneurs frivoles, / Ils n'ont que des effets, j'ai les belles paroles" (ll. 849–50). Honorie's verbal irony is more caustic, but she does not direct it against Attila. Instead she attacks Valamir with sarcasm for refusing to avenge her honor: "De l'aimable façon qu'il [Attila] vous traite aujourd'hui / Il a trop mérité ces tendresses pour lui" (ll. 471–72). It is Attila, however, who dominates the verbal irony in the play.

Attila is tied to dramatic irony as well. In act 4, scene 4, the tyrant suggests a number of possible husbands for Ildione to Ardaric, feigning ignorance of the latter's feelings for the young woman. Like all examples of stage-centered dramatic irony, the author stands behind the character and addresses the audience. Typically in such a situation, the onstage source of the dramatic irony either has an onstage audience for that irony (Nicomède addressing Attale in Laodice's presence, *Nicomède* 1.1) or is completely unaware of the ironic dimension. Here, there is no onstage audience for Attila's irony—Ardaric and Attila are alone—yet Attila is knowingly ironic. Thus, Attila's intended dramatic irony makes him a kind of double for the playwright as the onstage function of his dramatic irony can only be for his own pleasure.

In several respects, however, Attila is more the victim of irony than its source. Casting himself as the scourge of God, chosen to cover the the earth in blood ("Et mon bras dont il fait aujourd'hui son tonnerre / D'un déluge de sang couvre pour lui la Terre," ll. 1581–82), Attila will instead be made the victim of the irony of fate: the blood in question will be his own as he, rather than his intended victims, is destroyed. While completely unaware of the fatal irony that awaits him, Attila does seem to acknowledge his own vulnerability, but only in the sentimental domain. He fears the fundamental differences between himself and Ildione and envisions her power in terms of ironic reversals:

> Quand je voudrai punir vous saurez pardonner,
> Vous refuserez grâce où j'en voudrai donner,
> Vous envoierez la paix où je voudrai la guerre,
> Vous saurez par mes mains conduire le tonnerre.
>
> (ll. 831–34)

Corneille broadens the ironic potential of Attila's feelings by making his lover's discourse glaringly incongruous in the mouth of the wily and aging warrior.

The irony in this play is not limited to Attila as its source or its victim. Although irony of fate is Attila's alone to suffer, situational irony is widespread. Valamir does not acknowledge the irony of his description of the Roman kings Arcadius and Honorius who, having each received half of the Roman empire, give it over to others to rule, "À ces deux Majestés ne laissant que le nom" (l. 200). Despite the prophecies concerning their glorious futures, Ardaric and Valamir bear a telling resemblance to Arcadius and Honorius, as even their names suggest. Nor does Honorie acknowledge the situational irony in the fact that she reacts to the constraints that Attila's tyrannical power puts on her ability to marry Valamir by demanding Octar's betrayal of his master if the latter hopes to marry the woman he loves (4.1). She is thus just as tyrannical as her tyrant. Furthermore, the repeated allegorical allusions to Louis IV in the prophecies concerning Méroüée give an ironic cast to *Attila* in a completely different fashion. These allusions function not within the play's action, but in the margin between it and the world in which it was performed. Similarly, Attila's consultation scene with the two kings during which he asks for their advice about whom to marry (1.2) echoes, in a parodic fashion, the famous scene in *Cinna* where Auguste asks his advisors whether he should abdicate the throne.

While certainly not limited to Attila, the irony in this play centers around him in three respects. First, he is the central pole around which the complex symmetry of the characters is arrayed. The high degree of symmetrical patterning suggests irony. Surrounded by two kings, two fiancées, three sets of lovers, Attila has all the power but is ironically the odd man out. Second, the plot hinges on the tragic irony of his massive hemorrhage. Finally, Attila is an ironic figure through his embodiment of excess and exaggeration. He speaks an exceptionally large number of lines (555.3 or thirty-one percent of the total), and dominates the stage as well as the action. He makes outsized claims to be the arm of divine retribution, in a line of descent that stretches from the biblical flood to the final judgment day to come. Incongruously, Attila's surprising occasional resemblance to Matamore bespeaks exaggeration as well.[174]

In his ironic distance from the other characters, in his superior power, in his manipulation of the symmetrical patterns that surround him, Attila bears a striking resemblance to the playwright. When we look more closely we can see the outlines, not of two, but of three competing ironists: Attila, Corneille, and God. All three judge, all three mock their creations. The divine presence is manifest in this play as it is in few others: only *Polyeucte* and perhaps *Cinna* could be considered comparable in Corneille's œuvre. Even *Théodore*, which Corneille calls a *tragédie chrétienne*, gives no clear sign of divine intervention beyond Didyme's perhaps inspired use of disguise to save Théodore from rape. In *Attila*, God's hand is clearly seen in the blood that flows from Attila's nose. Considering who is in charge of events here reveals much about the play's irony. Attila, in his tyrannical manipulation of the two kings and the two fiancées, gives every sign of being in charge. It is only in the ironic reversal of the dénouement that Attila's power is thwarted: one of the greatest ironists of Corneille's theater becomes the victim of irony, a *trompeur trompé*. God patently operates as an ironist in *Attila* as He takes control of the action from the tyrant with the very tool—blood—that Attila claimed God had delegated to him in order to do divine work. On another level entirely, however, Corneille himself is the supreme ironist of the play. The playwright creates the ironic tyrant and the ironic God, as well as the ironies that the second imposes on the first. I contend that the relationship between these three figures is a reflection of the role of irony in Corneille's theater, the extent of its reach, and its close ties to the playwright's central preoccupation with power. Irony enables Corneille to occupy the role of the cruel tyrant and the supreme divine being simultaneously.

*

Irony is not a systematic feature of Corneille's dramaturgy.[175] In *Attila* as throughout the playwright's plays and writings on the theater, irony appears in different forms and takes on a smaller or larger role depending on the context. *Attila* is unusual insofar as it incorporates many types of irony, but despite such variety certain kinds of irony predominate, specifically, verbal and situational irony, which work to construct a double role for Attila as ironist and victim of irony. While not as widespread as in *Attila*, irony permeates Corneille's theater; every one of his plays avails itself of at least some of the resources irony affords.

We have considered at great length the double at the heart of all irony, the relationship of intent and reception, and the degree to which doubt is inherent to all but the most blatant forms of irony. It is important to keep in mind as well two other features of irony that may help to explain why Corneille would have been attracted to it, one benefiting the spectator and the other the author. The first is the pleasure afforded by irony. The spectator is made to feel intelligent for "getting" the double meaning, grasping the double situation or context. The audience experiences the pleasure of collusion whenever it perceives irony; the playwright seems to be winking knowingly at us, making an allusion for our personal benefit almost as a kind of aside. The critical, unameliorative tenor of most irony only increases the spectators' and the readers' pleasure by allowing us to share a moment of superiority with the playwright. Irony thus draws the audience in, giving them the significant role of receiver in the triangular structure of irony. While the ability to engage one's audience certainly benefits the author, irony offers the playwright an even greater advantage, that of freedom. Berrendonner says that irony appears "dans l'ordre de la parole, comme le dernier refuge de la liberté individuelle" (239). Corneille uses irony as a gesture of liberation from a broad range of constraints, from univocal discourse, to the ponderous seriousness of certain subjects, to the at times onerous rules of seventeenth-century French theater. Irony frees the playwright to attack his enemies in his prefatory texts while providing the cover of plausible deniability; it also makes room for *raillerie* in areas that are generally taken very seriously. That freedom was an abiding concern for Corneille is evident in the numerous discussions he undertakes regarding dramatic practice. Irony offers the freedom to speak while cloaking oneself with the doubt that it engenders and thereby protecting oneself from the full consequences of such liberty.

*

Considering irony within the scope of Corneille's career, we find that it is a component of his theater throughout his many years as a playwright, manifested to differing degrees and in varying forms. We may note, however, a relative paucity in the early plays and a general tendency towards a more sizable presence of irony with the passage of time. Indeed, that same development holds for both comedy and the serious plays, albeit shifted, given that Corneille's career as a comic playwright is concentrated in his early years; his last comedy is written almost thirty years before he stops writing for the theater. While there is little irony in *Mélite*, the presence of irony increases slowly in the first five comedies, becomes significant in *L'Illusion comique*, primarily through the shift of diegetic levels and the ironic heroism of Matamore, and takes on a major role in *Le Menteur* and *La Suite du Menteur* as well as in the relationship between these last two. The same general line of development holds true for the tragedies and other non-comedies, although in a far less linear or incremental fashion. The tetralogy contains significant *possible* irony, from Sabine's demands to be sacrificed, to Auguste's refusal of Livie's advice, to the competing registers in *Polyeucte*. Once we move beyond that group of plays, however, beginning with *Pompée*, irony becomes far more frequently *evident* as well as *possible*. The global movement from absence to presence of irony is indicative of Corneille's increased experience and sophistication as a playwright. The development I am suggesting is by no means a steady one, as Corneille experiments with different kinds of irony, in different proportions, and for different ends. Irony plays a decidedly larger role in certain of the post-tetralogy group of plays—*Pompée, Rodogune, Nicomède, Œdipe, Attila*—than in others. Certain types of irony dominate as well: situational irony attends a number of deaths (e.g., Sertorius, Attila, Suréna) and it plays a role in the reversals of several less violent dénouements (e.g., *Don Sanche d'Aragon, Nicomède, Tite et Bérénice*). Dramatic irony, whether stage-centered—a major source of tension in P*olyeucte, Rodogune,* and *Héraclius*—or authorial, with a large role in *Pompée, Œdipe,* and *Sophonisbe,* is widespread. Verbal irony is a universal feature of Corneille's theater, conveying a broad range of attitudes, from playful teasing and *raillerie* to hostile aggression. In its flexibility and in the ambiguity of its invariably double discourse, verbal irony is a potent vehicle for conveying the complex tensions between characters. The significant presence of irony coming from the three categories I have identified as "evident" establishes the sizable role of irony in Corneille's dramaturgy, belies the image of the playwright as a stolid dullard bequeathed to us by Fontenelle, and strengthens the claims of the possible ironies that we have examined in the second part of this study.

Certain specific types of irony are particularly characteristic of Corneille. He uses verbal echoic mention widely. The device of one character's words closely echoing another's has dramatic force in his hands, as the tension and hostility between the characters are enacted through the double voicing of the ironic echo. Corneille also employs irony at his own expense, making explicit and deprecating references to his own work in several comedies, parodying his own discourse and dramatic high points, and at times taking an excessively humble stance in his prefatory material. A third particularly Cornelian variety of irony is the denigration of the figure of the hero through exaggeration and parody. The emblematic figure of Rodrigue has a double in Matamore and this double representation of heroism, endowed with ironic similarities, reverberates through a number of the plays that follow. This particular variety of irony is anchored at the heart of Cornelian thematics: the subject of the hero and heroism runs through much of his theater and has been an abiding preoccupation of scholars of his work.

Revealing too are those points where there is friction between Corneille's dramaturgic or thematic preoccupations and an ironic turn of mind. Corneille's affinity for surprise both abets and runs counter to irony. Surprise and irony are compatible when the surprise in question entails incongruity of any sort, as in the cases of the outrageous demands made by Sabine, Rodogune, and Rodelinde, because the incongruity itself is surprising. Situational irony thrives on elements of surprise: witness Attila's final fatal nosebleed. Chronologically based character contradiction often entails surprise at the moment of reversal, as for example when Bérénice, in the last scene of *Tite et Bérénice,* suddenly decides to leave Rome and abandon her love for Tite. Irony through exaggeration overlaps comfortably with surprise because both involve the dramatist's desire to go too far. Like irony, surprise destabilizes, throws one off balance. Surprise and dramatic irony, however, appear to be incompatible. Dramatic irony is based on knowledge and surprise requires inadequate knowledge, yet Corneille alternates the two in a daring fashion in *Œdipe*. He makes frequent use of what the audience already knows to create dramatic irony and also repeatedly astonishes the audience with elements that are altered from their traditional versions and thus completely unexpected. In contrast, the irony of fate is profoundly incompatible with surprise. The presence of a controlling superior force makes events inevitable. Certainly the characters are surprised, but not the audience, and the latter is Corneille's intended target for surprise. The friction between surprise and the irony of fate helps to explain why the latter is relatively rare in Corneille's theater. For Racine, who is intrigued by the implacable hand of destiny—whether historical, mythological, or religious—irony of fate is, on the contrary, central. It is on this point that the two playwrights' use of irony differs most profoundly.

Significant friction between irony and Corneille's dramatic practice is not limited to the issue of surprise. The playwright's affection for the sublime is often incompatible with irony, particularly if the latter involves *raillerie*. Just like hyperbole, the sublime shares with certain forms of irony a strong element of exaggeration and thus may lead to uncomfortable interpretive uncertainty. This is related to the case of ironic heroism disussed above as being particularly characteristic of Corneille's irony. It is hardly controversial to assert that Corneille seeks to have certain of his heroic figures attain the sublime. However, it goes against the grain of conventional views of heroism to consider such heroes in ironic terms. The more these heroes leave themselves open to an ironic interpretation, through resemblance to Matamore or in some other fashion, the more their sublimity or their heroic status is called into question. Even more friction is raised by the relationship between irony and religion. While it is not within my purview to question or even discuss the sincerity of Corneille's religious convictions, I note the significant gap between the devout believer and the ironist. This friction is manifested most clearly in the gaps we explored in the two religious plays, *Polyeucte* and *Théodore*.

It is not an accident that irony provides appreciable friction with significant features of Corneille's dramaturgy. In the paradox of that friction and those seemingly patent oppositions the true power of irony can be espied. I propose that we understand these types of irony in Corneille's theater within a paradigm not of either/or, but rather of both/and, itself characteristic of irony. Corneille and his theater occupy both positions, at times simultaneously. Corneille seeks the sublime *and* mocks the sublime; his characters embody serious explorations of the nature of heroism *and* the playwright turns an ironic eye on heroism itself; Corneille is serious *and* he winks ironically at the audience. This paradoxical quality of irony, I believe, contributes strongly to Corneille's enduring fascination as a playwright. Irony, in its play of paradox and double meaning, intent and reception, aggression and *raillerie*, both embodies and serves as a metaphor for Corneille's complexity, subtlety, and undecidability.

Notes

[174]Aside from other examples considered in chapter 6, we also find his words to Ildione: "Quels climats voulez-vous sous votre obéissance? / Si la Gaule vous plaît, vous la partagerez, / J'en offre la conquête à vos yeux adorés" (ll. 874–76).
[175]It is not in the nature of irony to be systematic (see Jankélévitch, *L'Ironie* [1964] 176).

BIBLIOGRAPHY

Abraham, Claude. "L'Envers de la médaille: Dialectique et parodie chez Corneille." *PFSCL* 11.21 (1984): 349–76.

———. *Pierre Corneille*. New York: Twayne, 1972.

Abrams, M. H. *A Glossary of Literary Terms*. New York: Holt, Rinehart and Winston, 1971.

Adam, Antoine. *Histoire de la littérature française au XVIIᵉ siècle*. 5 vols. Paris: Del Duca, 1962.

Allemann, Beda. "De l'ironie en tant que principe littéraire." *Poétique* 36 (1978): 385–98.

Allentuch, Harriet Ray. "Reflections on Women in the Theater of Corneille." *Kentucky Romance Quarterly* 21 (1974): 97–111.

Aristotle. *Poetics*. New York: Hill and Wang, 1961.

Aston, Elaine and George Savona. *Theatre as Sign-System*. London: Routledge, 1991.

Baker, Susan Read. *Dissonant Harmonies*. Tübingen: Gunter Narr, 1990.

———. "Sounds of Silence: Faltering Speech in Racine's *Bérénice* and Corneille's *Tite et Bérénice*." *Racine et/ou le classicisme*. Ed. Ronald Tobin. Tübingen: Gunter Narr, 2001. 223–32.

———. "Strategies of Seduction in *Cinna*." *Homage to Paul Bénichou*. Ed. Sylvie Romanowski and Monique Bilezikian. Birmingham, AL: Summa, 1994. 75–91.

———. "*Théodore, Vierge et Martyre* (1645): A Case of Prostitution." *Degré second* 10 (1986): 1–15.

Barnwell, H.T. "Appendix C: Towards an Appreciation of *Pompée* as Tragedy." *Pompée*. By Pierre Corneille. Oxford: Oxford University Press, 1971. 200–205.

———. "Introduction." *Pompée*. By Pierre Corneille. Oxford: Oxford University Press, 1971. 7–66.

Bénichou, Paul. "Formes et significations dans la *Rodogune* de Corneille." *Le Débat* 31 (1984): 82–102.

Bergson, Henri. *Le Rire. Essai sur la signification du comique*. 1900. Paris: Presses Universitaires de France, 1940.

Berrendonner, Alain. *Éléments de pragmatique linguistique*. Paris: Minuit, 1981.

Biet, Christian. "Œdipe dans la tragédie du XVIIᵉ siècle: Mémoire mythologique, mémoire juridique; mémoire généalogique." *PFSCL* 21.41 (1994): 499–518.

Boorsch, Jean. "Remarques sur la technique dramaturgique de Corneille." *Yale Romanic Studies* 18 (1941): 101–62.

Booth, Wayne. *The Rhetoric of Irony*. Chicago: University of Chicago Press, 1974.

Bouvet, Alphonse. "Hommage à Sabine." *Australian Journal of French Studies* 1 (1964): 119–33.

Budra, Paul and Betty A. Schellenberg. "Introduction." *Part Two: Reflections on the Sequel.* Ed. Paul Budra and Betty A. Schellenberg. Toronto: University of Toronto Press, 1998. 3–18.

Cairncross, John. "*Polyeucte*: Pièce ambiguë." *PFSCL* 11.21 (1984): 559–73.

Canova-Green, Marie-Claude. "Melpomène, Thalie, Euterpe, et Clio: La Guerre des muses dans les prologues des opéras louisquatorziens, 1672–1715." *Continuum* 5 (1993): 143–56.

Carlin, Claire. *Pierre Corneille Revisited*. New York: Twayne, 1998.

Carmichael, Thomas. "'After the Fact': Marx, the Sequel, Postmodernism, and John Barth's *LETTERS*." *Part Two: Reflections on the Sequel.* Ed. Paul Budra and Betty A. Schellenberg. Toronto: University of Toronto Press, 1998. 174–88.

Chatman, Seymour. "Ironic Perspective: Conrad's *Secret Agent*." *New Perspectives on Narrative Perspective*. Ed. Willie Van Peer and Seymour Chatman. Albany: State University of New York Press, 2001. 117–31.

Chauviré, R. "Doutes à l'égard de *Polyeucte*." *French Studies* 2 (1948): 1–34.

Cherpack, Clifton. "The Captive Audience in *L'Illusion Comique*." *MLN* 81 (1966): 342–44.

Clarke, D. R. "Heroic Prudence and Reason in the 17th Century: Auguste's Pardon of Cinna." *Forum for Modern Language Studies* 1 (1965): 328–38.

———. "Plutarch's Contribution to the Invention of Sabine in Corneille's *Horace*." *Modern Language Review* 89 (1994): 39–49.

Corlouer, Marine. "*Don Sanche d'Aragon*: Ambiguïtés d'une leçon politique." *Pierre Corneille: Ambiguïtés*. Ed. Michel L. Bareau. Edmonton, AB: Alta, 1989. 55–68.

Corneille, Pierre. *Œuvres complètes*. Ed. Georges Couton. 3 vols. Paris: Gallimard, 1980–87.

Cornic, Sylvain. "*Ad limina templis Polymniae*: Les Fonctions du prologue d'opéra chez Quinault." *Recherches des jeunes dix-septiémistes*. Ed. Charles Mazouer. Tübingen: Gunter Narr, 2000. 47–62.

Couleau, Christèle. "L'Ironie, principe de réversibilité du récit." *Envers Balzaciens*. Poitiers: Licorne, 2001. 151–64.

d'Aubignac, François Hédelin. *La Pratique du théâtre*. 1657. Geneva: Slatkine Reprints, 1971.

Dalla Valle, Daniela. "Le Mythe d'Œdipe dans le théâtre français jusqu'à l'*Œdipe* de Corneille." *XVIIᵉ siècle* 190 (1996): 89–101.

Defaux, Gérard. "*Cinna*, tragédie chrétienne? Essai de mise au point." *MLN* 119 (2004): 718–65.

Delmas, Christian. "Introduction." *Andromède*. By Pierre Corneille. Paris: Didier, 1974. xi–civ.

Desfougères, Anne-Marie. "L'Echec de *Pertharite*." *Pierre Corneille: Actes du colloque tenu à Rouen*. Ed. Alain Niderst. Paris: Presses Universitaires de France, 1985. 501–6.

Doubrovsky, Serge. *Corneille et la dialectique du héros*. Paris: Gallimard, 1963.

Dupriez, Bernard. *Les Procédés littéraires (Dictionnaire)*. Paris: Union Générale d'Éditions, 1984.

Ekstein, Nina. "Metaphors of Mathematics in Corneille's Theater." *Neophilologus* 86 (2002): 197–214.

———. "Pompée's Absence in *La Mort de Pompée*." *Rivista di Letturature Moderne e Comparate* 56 (2003): 259–74.

———. "Sophonisbe's Seduction: Corneille Writing Against Mairet." *EMF: Studies in Early Modern France* 8 (2002): 104–18.

———. "Staging the Tyrant on the Seventeenth-Century French Stage." *PFSCL* 26.50 (1999): 111–29.

———. "Women and Marriage in Corneille's Theater." *La Femme au XVIIe siècle*. Ed. Richard G. Hodgson. Tübingen: Gunter Narr, 2002. 391–405.

Epstein, Nancy P. "Rethinking the Study of Irony in La Fontaine." *Dalhousie French Studies* 37 (1996): 31–39.

Fontenelle, Bernard de. "Vie de M. Corneille." *Œuvres complètes*. Vol. 3. Paris: Fayard, 1989. 83–109.

Forestier, Georges. "Corneille poète d'histoire." *Littératures classiques* 11 supplément (1989): 37–47.

———. "Une Dramaturgie de la gageure." *Revue d'Histoire Littéraire de la France* 5 (1985): 811–19.

———. *Essai de génétique théatrale: Corneille à l'œuvre*. Paris: Klincksieck, 1996.

———. "Ironie et déguisement chez Rotrou: Une Richesse de moyens exemplaire." *PFSCL* 9.17 (1982): 553–70.

———. "Structure de la comédie classique." *Littératures classiques* 27 (1996): 243–57.

Freud, Sigmund. *Le Mot d'esprit et ses rapports avec l'inconscient*. Paris: Gallimard, 1971.

Frye, Northop. *Anatomy of Criticism*. Princeton: Princeton University Press, 1957.

Fumaroli, Marc. "Du *Cid* à *Polyeucte*: Une Dramaturgie du couple." *Héros et orateurs*. Geneva: Droz, 1996. 399–413.

———. "L'Héroïsme cornélien et l'éthique de la magnanimité." *Héros et orateurs*. Geneva: Droz, 1996. 323–49.

———. "Pierre Corneille, fils de son œuvre." *Héros et orateurs*. Geneva: Droz, 1996. 17–61.

———. "Rhétorique et dramaturgie: Le Statut du personnage dans la tragédie cornélienne." *Héros et orateurs*. Geneva: Droz, 1996. 288–322.

Furetière, Antoine. *Dictionnaire universel.* 1690. Ed. Alain Rey. Paris: Robert, 1978.

Garapon, Robert. *La Fantaisie verbale et le comique dans le théâtre français du moyen âge à la fin du dix-septième siècle.* Paris: Armand Colin, 1957.

Gay-Crosier, Raymond. "Régistres de l'ironie gidienne: Le Cas des *Faux-Monnayeurs.*" *Revue des lettres modernes* 1033–1038 (1991): 83–108.

Genette, Gérard. *Palimpsestes.* Paris: Seuil, 1982.

Georges, André. "Importance et signification du rôle de Livie dans *Cinna* de P. Corneille." *Romanic Review* 79 (1988): 269–82.

Gérard, Albert. "'Vice Ou Vertu': Modes of Self-Assertion in Corneille's *La Mort de Pompée.*" *Revue des langues vivantes* 31 (1965): 323–52.

Géraud, Violaine. "L'Ironie dans *Les Illustres Françaises* de Robert Challe." *L'Information grammaticale* 57 (1996): 16–20.

Goode, William O. "*Médée* and Jason: Hero and Nonhero in Corneille's *Médée.*" *French Review* 51 (1978): 804–15.

Goodkin, Richard E. *Birth Marks: The Tragedy of Primogeniture in Pierre Corneille, Thomas Corneille, and Jean Racine.* Philadelphia: University of Pennsylvania Press, 2000.

Gossip, C. J. "*Attila* and Tragedy." *Seventeenth-Century French Studies* 9 (1988): 152–65.

———. *Corneille: Cinna.* London: Grant & Cutler, 1998.

Green, D. H. *Irony in the Medieval Romance.* Cambridge: Cambridge University Press, 1979.

Greenberg, Mitchell. *Corneille, Classicism and the Ruses of Symmetry.* Cambridge: Cambridge University Press, 1986.

———. "*Horace*, Classicism and Female Trouble." *Romanic Review* 74 (1983): 271–92.

Hamon, Philippe. *L'Ironie littéraire.* Paris: Hachette, 1996.

Harvey, Lawrence E. "Corneille's *Horace*, a Study in Tragic and Artistic Ambivalence." *Studies in Seventeenth-Century French Literature Presented to Morris Bishop.* Ed. Jean-Jacques Demorest. Ithaca, NY: Cornell University Press, 1962. 65–97.

Hémon, Félix. *Théâtre de Pierre Corneille.* Paris: Librairie Ch. Delagrave, 1886–87.

Herland, Louis. *Horace ou la naissance de l'homme.* Paris: Minuit, 1952.

———. "L'Imprévisible et l'inexplicable dans la conduite du héros comme ressort tragique chez Corneille." *Le Théâtre tragique.* Ed. Jean Jacquot. Paris: CNRS, 1962. 239–49.

Horace. *Satires, Epistles and Ars Poetica.* 1926. Cambridge, MA: Harvard University Press, 1978.

Hubert, Judd D. *Corneille's Performative Metaphors.* Charlottesville: Rookwood, 1997.

———. "The Function of Performative Narratives in Corneille's *La Mort de Pompée.*" *Semiotica* 51 (1984): 115–31.

Hutcheon, Linda. *Irony's Edge: The Theory and Politics of Irony.* London: Routledge, 1994.

———. *A Theory of Parody.* New York: Methuen, 1985.

Jankélévitch, Vladimir. *L'Ironie.* Paris: Félix Alcan, 1936.

———. *L'Ironie.* Paris: Flammarion, 1964.

Jaouën, Françoise. "La Faute à Corneille." *Les Cahiers* 21 (1996): 58–68.

Kaufer, David S. "Irony, Interpretive Form, and the Theory of Meaning." *Poetics Today* 4.3 (1983): 451–64.

Kawin, Bruce F. *Telling It Again and Again: Repetition in Literature and Film.* Ithaca, NY: Cornell University Press, 1972.

Kerbrat-Orecchioni, Catherine. "Ironie comme trope." *Poétique* 41 (1980): 108–27.

———. "Problèmes de l'ironie." *Linguistique et Sémiologie* 2 (1976): 9–46.

Kierkegaard, Søren. *The Concept of Irony.* 1841. Princeton: Princeton University Press, 1989.

Knight, R. C. "*Andromaque* et l'ironie de Corneille." *Actes du premier congrès international racinien.* Uzès: Peladan, 1963. 21–27.

———. *Corneille's Tragedies. The Role of the Unexpected.* Savage, MD: Barnes and Noble, 1991.

———. "Othon the Unheroic Hero." *PFSCL* 11.21 (1984): 593–609.

———. "*Quand un héros soupire*: The Sad Case of Sertorius." *Humanitas.* Ed. Davis, R. Leslie, John H. Gillespie, and Robert McBride. Coleraine: New University of Ulster, 1984. 23–33.

Knox, Norman. "On the Classification of Ironies." *Modern Philology* 70 (1972): 53–62.

La Charité, Raymond C. and Virginia A. La Charité. "Corneille's *Suréna*: An Option for a New Dramaturgy." *Romance Notes* 10 (1968): 103–5.

Lagarde, François. "Le Sacrifice de la femme chez Corneille." *Stanford French Review* 12.2-3 (1988): 187–204.

La Harpe, Jean-François de. *Poésie, Eloquence.* Vol. 2 of *Lycée, ou Cours de littérature ancienne et moderne.* Paris: H. Agasse, 1799–1805.

Lancaster, Henry Carrington. *A History of French Dramatic Literature in the Seventeenth Century.* 5 pts. New York: Gordian Press, 1966.

Lang, Candace D. *Irony / Humor.* Baltimore: Johns Hopkins University Press, 1988.

Lanson, Gustave. *Corneille.* Paris: Hachette, 1898.

Leggatt, Alexander. "Killing the Hero: Tamburlaine and Falstaff." *Part Two: Reflections on the Sequel.* Ed. Paul Budra and Betty A. Schellenberg. Toronto: University of Toronto Press, 1998. 53–67.

Lemaître, Jules. "Pierre Corneille." *Histoire de la langue et de la littérature française des origines à 1900.* Ed. L. Petit de Julleville. Paris: Armand Colin, 1897. 262–345.

Lockert, Lacy. *Studies in French-Classical Tragedy.* Nashville, TN: Vanderbilt University Press, 1958.

Louvat, Bénédicte and Marc Escola. "Le Statut de l'épisode dans la tragédie classique." *XVIIe siècle* 50 (1998): 453–70.

Louvat-Molozay, Bénédicte. "De l'oracle de tragédie comme procédé dramaturgique: L'Exemple de Corneille." *Mythe et histoire dans le théâtre classique: Hommage à Christian Delmas.* Ed. Fanny Népote-Desmarres. Paris: Champion, 2002. 395–416.

Lyons, John D. *Kingdom of Disorder: The Theory of Tragedy in Classical France.* West Lafayette, IN: Purdue University Press, 1999.

———. *A Theatre of Disguise: Studies in French Baroque Drama, 1630–1660.* Columbia, SC: French Literature Publications, 1978.

———. *The Tragedy of Origins: Pierre Corneille and Historical Perspective.* Stanford: Stanford University Press, 1996.

Magné, Bernard. "L'Ironie dans *Iphigénie* de Racine." *PFSCL* 9.16 (1982): 237–52.

Mairet, Jean. *La Sophonisbe.* Ed. Jacques Scherer. Paris: Gallimard, 1975. Vol. 1 of *Théâtre du XVIIe siècle.*

Mallinson, G. J. *The Comedies of Corneille.* Manchester: Manchester University Press, 1984.

Margitic, Milorad R. *Essai sur la mythologie du Cid.* University, MS: Romance Monographs, 1976.

Marin, Louis. *Des pouvoirs de l'image.* Paris: Seuil, 1993.

Marty-Laveaux, Charles. *Œuvres de Pierre Corneille.* 12 vols. Paris: Hachette, 1862–68.

Maskell, David. "Corneille's *Examens* Examined: The Case of *Horace.*" *French Studies* 51 (1997): 267–80.

Matzat, Wolfgang. "Mythe et identité dans le théâtre classique: L'*Œdipe* cornélien et l'*Iphigénie* racinien." *Les Lieux de mémoire et la fabrique de l'œuvre.* Ed. Volker Kapp. Tübingen: *PFSCL,* 1993. 161–72.

Mauron, Charles. *Des Métaphores obsédantes au mythe personnel.* Paris: Corti, 1962.

May, Georges. *Tragédie cornélienne, tragédie racinienne: Étude sur les sources de l'intérêt dramatique.* Urbana: University of Illinois Press, 1948.

McDermott, Helen Bates. "The Uses of Irony in *Othon.*" *French Review* 51 (1978): 648–56.

McFarlane, I. D. "Corneille's *Œdipe.*" *Myth and Its Making in the French Theatre.* Ed. E. Freeman, H. Mason, M. O'Regan, and S. W. Taylor. Cambridge: Cambridge University Press, 1988. 44–56.

———. "Notes on the Rhetoric of *Horace.*" *The French Language.* Ed. T. G. S. Combe and P. Rickard. London: Harrap, 1970. 182–210.

Merlin-Kajman, Hélène. *L'Absolutisme dans les lettres et la théorie des deux corps.* Paris: Honoré Champion, 2000.

Minel, Emmanuel. "Du *Menteur* à sa *Suite*: De la valeur comme vaine sociabilité à la valeur en liberté surveillée ou d'une théâtralité problématique à une théâtralité autonome." *PFSCL* 25.48 (1998): 213–24.

Molière. *Œuvres complètes.* Ed. Georges Couton. 2 vols. Paris: Gallimard, 1971.

Monson, Don A. "Andreas Capellanus and the Problem of Irony." *Speculum* 63 (1988): 539–72.

Montaigne. *Œuvres complètes*. Paris: Gallimard, 1962.

Morel, Jacques. "La Bruyère écrivain ironique." *Littératures classiques* 13 supplément (1989): 55–62.

Morrison, Ian R. "Un Aspect de *Cinna*: Cinna orateur." *Les Lettres romanes* 50 (1996): 181–91.

Muecke, D. C. "Analyses de l'ironie." *Poétique* 36 (1978): 478–94.

———. *Irony and the Ironic*. London: Methuen, 1982.

Nadal, Octave. *Le Sentiment de l'amour dans l'œuvre de Pierre Corneille*. Paris: Gallimard, 1948.

New Shorter Oxford English Dictionary. Oxford: Oxford University Press, 1996.

Newmark, Peter. "A New View of Horace." *French Studies* 10.1 (1956): 1–10.

Niderst, Alain. "Notice à *La Toison d'or*." *Théâtre Complet*. By Pierre Corneille. Vol. 3, Pt. 1. Rouen: Publication de l'Université de Rouen, 1986. 93–97.

Norman, Buford. *Touched by the Graces: The Libretti of Philippe Quinault in the Context of French Classicism*. Birmingham, AL: Summa, 2001.

Nurse, Peter. "Introduction." *Horace*. By Pierre Corneille. London: Harrap, 1963.

Oxford English Dictionary Online. 2nd Ed. Oxford: Oxford University Press, 2006.

Paillet-Guth, Anne-Marie. "L'Ironie dans *Nicomède*." *L'Information grammaticale* 76 (1998): 20–24.

Pascal, Blaise. *Pensées*. Ed. Philippe Sellier. Paris: Livre de Poche, 2000.

Pavel, Thomas G. *La Syntaxe narrative des tragédies de Corneille*. Paris: Klincksieck, 1976.

Perrin, Laurent. *L'Ironie mise en trope*. Paris: Kimé, 1996.

Petit de Julleville, L. *Théâtre choisi de Corneille*. Paris: Hachette, 1896.

Picciola, Liliane. "Notice." *La Suite du Menteur. Théâtre complet*. By Pierre Corneille. Vol. 2. Paris: Garnier, 1996. 291–303.

Prigent, Michel. *Le Héros et l'état dans la tragédie de Pierre Corneille*. Paris: Presses Universitaires de France, 1986.

Racine, Jean. *Théâtre complet*. Paris: Garnier Frères, 1980.

Ramazani, Vaheed K. "Lacan / Flaubert: Towards a Psychopoetics of Irony." *Romanic Review* 80 (1989): 548–59.

Rat, Maurice, ed. *Théâtre complet*. By Pierre Corneille. 3 vols. Paris: Garnier, 1960.

Rathé, Alice. "Le Cercle de famille: Rapports de forces sur la scène cornélienne." *PFSCL* 16.31 (1989): 505–28.

———. "Distribution des rôles dans *Pulchérie*." *Pierre Corneille: Ambiguïtés*. Ed. Michel L. Bareau. Edmonton, AB: Alta, 1989. 97–104.

———. *La Reine se marie: Variations sur un thème dans l'œuvre de Corneille*. Geneva: Droz, 1990.

Reed, Gervais. "The Unity of Thought, Feeling, and Expression in Corneille's *Cinna*." *Symposium* 44 (1990): 206–21.

Reiss, Timothy J. "La Voix royale: De la violence étatique ou, du privé à la souveraineté dans *Cinna*." *Pierre Corneille: Ambiguïtés*. Ed. Michel L. Bareau. Edmonton, AB: Alta, 1989. 41–53.

Rimmon-Kenan, Shlomith. "The Paradoxical Status of Repetition." *Poetics Today* 1.4 (1980): 151–59.

Rosenmeyer, Thomas. "Irony and Tragic Choruses." *Ancient and Modern: Essays in Honor of Gerald F. Else*. Ed. John H. D'Arms and John W. Eadie. Ann Arbor: Center for Coordination of Ancient and Modern Studies, 1977. 30–44.

Rostand, François. *L'Imitation de soi chez Corneille*. Paris: Boivin, 1946.

Rousset, Jean. *Forme et Signification*. Paris: José Conti, 1962.

———. *La Littérature de l'âge baroque en France*. Paris: José Corti, 1953.

Scherer, Jacques. *Le Théâtre de Corneille*. Paris: Nizet, 1984.

Schlumberger, Jean. *Plaisir à Corneille*. Paris: Gallimard, 1936.

Schoentjes, Pierre. *Poétique de l'ironie*. Paris: Seuil, 2001.

Scott, J. W. "The 'Irony' of *Horace*." *French Studies* 13 (1959): 11–17.

Scott, Paul. "Manipulating Martyrdom: Corneille's (Hetero)Sexualization of *Polyeucte*." *Modern Language Review* 99 (2004): 328–38.

Sellstrom, A. Donald. "*La Mort de Pompée*: Roman History and Tasso's Theory of Christian Epic." *PMLA* 97 (1982): 830–43.

Serroy, Jean. "Notice." *Le Menteur et La Suite du Menteur*. By Pierre Corneille. Paris: Folio, 2000. 295–308.

———. "Préface." *L'Illusion comique*. By Pierre Corneille. Paris: Folio, 2000. 7–39.

———. "Préface." *Le Menteur et La Suite du Menteur*. By Pierre Corneille. Paris: Folio, 2000. 7–34.

———. "La Sincérité du Menteur." *Travaux de littérature* 7 (1994): 125–34.

Smith, Christopher. "Towards Coherence in Comedy: Corneille's *Le Menteur*." *Form and Meaning: Aesthetic Coherence in Seventeenth-Century French Drama*. Ed. William D. Howarth, Ian McFarlane, and Margaret McGowan. Amersham: Avebury, 1982. 63–74.

Soare, Antoine. "*Pompée* ou le machiavélisme de l'innocence." *French Forum* 13 (1988): 187–203.

Sperber, Dan and Deirdre Wilson. "Les Ironies comme mentions." *Poétique* 36 (1978): 399–412.

———. *Relevance: Communication and Cognition*. Cambridge: Harvard University Press, 1986.

Staves, Susan. "Liars and Lying in Alarcon, Corneille, and Steele." *Revue de Littérature comparée* 46 (1972): 514–27.

Stegmann, André. *L'Héroïsme cornélien*. Paris: Armand Colin, 1968.

———. "L'Humour et l'ironie tragiques de Corneille." *PFSCL* 7 (1977): 323–48.

————. ed. *Œuvres complètes*. By Pierre Corneille. Paris: Seuil, 1963.

Stringfellow, Frank, Jr. *The Meaning of Irony: A Psychoanalytic Investigation*. Albany: State University of New York Press, 1994.

Sutcliffe, F. E. "Le Pardon d'Auguste: Politique et morale dans *Cinna*." *Modern Miscellany Presented to Eugène Vinaver*. Ed. T. E. Lawrenson et al. Manchester: Manchester University Press, 1969. 243–53.

Sweetser, Marie-Odile. *La Dramaturgie de Corneille*. Geneva: Droz, 1977.

————. "Niveaux de la communication et de la création dans les récits du *Menteur*." *PFSCL* 12.23 (1985): 489–502.

Theile, Wolfgang. "La Réception des mythes au XVIIᵉ siècle: L'*Œdipe* de Corneille." *Horizons européens de la littérature française au XVIIᵉ siècle*. Ed. Wolfgang Leiner. Tübingen: Gunter Narr, 1988. 119–25.

Tiefenbrun, Susan. "Blood and Water in *Horace*: A Feminist Reading." *PFSCL* 10.19 (1983): 617–34.

————. *Signs of the Hidden: Semiotic Studies*. Amsterdam: Rodopi, 1980.

Toczyski, Suzanne C. "Two Sisters' Tears: Paralinguistic Protest in *Horace*." *La Rochefoucauld, Mithridate, frères et sœurs*. Ed. Claire Carlin. Tübingen: Gunter Narr, 1998. 221–29.

Triau, Christophe. "*Cinna*: Catastrophe finale et catastrophe initiale." *Seventeenth-Century French Studies* 23 (2001): 81–89.

Ubersfeld, Anne. *Lire le théâtre*. 1978. Paris: Editions Sociales, 1982.

Verhœff, Han. *Les Comédies de Corneille: Une Psycholecture*. Paris: Klincksieck, 1979.

————. *Les Grandes Tragédies de Corneille: Une Psycholecture*. Paris: Lettres Modernes, 1982.

Voltaire. *Commentaires sur Corneille*. Ed. David Williams. *Les Œuvres complètes de Voltaire*. 53–55. Banbury: Voltaire Foundation; Thorpe Mandeville House, 1975.

Wagner, Marie-France. "Évocation de Louis XIV sous le masque dramatique de Jason triomphant de l'oracle." *PFSCL* 15.28 (1988): 201–19.

————. "Introduction." *La Conquête de la Toison d'or*. By Pierre Corneille. Paris: Honoré Champion, 1998. 11–81.

————. "'Le Miroir sans tache' dans l'*Andromède* de Pierre Corneille." *French Literature Series* 22 (1995): 163–75.

Webster's New World Dictionary and Thesaurus. Version 2.0. New York: Macmillan, 1998.

Wood, Allen G. "*Décor* and Decorum in *Andromède*." *PFSCL* 15.29 (1988): 685–99.

Woshinsky, Barbara R. *The Linguistic Imperative in French Classical Literature*. Saratoga, CA: ANMA Libri, 1991.

Wygant, Amy. "Pierre Corneille's Medea-Machine." *Romanic Review* 85 (1994): 537–52.

Yarrow, P. J. *Corneille*. New York: St. Martin's, 1963.

————. "Réflexions sur le dénouement de *Cinna*." *PFSCL* 11.21 (1984): 547–58.

Yelland, H. L. et al. *A Handbook of Literary Terms*. New York: Citadel, 1966.

Zanger, Abby E. *Scenes from the Marriage of Louis XIV*. Stanford: Stanford University Press, 1997.

Zimmermann, Eléonore M. "La *Bérénice* de Pierre Corneille: *Pulchérie*." *Homage to Paul Bénichou*. Ed. Sylvie Romanowski and Monique Bilezikian. Birmingham, AL: Summa, 1994. 93–111.

Index of Corneille's Works

Agésilas, 37-38, 39, 79, 80-81, 88, 98n74, 99n84, 108, 132-33; *au lecteur,* 174-75

Andromède, 62, 65-67, 70, 72n62, 159-60, 175; *argument,* 34-35, 115-16, 175; *épître dédicatoire,* 120; *examen,* 179n167

Attila, 18, 34, 38, 41, 51, 53n39, 59, 61, 69-70, 78, 79, 81, 98n78, 99n83-84, 101, 103, 104, 108, 111, 112, 133-34, 139, 140, 142-43, 149n131, 166-67, 178n159, 178n161, 180-83, 184, 185, 187n174

Cid, Le, 10, 14, 19, 29n25, 55, 89, 90, 96, 99n81, 100n94, 103, 107-8, 109, 110, 111, 112, 114, 121n101, 122n109, 126, 135, 140, 143, 150-51, 157, 158, 176n140, 177n149, 185; *examen,* 173

Cinna, 9, 21, 24, 47-48, 56-57, 58, 59, 60, 62, 63, 71n56, 71n58, 72n59, 78, 88, 89, 108, 114, 116, 135, 143-46, 149n128, 149nn135-38, 158, 182, 184; *épître dédicatoire,* 117-18, 123n113; *examen,* 175

Clitandre, 79, 80; *examen,* 79, 118; *préface,* 116, 170-71, 175

Conquête de la Toison d'or, La, 2, 20, 37, 39-40, 62, 72n59, 132, 159-65, 177n152

Don Sanche d'Aragon, 27-28, 35, 55-57, 71n58, 117, 164, 185; *épître dédicatoire,* 115, 174; *examen,* 173

Galerie du palais, La, 18, 78; *examen,* 175

Héraclius, 17, 22, 24-25, 36, 71n58, 78, 96, 98n71, 98n78, 99n83, 125, 140, 185; *au lecteur,* 142; *examen,* 22, 114

Horace, 20, 24, 57-58, 64-65, 66, 70, 71n53, 71n58, 72nn60-61, 80, 81, 86, 87-88, 90-97, 98n75, 99n83, 99nn86-91, 100nn92-94, 101, 102, 114, 121n101, 122n103, 127, 135, 140, 158, 179n166, 184, 185; *épître dédicatoire,* 117, 118; *examen,* 64, 116, 172, 179n166

Illusion comique, L', 12, 25, 30nn29-30, 51, 62, 69, 70, 101, 104, 109-13, 122nn106-11, 134, 150-51, 170, 179n172, 184, 185; *examen,* 172, 179n172

Médée, 20, 23, 38, 40, 59, 62, 78, 101, 104, 165, 167; *épître dédicatoire,* 117

Mélite, 34, 104, 184; *au lecteur,* 116; *épître dédicatoire,* 116; *examen,* 79

Menteur, Le, 10, 18, 29n23, 42, 54n47, 54n49, 58, 60, 71n54, 85-86, 99n81, 101, 104-5, 107, 109, 112, 121n101, 138, 150, 151-58, 159, 165, 166, *interesting*

176n139, 176n142, 176nn144-45, 177nn146-49, 184; *au lecteur*, 114, 154; *épître dédicatoire*, 35, 60, 150; *examen*, 156

Nicomède, 3, 19, 22, 23, 41-48, 52, 53n40, 53n42, 54nn43-44, 54n46, 59, 88, 97, 99n83, 103, 106-7, 114, 166, 181, 184, 185

Œdipe, 17, 19, 22, 25-29, 30nn31-33, 54n45, 55, 60, 61, 62, 67-69, 70, 71n55, 71n57, 72nn63-66, 89, 99n81, 99n84, 105-6, 108, 114, 117, 132, 140-42, 143, 167-68, 184, 185, 186; *au lecteur*, 114, 115, 168; *épître dédicatoire*, 123n112; *examen*, 26, 115

Othon, 37, 40, 71n58, 103, 109, 138, 142, 146, 166; *préface*, 114

Pertharite, 21, 56, 57, 59, 78, 98n78, 124-26, 127, 128, 135, 140, 143, 185; *examen*, 63

Place Royale, La, 16, 18, 34, 58, 99n83, 134

Polyeucte, 3, 17, 21, 55, 61-62, 64, 72n59, 108, 121n101, 128-30, 134, 135, 137, 147n118, 148n119, 149n127, 176n140, 182, 184, 185, 186; *examen*, 35, 130, 148n120

Pompée, 8, 19-20, 22-23, 37, 60, 72n59, 105, 109, 111, 112, 122n104, 135-38, 139, 149nn130-31, 150, 176n139, 178n158, 184, 185; *épître dédicatoire*, 118, 142; *examen*, 137

Psyché, 70; *libraire au lecteur, Le*, 72n67

Pulchérie, 24, 38, 41, 48-52, 54n45, 54n47, 79, 99n81, 111-12

Rodogune, 17-18, 21, 22, 33, 58-59, 81-83, 96, 98n76, 99n84, 101, 104, 114, 116, 125, 126-28, 135, 147n116, 151, 170, 184, 185; *examen*, 127-28

Sertorius, 22, 33, 37, 38, 56, 57, 62, 78, 89, 178n158, 184; *préface*, 115

Sophonisbe, 20, 23, 35, 37, 55, 78, 86-87, 98n78, 99n82, 114, 119, 168, 178n162, 179n168, 185; *préface*, 119-20, 168, 171

Suite du Menteur, La, 14, 18, 21, 29n23, 29n27, 31, 32, 35-36, 53n36, 54n49, 58, 78-79, 88, 98nn72-73, 99n83, 106, 107, 150, 151-58, 159, 165, 176nn141-44, 177nn146-48, 177n150, 184; *épître dédicatoire*, 153, 172, 177n146; *examen*, 153, 176n144

Suivante, La, 18, 19, 59-60; *épître dédicatoire*, 172

Suréna, 33, 59, 61, 108, 143, 184

Théodore, 3, 53n35, 61-62, 98n78, 108, 128, 131, 134, 148n123, 173, 182-83, 186; *épître dédicatoire*, 116, 148n122, 173, 179n173; *examen*, 108, 114, 179n173

Tite et Bérénice, 21, 23-24, 37, 40, 80-81, 98n79, 133, 135, 170, 185

Trois Discours sur le poème dramatique, 13, 116, 169, 170, 171, 175; *Discours de la tragédie*, 102-3; *Discours de l'utilité et des parties du poème dramatique*, 102, 134, 148n125; *Discours des trois unités*, 175

Veuve, La, 8, 18, 34, 58, 99n83

General Index

Abraham, Claude, 84, 99n87, 122n105, 122n109
Abrams, M. H., 60
Adam, Antoine, 153, 157
aggression, irony as, 41, 93, 119, 142, 150, 185, 187. *See also* attack; hostility; weapon
Alarcón (Juan Ruiz de Alarcón), 154, 166, 176n145, 178n160; *Verdad sospechosa, La,* 154, 156, 166, 176n145, 178n160
alazon, 113-15, 118-20
allegory, 5, 111, 160, 133-34, 182
Allemann, Beda, 77, 97n68
Allentuch, Harriet, 84
ambiguity, 5, 39, 44, 64, 91; and Araspe (*Nicomède*), 47; dénouement of *Don Sanche,* 56; of double discourse, 185; *eirôn,* 115; inherent to irony, 6, 7, 8, 32, 75; intended, 35; oracles, 63, 66, 68, 69, 70; parody, 105; relationship between prologue and play, 159; and Rodogune, 128; and Sabine (*Horace*), 90, 95; and situational irony, 57. *See also* doubt; uncertainty
antiphrasis, 4, 16, 34, 53n38, 101, 140; *contre-vérité,* 32; in *Nicomède,* 43, 45, 46; and Sabine (*Horace*), 93, 94, 97; and sarcasm, 39, 40; and Théodore, 131; and verbal irony, 33, 139
antithesis, 2, 65, 91, 97, 129, 138, 139-42, 143; and logical order,

57; in relationship between *Pompée* and *Le Menteur,* 60; and verbal gaps, 124
Appian of Alexandria, 170
Arguments: Andromède, 34-35, 115-16, 175
Aristotle, 171, 178n163; authority of, 62, 119, 170, 172, 174, 177n146, 178n165, 179n170; and classical tragedy, 29, 57; and *Œdipus Rex,* 168; *Poetics,* 168, 170, 172, 178n165
Aston, Elaine, 19
attack, irony as, 5, 38, 53, 169, 172, 184; and *eirôn,* 119; in *Nicomède,* 41, 43, 44, 46-47; and Sabine (*Horace*), 92, 96. *See also* aggression; hostility; weapon
au lecteur: Agésilas, 174-75; *Héraclius,* 142; *Mélite,* 116; *Menteur, Le,* 114, 154; *Œdipe,* 67, 114, 115, 168; *Psyché,* 72n67
authority, 147, 150, 151-152, 168, 169-176; of the *doctes,* 115, 166, 171-73, 175; parody, 106, 107; of the rules of theater, 83, 118, 119, 124, 169, 171, 172, 173-74, 175, 179n165, 179n169, 184; in sequels, 151; of sources, 146
auto-irony, 36, 53n37
Averroès (Ibn Rushd), 174

Baker, Susan Read, 98n79, 109, 121n100, 131, 144, 147nn114-15

Barnwell, H. T., 23, 172

Bénichou, Paul, 98n76

Benserade, Isaac de, 171

Bergson, Henri, 38

Berrendonner, Alain, 14n3, 32, 84, 184

Biet, Christian, 142

Boileau-Despréaux, Nicolas, 110

Boisrobert, seigneur de (François Le Metel), 171

Boorsch, Jean, 36, 140

Booth, Wayne, 14n6, 15n12, 15n18

Bouvet, Alphonse, 94, 95, 99n87, 99n91

Brahm, Alcanter de, 15n17

Budra, Paul, 176n141

Cairncross, John, 130

Canova-Green, Marie-Claude, 177n151

Carlin, Claire, 108

Carmichael, Thomas, 151, 152

Cassius, Dio, 143, 178n164

certainty, 6, 10, 13, 15n14, 33, 115, 158. *See also* doubt; uncertainty

channels of communication, 13, 16, 17, 25, 29, 156-58; between characters, 12, 16, 31, 157; from playwright to audience, 12, 16, 21, 157; separation between, 12

Chatman, Seymour, 31

Chauviré, R., 149n127

Cherpack, Clifton, 112

Clarke, D. R., 99n89, 149n128

coincidence, 1, 23, 57, 69, 77, 79-81, 97; and generic expectations, 80; incongruity, 56, 80; and marriage, 78; in *Rodogune*, 83, 104; and situational irony, 7, 56, 71

comedy, 12, 25, 54n50, 58, 138, 153, 159, 185; excessive characters in, 104-5; generic designation, 174; generic shift, 153, 178n160; and ironic play-acting, 18; and marriage, 78-79, 98n73, 156; and parody, 108, 109; position of in Corneille's *œuvre*, 151, 184; and *raillerie*, 34; and stage-centered dramatic irony, 18

comic, the, 36, 47, 98n70, 103, 184; and dramatic irony, 16, 19; and exaggeration, 105; and the *Menteur* plays, 88, 105, 106, 112, 138, 152, 155; and parody, 121n98; and verbal echoes, 38

complicity, 18; between author and audience, 19, 21, 22, 23, 29, 45; and dramatic irony, 25; between ironist and receiver onstage, 9

consistency of character, 95, 124, 128, 134, 136, 149n128, 152; contradiction of character, 134-39, 152, 185

contagion, 8, 47, 95

contradiction, 1, 5, 14n5, 46, 53n38, 124, 139, 149n132; in *Andromède*, 66; in *au lecteur* to *Agésilas*, 174-75; character. *See under* consistency of character; in *Cinna*, 144; and paradox, 142; and Rodogune, 127, 128; as signal of irony, 10, 116; and situational irony, 4, 55, 59, 66; and verbal irony, 33

Corlouer, Marine, 164
Cornic, Sylvain, 159
Couleau, Christèle, 34
Couton, Georges, 15n13, 27-28, 38, 54n50, 109, 111, 120, 123n113, 133, 134, 136, 147n116, 148n121, 157, 162, 167, 170, 178n155, 178n159, 178n161, 178n164

Dalla Valle, Daniela, 142
d'Aubignac, François Hédelin, 3, 11, 72n61, 148n122, 171, 179nn166-67
Defaux, Gérard, 71n56, 149n137
Delmas, Christian, 116, 120
Desfougères, 125, 147n114
disjunction, 66, 69, 104, 137; between author's and characters' voices, 17, 31; and Dorante (*Le Menteur*), 154, 155; and double registers, 134; and Sabine (*Horace*), 95, 96, 97; and *Toison d'or, La*, 161; and verbal irony, 31, 32, 42, 48. *See also* gaps
dissimulation. *See under* lies
distance, 4, 6, 7, 8, 53, 129, 168, 169, 182; between channels of communication, 13; between ironist and victim, 25; and Nicomède, 41, 42, 43, 45, 53n40; in *Œdipe*, 61, 72n64, 72n66; between ostensible and intended meanings, 32, 33; and parody, 105; between receiver and victim, 25; between statement and echoic mention, 36, 37, 84, 85
doctes. See under authority
double entendre, 17, 18, 24, 35-36, 46, 53n35

doubling, 4, 5, 7, 31, 68, 79, 129, 136, 139, 183, 186-87; and *Attila*, 181, 183; Corneille's double position, 97; double discourse, 49, 50, 51, 52, 53n38, 185; double register. *See* register, double; double voicing. *See under* voice; in *épîtres dédicatoires*, 117; and exaggeration, 101; and parody, 106; in *Rodogune*, 82, 83, 104; in theater, 11-13, 133; in *Toison d'or, La*, 160, 162
Doubrovsky, Serge, 62, 94, 111, 136, 147n114, 149n131
doubt, 5, 7-9, 29, 33, 35, 77, 78, 86, 121, 138, 147, 183, 184; and exaggeration, 101, 103; in *Nicomède*, 52; and paradox, 142; and possible irony, 13, 53, 75, 76; in *Pulchérie*, 52; and sarcasm, 6, 39; and situational irony, 71. *See also* ambiguity; uncertainty
dramatic irony, 1, 13, 16-30, 62, 69; in *Attila*, 181; authorial, 17, 19-24, 29, 31, 35, 45, 185; and channels of communication, 16, 17; in *Cid, Le*, 19; in *Cinna*, 24; and comedy, 18; in *Don Sanche*, 27-28; in *Héraclius*, 17, 22, 24-25, 36; in *Illusion comique, L'*, 25, 30n29; and irony of fate, 20, 61; in *Nicomède*, 19, 45; in *Œdipe*, 16, 25-29, 68; oracles, 70; in *Polyeucte*, 17; in *Pompée*, 22-23; in *Rodogune*, 17-18, 82; and situational irony, 60, 71; in *Sophonisbe*, 20-21; stage-centered, 17-19, 24, 29, 181, 185; and surprise, 20, 26, 185-86
duplicity, 18, 48-52, 72n65
Dupriez, Bernard, 5

echoic mention, 1, 10, 13, 36-
38, 83-89, 97, 98n80, 99n84,
169; and the comic, 38; and
Corneille's writing habits, 184-
85; and the dramatic, 53; in
Horace, 86; in *Menteur, Le*,
85-86; in *Nicomède*, 45-46; and
parody, 105, 107, 108, 182; in
Pulchérie, 50; and sarcasm, 38;
in *Sophonisbe*, 86-87
edge, ironic, 5, 38, 56, 58, 80, 91,
126, 133, 162, 166, 175
eirôn, 53n37, 115-20
épîtres dédicatoires, 117, 118, 120;
Andromède, 120-21; *Cinna*,
117-18, 123n113; *Don Sanche*,
115, 174; *Horace*, 117, 118;
Médée, 117; *Mélite*, 116; *Menteur, Le*, 35, 60, 150; *Oedipe*,
123n112; *Pompée*, 118, 142;
Suite du Menteur, La, 153, 172,
177n146; *Suivante, La*, 172;
Théodore, 116, 148n122, 173,
179n173
Epstein, Nancy P., 15n9
Escola, Marc, 25, 29, 132, 142,
167
être et paraître, 12, 60, 71n55, 107,
134
Euripedes, 167
exaggeration, 1, 10, 39, 76, 80, 101-
21, 124, 129, 142, 173; and the
alazon, 113; in *Attila*, 103, 180,
182; and Cléopâtre (*Rodogune*),
104; and Dorante (*Le Menteur*),
104-5; flattery, 117-18; and
heroism, 108-13, 185; hyperbole, 102; *invraisemblance*,
102-3, 105; and Matamore
(*L'Illusion comique*), 104, 109-
13; in *Nicomède*, 43; in *Othon*,

40; and parody, 105, 108, 113;
and Sabine (*Horace*), 91; and
self-denigration, 116-17; and
self-evaluation, 114-15; and the
sublime, 186; and surprise, 125,
128, 185. *See also* hyperbole
examens, 13, 15n22, 118, 171;
Andromède, 179n167; *Cid, Le*,
173; *Cinna*, 175; *Clitandre*, 79,
118; *Don Sanche*, 173; *Galerie
du palais, La*, 175; *Héraclius*,
22, 114; *Horace*, 64, 116, 172,
179n166; *Illusion comique*, 172,
179n172; *Mélite*, 79; *Menteur,
Le*, 156, 176n145; *Œdipe*, 26,
115; *Pertharite*, 63; *Polyeucte*,
35, 130, 148n120; *Pompée*,
137; *Rodogune*, 127, 128; *Suite
du Menteur, La*, 153, 176n144;
Théodore, 108, 114, 179n173

fate, irony of, 1, 2, 3, 14, 15n10, 55,
60-63, 71, 80, 87, 186; in *Attila*, 61, 181, 182; Corneille as
victim of, 63, 75, 154; and dramatic irony, 20; free will, 28, 61,
140-42; and *Œdipe*, 7, 26, 28,
61; and oracles, 63; and prophecies, 69; in *Rodogune*, 83
Fontenelle, Bernard de, 185
Forestier, Georges, 1, 29n26, 59,
71n55, 79, 98n73, 99n86,
108, 109, 121n97, 142, 145,
147nn115-16, 149n129, 165,
166, 168, 172, 175
free will. *See under* fate
Freud, Sigmund, 75
Frye, Northrop, 113, 115
Fumaroli, Marc, 14n2, 41, 54n46,
148n119
Furetière, Antoine, 4, 14n4, 44

gaps, ironic, 4, 5, 76, 93, 102, 124-49, 150, 159, 170, 172, 175, 176, 186; between addressees, 117; in *Agésilas*, 132-33; and antithesis, 139-42; in *Cinna*, 143-46; between Corneille's version and the source, 165-69; created or camouflaged, vis-à-vis authorities, 169-76; in dates, 118; between language and action, 100n93, 104, 125, 137; between *Le Menteur* and *La Suite du Menteur*, 151, 153-55, 177n147; in *Œdipe*, 132, 140-42; between ostensible and intended meanings, 114, 173; in *Othon*, 138; and paradox, 142-43; in *Pertharite*, 125-26; in *Polyeucte*, 129-30; in *Pompée*, 135-38; between prologue and play, 158; between registers, 128-134; in *Rodogune*, 126-28; and surprise, 125; in *Théodore*, 131; in *Toison d'or, La*, 160-64; between voices, 12. *See also* disjunction

Garapon, Robert, 110-11

Gay-Crosier, Raymond, 15n8

Genette, Gérard, 113

Georges, André, 144, 145, 146, 149n134

Gérard, Albert, 149n129

Géraud, Violaine, 12

Goode, William O., 167

Goodkin, Richard, 8, 26, 136

Gossip, C. J., 149n131, 149n135

Green, D. H., 2, 11

Greenberg, Mitchell, 71n52, 98n75, 129

Hamon, Philippe, 3, 12, 13, 36, 38, 77, 112, 139, 169

Hardy, Alexandre, 171

Harvey, Lawrence E., 99n87

Heinsius, Daniel, 174

Hémon, Félix, 159

Herland, Louis, 94, 127, 147n116, 148n126

hero. *See* heroism

heroism, 25, 47, 88, 99n84, 103, 108-13, 119, 120, 121n102, 128, 151, 154, 159, 161, 167; of César (*Pompée*), 137, 138, 149n129, 149n131; centrality in discussion of Corneille's plays, 2, 185; of Horace, 58, 71n53, 86; of Matamore, 109-13, 184, 185; of Nicomède, 41, 42, 53n40; of Othon, 138; and parody of, 108-13, 122n105, 185; of Ptolomée (*Pompée*), 136; relationship to irony, 2, 14n1, 28, 41, 186; Sabine's (*Horace*) attack on, 91, 92, 96, 97

Homer, 4

Horace (Quintus Horatius Flaccus), 119, 128, 134, 148n125, 170, 172, 174-75, 177n146; *Ars Poetica*, 170, 179n171

hostility, irony as, 36, 53, 87; and echoic mention, 185; and sarcasm, 38, 39, 40, 42, 44. *See also* aggression; attack; weapon

Hubert, Judd D., 15n21, 137, 141, 148n124, 149n129

Hutcheon, Linda, 3, 4, 5, 6, 7, 9, 10, 15n8, 15n15, 15n18, 53n41, 55, 58, 105, 106, 121n98, 133, 164

hyperbole, 33, 43, 121n95, 128, 131, 186; infelicitous hyperbole, 102, 104, 125; and Matamore (*L'Illusion comique*), 112;

relationship to exaggeration, 102; in *Rodogune*, 104. *See also* exaggeration

inclusiveness. *See under* undecidibility
incongruity, 1, 4, 15n12, 26, 61, 76, 118, 132, 133, 135, 140, 146, 150, 175, 185; in *Agésilas*, 132-33; in *Attila*, 166, 180, 181, 182; coincidence, 80; and Dorante (*Le Menteur*), 138; and *invraisemblance*, 57; and the *Menteur* plays, 151, 155, 157, 165; in *Œdipe*, 142; and Othon, 138; and Rodelinde (*Pertharite*), 124-26; and Rodogune, 59, 126-28; and Sabine (*Horace*), 96, 97; as signal of irony, 10, 13, 166; and situational irony, 55-57, 59, 60; and *Théodore*, 131; between *La Toison d'or* and its prologue, 160, 161, 162, 164, 165
intertextual reference, 10, 23, 89, 151-52, 168
inversion. *See under* reversal
invraisemblance, 57, 79, 102-3, 105, 125, 145, 147n114. See *also* *vraisemblance*

Jankélévitch, Vladimir, 14nn6-7, 105, 187n175
Jaouën, Françoise, 15n22, 114, 129
Josephus, Flavius, 170
Justinian, 170
Juvenal, 170

Kaufer, David S., 39
Kawin, Bruce F., 97n69
Kerbrat-Orecchioni, Catherine, 5, 6, 15n20, 42, 75, 101

Kierkegaard, Søren, 76
Knight, R. C., 3, 92, 99n88, 115, 125, 138
Knox, Norman, 15n10, 15n20

La Charité, Raymond C., 108
La Charité, Virginia A., 108
Lagarde, François, 92, 99n87
La Harpe, Jean-François de, 146
Lancaster, Henry Carrington, 90, 94, 151, 156, 160, 161, 162, 178n157
Lang, Candace D., 6
Lanson, Gustave, 178n165
Lefranc, Abel, 120
Leggatt, Alexander, 157
Lemaître, Jules, 9, 34, 41, 130, 149n129
lies (in relation to irony), 42, 48, 49, 53n41; dissimulation, 6, 14n8, 115
litotes, 33, 115, 120. *See also* understatement
Livy (Titus Livius), 65, 90, 99n86
Lockert, Lacy, 100n93
Longinus, Dionysius, 102
Louis XIV: in *Andromède*, 159-60; in *Attila*, 111, 133, 134, 182; and *Don Sanche*, 164; in *Tite et Bérénice*, 133-34; in *Toison d'or, La*, 159-60, 161-62, 163-64, 165, 177n152, 178n155, 178n157
Louvat (-Molozay), Bénédicte, 25, 28, 63, 65, 66, 72nn61-62, 72n65, 132, 142, 167
Lully, Jean-Baptiste, 159
Lyons, John D., 53n39, 71n58, 108, 122n103, 169, 171, 172, 179n169

Magné, Bernard, 63

Mairet, Jean, 20, 21, 119, 168, 171, 178n162, 179n168; *Sophonisbe, La*, 20, 168

Mallinson, G.J., 153, 154

margins, 140, 147, 150-179, 182; between *Le Cid* and *L'Illusion comique*, 150-51; between Corneille and authority of Ancients, 170-71; between Corneille and authority of rules and *doctes*, 171-76; between *Médée* and its sources, 167; between *Le Menteur* and its sources, 166; between *Le Menteur* and *La Suite du Menteur*, 151-58, 159, 165; between *Le Menteur* and *Pompée*, 150; between *Nicomède* and its sources, 166; between *Œdipe* and its sources, 167-68; between *Othon* and its sources, 166; between prologue and play: *Andromède*, 159-60; between prologue and play: *La Toison d'or*, 160-65; between *Sophonisbe* and its sources, 168;

Margitic, Milorad R., 135, 137

Marie-Thérèse d'Autriche, 160, 161-62, 163, 164, 178n157

Marin, Louis, 136

Marivaux, Pierre Carlet de Chamblain de, 121n99

Marty-Laveaux, Charles, 120

Maskell, David, 116, 172

Matzat, Wolfgang, 25, 62, 142

Mauron, Charles, 110, 176n140

May, Georges, 114

Mazarin, Jules, 118, 163

McDermott, Helen Bates, 138

McFarlane, I. D., 3, 77, 81

Merlin-Kajman, Hélène, 41, 100n94, 118

Minel, Emmanuel, 155, 177n147

mockery, 3, 5, 19, 27, 34, 56, 86, 96, 107, 111, 121, 132, 139, 151, 152, 186; in *Attila*, 34, 38, 103, 180, 182; and dramatic conventions, 79, 80, 81, 83, 118, 159; and exaggeration, 103, 104-5; and irony of fate, 60, 62; and prefatory texts, 34, 120, 142, 146, 170, 172, 173, 175; and verbal echoes, 36, 37, 38. *See also* playfulness; *raillerie*

Molière (Jean-Baptiste Poquelin), 2, 72n67, 89; *Bourgeois gentilhomme, Le*, 122n105; *École des femmes, L'*, 89; *Misanthrope, Le*, 36

Monson, Don A., 147n117

Montaigne, 143, 144

Morel, Jacques, 15n18

Morrison, Ian R., 62

Muecke, D. C., 2, 8, 10, 15n19, 19, 56, 115

Nadal, Octave, 15n22, 110, 177n146

Napoleon Bonaparte, 9, 47, 76, 135, 149n128

Newmark, Peter, 90, 91, 92, 96-97, 99n87, 140, 149n132

Niderst, Alain, 2, 162, 178n153

Norman, Buford, 159

Nurse, Peter, 91, 92, 99n88

Œdipus, 2, 3, 7, 16, 25, 26, 28, 68, 89, 115, 140, 142

oracles, 57, 63-70; in *Andromède*, 65-67, 72n62; in *Attila*, 69-70; in *Horace*, 64-65, 72n61; in *L'Illusion comique*, 69; and irony of fate, 63; in *Œdipe*,

25, 30nn31-32, 67-69, 71n57, 72nn64-65, 140, 141, 142, 167; in *Psyché*, 70. *See also* prophecy

Ovid, 35, 65-66

Paillet-Guth, Anne-Marie, 12, 14nn1-2, 29n26, 36, 43, 44, 48, 101

parabase, 12, 29n23

paradox, 25, 44, 53n38, 59, 66, 67, 75, 97n69, 120, 124, 139, 141, 142-43, 144, 146, 174, 186-87; and Auguste's reaction to Livie (*Cinna*), 144, 146; and relation to antithesis, 124, 139, 142

parody, 1, 30n34, 89, 105-13, 121n100, 122n103, 130, 152, 185; in *Attila*, 108, 182; in *Le Cid*, 107-8; of the Cornelian hero through Matamore, 108-13, 122n105, 185; and exaggeration, 105, 113, 185; and irony, 106, 113; of love, 106-7; in *Le Menteur*, 107-8, 121n101; in *Œdipe*, 27, 108, 168; pastiche, 105; self-parody, 105, 107; and repetition, 105; and ridicule, 105, 106, 121n98; in *Rodogune*, 83; in *Théodore*, 108, 131

Pascal, Blaise, 2, 97n70

Pavel, Thomas G., 90

Perrin, Lauent, 3, 14n6, 15n16, 15n18, 32, 33, 39, 53n38, 101, 102, 121n95, 142

Petit de Julleville, L., 47, 90, 99n88, 122n107, 154

Picciola, Liliane, 154

Plautus, 174

playfulness, 3, 5, 23-24, 29, 39, 78, 82, 121, 127, 158, 159, 185;

and allusions, 21-22, 23; and echoic mention, 38, 50; and metatheatrical references, 157; in *Œdipe*, 27, 89; and parody, 105; in prefatory texts, 35, 116, 120, 170; and self-deprecation, 158; and surprise, 126. *See also* mockery; *raillerie*

Plutarch, 99n89

préfaces, 13; *Clitandre*, 116, 170-71, 175; *Othon*, 114, 142; *Sertorius*, 115; *Sophonisbe*, 20-21, 119-20, 168, 171

Prigent, Michel, 41, 53n40

prologues, 2, 72, 147, 150, 158-65, 177n151; of *Andromède*, 159-60; and opera, 159; of *Toison d'or, La*, 159, 160-64, 165, 177n152, 178n153, 178n156

prophecy, 20, 22, 72n59; in *Attila*, 61, 69, 70, 182; and Livy (*Cinna*), 62, 72n59, 144, 145-46, 182; in relation to oracles, 64. *See also* oracles

Pure, l'abbé de, 116, 171

querelle du Cid, la, 111, 126, 171, 179n170

Quinault, Philippe, 159

Racine, Jean, 1, 2, 63, 76, 89, 108, 186; *Plaideurs, Les*, 89

raillerie, 1, 5, 14n4, 34, 53, 150, 158, 176, 184, 185, 186, 187; and *Attila*, 34, 180; in *Nicomède*, 43, 44; and prefatory texts, 34, 175; in *Pulchérie*, 50. *See also* mockery; playfulness

Ramazani, Vaheed K., 32, 36

Rat, Maurice, 120

Rathé, Alice, 3, 54n50, 111

Reed, Gervais, 149n136, 149n138
register, change of, 1, 10, 33, 157
register, double, 128-134, 175; in
  Agésilas, 132-33; and allegory,
  133; and concealed gaps, 134; in
  Œdipe, 131-32, 167-68; in *Poly-*
  eucte, 129-30, 135, 148n119,
  184; in *Théodore*, 130
Reiss, Timothy J., 90, 145
repetition, 10, 13, 76, 77-79, 81,
  88, 97, 97nn69-70, 102, 108,
  120, 124, 140, 152, 165, 170;
  in *Le Menteur*, 85-86; and
  Nicomède, 43, 45; and parody,
  105; in *Rodogune*, 82; and Sabine (*Horace*), 91, 95, 96, 97;
  in *Sophonisbe*, 86-87; and verbal
  echo, 37, 84-86
reversal, 37, 52, 53n36, 56, 67, 101,
  110, 118, 119, 123n113, 124,
  135, 147, 185; in *Attila*, 180,
  181, 183; in *Cinna*, 143-44,
  146; of endings in source material, 156, 166; inversion, 34, 37,
  56, 68, 85, 86, 88, 105, 106,
  140; and oracles, 64-65; reversal of fortune, 1, 4, 56, 57-58,
  87; and situational irony, 71;
  in *Sophonisbe*, 86-87; *trompeur*
  trompé, 58
Richelieu, cardinal et duc de, (Ar-
  mand-Jean du Plessis), 8-9,
  15n14, 117, 118
Rimmon-Kenan, Shlomith, 97n69
role-playing, 12, 18, 19, 45
Romantic irony, 4
Rosenmeyer, Thomas, 13, 158
Rostand, François, 84-85, 98n77,
  99n85
Rotrou, Jean de, 29n26; *Heureux*
  naufrage, L', 29n26

Rousset, Jean, 15n21, 81
rules of theater. *See under* authority

St. Ambroise, 170, 173
sarcasm, 1, 38-41, 53n39, 86; in
  Attila, 180, 181; and doubt, 6,
  10, 39; in *Nicomède*, 42, 44-45;
  in *Pulchérie*, 48, 50, 51-52; and
  Sabine (*Horace*), 91, 92, 94,
  99n90
Schellenberg, Betty A., 176n141
Scherer, Jacques, 82, 83
Schlumberger, Jean, 41, 105
Schoentjes, Pierre, 3, 4, 5, 6, 7, 13,
  14n5, 29n24, 33, 53n37, 58,
  85, 106, 139
Scott, J. W., 96-97
Scott, Paul, 129, 130, 147n118
Scudéry, Georges de, 111, 171,
  179n170
self-deprecation, 5, 40, 87; on Corneille's part, 115-18, 158, 185
Sellstrom, A. Donald, 149n129
Seneca: *De Clementia*, 143, 144,
  149n128; *Œdipus*, 28, 105,
  167-68
Serroy, Jean, 108, 109, 110, 113,
  121n102, 153, 154, 155,
  176n140, 177n148
Shakespeare: *Julius Caesar*, 10, 77
situational irony, 4, 6-7, 8, 13, 48-
  49, 55-72, 87, 101, 182, 183,
  184, 185; and coincidence, 7,
  56, 79; and incongruity, 56,
  57, 59; and intending source,
  7, 15n10, 55; and irony of fate,
  2, 60, 62; and logical order, 56,
  57, 81
Smith, Christopher, 178n160
Soare, Antoine, 149n129
Socrates, 14n6, 115

Sophocles, 25, 26, 67, 68, 167; *Œdipus Rex*, 16, 25, 27, 28, 67, 69, 70, 105, 140, 142, 167-68
Sperber, Dan, 36, 53n38, 98n80, 169
stage directions, 10, 25, 32
Staves, Susan, 121n101, 177n149
Stegmann, André, 29n28, 41, 54n48, 54n50, 72n61, 120, 123n113, 147n114, 177n152, 179n166
Stringfellow, Frank, Jr., 15n11, 39
sublime, the, 102, 103, 121n97, 130, 146, 147n116, 186
surprise, 3, 22, 96, 115, 134, 137; and Chimène (*Le Cid*), 126; and dramatic irony, 20, 62, 185-86; and exaggeration, 125, 128, 185; and incongruity, 57, 125, 128, 185; in *Œdipe*, 26; and oracles, 64, 67; and Rodelinde (*Pertharite*), 125; and Rodogune, 128
suspense, 16, 18, 27, 36, 137
Sutcliffe, F. E., 144, 145, 149n136
Sweetser, Marie-Odile, 71n54, 108, 149n129
symmetry, 13, 56, 57, 58, 76, 77, 97, 102, 140; in *Attila*, 81, 182; in *Horace*, 81; in *Rodogune*, 82-83, 104, 126

Tacitus, 166, 170
Theile, Wolfgang, 142
Tiefenbrun, Susan, 14n8, 15n9, 90, 99n87, 144
Toczyski, Suzanne C., 90
tragedy, 1, 14n1, 29, 58, 62, 80, 83, 98n74, 108, 124, 132, 138, 142, 151, 165, 174, 184; Greek tragedy, 4, 29, 57, 62, 140, 168; and irony of fate, 2, 60, 63; and marriage, 79

tragicomedy, 56, 80, 108, 153
Triau, Christopher, 60
trilogue, 44-45, 53n42
Tristan l'Hermite, François, 171
trompeur trompé, 58-59, 71, 71n54, 183

Ubersfeld, Anne, 12
uncertainty, 7, 9, 39, 60, 76, 84, 137, 147; and exaggeration, 102, 121; and intention, 24, 55; and interpretation, 5, 8, 33, 128, 186; and Sabine (*Horace*), 91, 92, 102. *See also* ambiguity; doubt
undecidability, 5, 6, 12, 35, 47, 52, 53, 105, 147, 187; and inclusiveness, 4, 5, 128, 142, 186; and incongruity, 128; and paradox, 142
understatement, 10, 14n8, 115. *See also* litotes

Vega, Lope de, 154, 176n145; *Amar sin saber a quién*, 154
verbal irony, 3, 4, 6-7, 12, 13, 15n18, 16, 17, 31-54, 55, 58, 60, 63, 71, 124, 131, 166, 185; and antiphrasis, 33-34, 139; in *Attila*, 180-81, 183; and double entendre, 35-36; and echoic mention, 36-38, 84, 185; and exaggeration, 101, 103; in *Nicomède*, 41-48, 103; in *Pulchérie*, 48-53; and *raillerie*, 34-35; and Sabine (*Horace*), 90, 93, 95; and sarcasm, 10, 38-41; signs of, 32-33; source of, 31
Verhœff, Han, 53,n36, 90, 92, 94, 156
victim of irony, 3, 12, 18, 24, 25,

26, 50, 69, 98n70, 115, 159; in *Attila*, 181, 182, 183; of author's irony, 19, 23; Corneille as, 63, 89, 154, 174; onstage, 16, 17, 19; and sarcasm, 38, 39, 40, 42, 44-45; and triangular structure, 23, 31, 44

voice, 9, 12, 32, 117; of author, 14, 17, 84, 175; of character, 17, 53, 84; double voicing, 17, 31, 88, 106, 113, 114, 185

Voltaire (François-Marie Arouet), 14n1, 116, 144, 147n114, 147n116, 159

vraisemblance, 57, 81, 83, 102-3, 124, 142, 155, 175. *See also invraisemblance*

Wagner, Marie-France, 116, 159,

161, 162, 178nn155-56

weapon, irony as, 93, 171, 176; and Attila, 180; and Nicomède, 41, 44, 48; and Sabine (*Horace*), 97; and verbal irony, 37, 53. *See also* aggression; attack; hostility

Wilson, Deirdre, 36, 53n38, 98n80, 169

Wood, Allen G., 116

Woshinsky, Barbara R., 90

Wygant, Amy, 162, 178n157

Yarrow, P. J., 14n2, 144, 145, 149nn135-36

Yelland, H. L., 38

Zanger, Abby E., 161, 162-64, 178nn153-54

Zimmermann, Eléonore M., 54nn50-51

Dad
call Steph
travel thing
Mike

Printed in the United States
88836LV00004B/243/A

9 781886 365254